MEN

REAL CONVERSATIONS

ANTHONY DENAHY AND **EMMA STIRLING**

with *Julian Czaplinski*

LEXICON

An imprint of Nautilus Media Group

LEXICON

Published by Lexicon, an imprint of Nautilus Media Group

Designers: Emma Stirling, Mitzi Mann and Emily Mathams

Cover photographs: Corey Wilson, Dan Vojtech, Julia Kuzmenko, Jennifer Cawley, Sergey Yusin, Reginald Thomas.

All photos in this book have been supplied with permission, and have been credited where possible.

Lexicon books are available at special discounts when purchased in bulk as well as for fund-raising or educational use. For details, contact Nautilus Media Group at info@nautilusmedia.com.au

www.nautilusmedia.com.au

ISBN 9780645107234

CONTENTS

INTRODUCTION

Two years ago, we had the crazy idea of contacting well-known men from around the world and asking them to divulge their innermost feelings and talk about everything from what makes them truly happy, their life purpose and success; to overcoming challenges, facing fear, vulnerability, dealing with anger, mental health, mindfulness, relationships, love, kindness, family and fatherhood.

That is to say, all the stuff that men don't normally talk about.

We contacted hundreds of men from all walks of life, and in all fields of endeavor – the one thing they all had in common was that they were known for being exceptional.

We didn't expect a lot – after all, who were we, a couple of unknown Australians, to expect these world-famous men to trust us with their thoughts and feelings?

There were plenty of men who didn't respond or who declined the invitation – and we totally understood that.

But, to our delight, 40 well-known men - ranging from the Dalai Lama, to astronauts, Navy SEALS, NBA players, NFL players, Paralympic gold medalists, physicians, coaches, race car drivers, extreme athletes, actors, CEOs, UFC and Muay Thai fighters, rappers, poets, philosophers, authors, artists and surfers – took a leap of faith and agreed to open their hearts and have very honest conversations about all these topics.

Men: Real Conversations is the result of all the discussions the men have had with Anthony and Julian, and some who have provided written responses to the questions, presenting the thoughts and feelings of this diverse group of men in their own words.

We chose to ask many of the same questions to the men, to gain insights into the different ways they would respond. "What does vulnerability mean to you?" certainly provided a wide variety of responses, as did "What is your favorite failure?"

There are strong themes in the conversations – many men have suffered from depression and mental health issues; some have strong relationships with their fathers, although many have had difficult relationships with them; many of the men have wonderful relationships with their mothers; happiness is found in simplicity; success is often not what they expected it would be; failure has often been the catalyst for great achievements; and there is a strong need for connection to nature and to protect the environment.

We have intentionally kept the conversations unedited, to ensure the integrity of the men's responses.

What do we hope to achieve with the book? We hope that anyone, facing the prospect of failure, will see what it means to persevere; that a young man might better understand the power, rather than weakness, of acknowledging his vulnerability; that a mother may better understand why talking about feelings can be harder for boys; and that women will see how respected they are for their strength, wisdom and compassion.

We hope that a young person, struggling with their identity, will know that they are not alone; that anyone who is confronting mental health challenges can see that it is so very common and will be encouraged to take steps to seek help; and that a father will recognize a side of himself he has not yet dared to share with his family.

Perhaps the most important outcome, however, is that it might encourage men of all ages to recognize the validity of their own feelings and to have real conversations about the things that matter to them most.

Many of the men we spoke with have told us that it was one of the best conversations they've ever had – to be asked about things that are deeply important to them personally, rather than their professional achievements.

We hope you find the honest and often raw insights from these men as compelling and beautiful as we do.

Anthony & Emma

WHY?

As a man I have failed many times, I have hit the bottom many times, I have contemplated my own existence many times; I have experienced grief, loss, sorrow and despair many times and I have failed people many times.

I have also exceeded my own expectations, enjoyed success, celebrated my children, had incredible highs and yearned for the possibilities that tomorrow brings and loved truly, madly, deeply.

In trying to always be a better version of myself, I knew there were people who I could turn to, to seek professional help that might help me feel like I am being a better man. However, the world is made up of extraordinary people - who better to ask than people with lived experiences?

Over the past two years, my incredible wife and I have undertaken a journey of discovery to find men who have a story, men who have integrity, passion, desires and have shared emotional success and failures with the people around them. Each of the men in this book has revealed something about themselves that I deeply admire.

Their lives have not been gilded; they have had their fair share of failures, disappointment, sorrow, loss and love. Yes, some are well-known and open about their lives, some you will know, others you may never have heard of - but all share one common trait and that is they are always trying to be the best versions of themselves.

This is not a book of how to succeed or a book that showers adulation on the men involved, many have already experienced that. It is a chance for these men's inner thoughts, dreams, and experiences to be shared and to answer questions that often they have never been asked.

The men have all given honestly, they have shown vulnerability in sharing their own unique stories so that I or anyone who picks up the book will find something that they can connect with, words that will resonate within themselves and let them know that they are doing a great job in today's chaotic and often rudderless society.

To all who have been in my life, sharing this book with you is my gift to you for all the gifts you have given me.

Love,
Anthony

THANKS

Our thanks go to our wonderful family and friends who have been incredibly supportive in our quest to bring *Men: Real Conversations* to life.

Love and appreciation go to Ros and Peter Stirling, Sandra and John Denahy, and Mitzi Mann. None of this would have been possible without you.

Our love to our children - Soph, Wynter and Elijah. You inspire us every day.

Thanks to Julian Czaplinski for the wonderful conversations you had – you have an amazing talent.

To Elias Altman, Paul Roos, Emily Mathams and Matt Stirling – thank you for all your hard work and support.

Thanks too to Tim Ferriss for one of the great questions which has gleaned some wonderfully insightful responses, *"How has failure, or apparent failure, set you up for later success? Do you have a "favorite failure" of yours?"*

Last but not least, our thanks to each of the men featured in these pages who have trusted us with their deepest thoughts and shown great faith in us to represent them authentically.

DISCLAIMER

HIS HOLINESS, THE 14TH DALAI LAMA OF TIBET

 @dalailama   @dalailama   Dalai Lama

His Holiness the 14th Dalai Lama, Tenzin Gyatso, describes himself as a simple Buddhist monk. He is the spiritual leader of Tibet. He was born on 6 July 1935, to a farming family, in a small hamlet located in Taktser, Amdo, northeastern Tibet. At the age of two, the child, then named Lhamo Dhondup, was recognized as the reincarnation of the previous 13th Dalai Lama, Thubten Gyatso.

The Dalai Lamas are believed to be manifestations of Avalokiteshvara or Chenrezig, the Bodhisattva of Compassion and the patron saint of Tibet. Bodhisattvas are realized beings inspired by a wish to attain Buddhahood for the benefit of all sentient beings, who have vowed to be reborn in the world to help humanity.

Do you have a favorite quote or philosophy you live by?

Generally speaking, I live by the philosophical view of dependent origination: This law of causality states that nothing exists on its own but arises from earlier circumstances and actions. Things arise in dependence upon causes and conditions. Everything affects everything else: everything is interconnected. Although dependent origination is at the heart of Buddhist teaching, it can be applied in our personal life without involving religion. The concept of dependent origination can also be applied on a larger and broader scale on a collective level, i.e., business, politics, society, culture, education. The practice of non-violence is essential if everything is interconnected. Self-discipline, compassion, kindness, forgiveness, etc, is all part of the practice of non-violence. With interdependence at its heart, the practice of non-violence is thus achievable.

An action is non-violent only when it is associated with the desire to refrain from harming others. The mere absence of violence is not considered non-violence. We all desire happiness and want to avoid suffering. If our motivation is to respect the rights of others and to refrain from harming others, even if we cannot help others, it is considered non-violence. If, however, we take a step further by thinking that our wellbeing depends on the wellbeing of our immediate family, society, nation and the whole world, and this concern for others results in relieving others' pain and contributes towards their happiness, then this becomes an act of compassion, a higher form of non-violence.

What is one personal characteristic that you are most proud of?

My determination to persevere in the face of difficulties is one personal characteristic that I am glad to possess. I have faced multiple challenges since my childhood. Whether these struggles were within the Tibetan society or more global in nature, I have always stood my ground and have never shied away from taking on these challenges.

What are the issues — whether social, environmental, political or economic — that you feel are most pressing and for which you feel the greatest personal concern and responsibility?

All of the issues that we are concerned about - social, environmental, political, economic - are all interconnected. The direction our world is heading towards depends to a great extent on our education system. All of our leaders in politics, business, and elsewhere are products of our existing education system.

The prevalent education curriculum is too centered on material development and ignores the basic human values that shape our own lives as well as society at large. I strongly believe inclusion of the nurture of basic human values into the educational curriculum will lead

to a more compassionate, non-violent world. Children receive love and affection from their mothers. This affection - the maternal instinct of a mother toward her newborn when she disregards her own comfort when caring for her child - is primarily biological. This unconditional loving attitude is what I mean when I talk about compassion as the source of all our shared ethical values. We can promote these basic human values through the development of common sense, common experience and scientific findings. This is what I call secular ethics.

Because of the religious diversity of its society, the Indian constitution promotes secularism. Secular in the context of the Indian understanding entails tolerance and respect not just for religious believers but also those who do not believe in religion. My use and understanding of "secular" is based on the way it is used in India. I am encouraged that Emory University has developed a new K-12 educational program with a curriculum called Social, Emotional and Ethical Learning (SEE Learning). It is guided by a shared vision for an education of heart and mind. The program conveys a science-based approach to bringing ethical development of the whole child into education.

What do you believe is the purpose of life?

One great question underlies our experience, whether we think about it consciously or not: What is the purpose of life? I have considered this question and would like to share my thoughts in the hope that they may be of direct, practical benefit to those who read them.

I believe that the purpose of life is to be happy. From the moment of birth, every human being wants happiness and does not want suffering. Neither social conditioning nor education nor ideology affects this. From the very core of our being, we simply desire contentment. I don't know whether the universe, with its countless galaxies, stars and planets, has a deeper meaning or not, but at the very least, it is clear that we humans who live on this earth face the task of making a happy life for ourselves. Therefore, it is important to discover what will bring about the greatest degree of happiness.

Who inspires you?

As a Buddhist practitioner, Buddha Shakyamuni inspires me. There are many ancient Indian masters - Nagarjuna, Chandrakirti, Dharmakirti - whose teachings and lives have inspired me greatly. World leaders - Mahatma Gandhi, Martin Luther King, His Holiness Pope John Paul II, Mother Teresa, Nelson Mandela, and Archbishop Desmond Tutu - are also great inspirations. Scientists I am inspired by include Newton and Einstein. I also greatly admire the German philosopher and physicist Carl von Weizsäcker, David Bohm and Francesco Varela. The list of people who have inspired me is long.

EMOTIONS

How do you believe we can achieve happiness?

For a start, it is possible to divide every kind of happiness and suffering into two main categories: mental and physical. Of the two, it is the mind that exerts the greatest influence on most of us. Unless we are either gravely ill or deprived of basic necessities, our physical condition plays a secondary role in life. If the body is content, we virtually ignore it. However, peace of mind is crucial for our wellbeing.

Hence, we should devote our most serious efforts to bringing about mental peace. From my own limited experience, I have found that the greatest degree of inner tranquility comes from the development of love and compassion.

The more we care for the happiness of others, the greater our own sense of well-being becomes. Cultivating a close, warm-hearted feeling for others automatically puts the mind at ease. This helps remove whatever fears or insecurities we may have and gives us the strength to cope with obstacles we encounter. It is the ultimate source of success in life.

As long as we live in this world, we are bound to encounter problems. If, at such times, we lose hope and become discouraged, we diminish our ability to face difficulties. If, on the other hand, we remember that it is not just ourselves but also everyone who has to undergo suffering, this more realistic perspective will increase our determination and capacity to overcome troubles. Indeed, with this attitude, each new obstacle can be seen as yet another valuable opportunity to improve our mind!

Thus, we can strive gradually to become more compassionate, that is we can develop both genuine sympathy for others' suffering and the will to help remove their pain. As a result, our own serenity and inner strength will increase.

What makes you laugh?

Foremost, I have peace of mind, and I truly believe in the oneness of all of the seven billion human beings. My mind is intellectually inclined, inquisitive, optimistic and cheerful. This state of mind is naturally conducive for smile and laughter.

My first commitment in life is the promotion of basic human values and the oneness of human beings. The main cause of conflicts in our society is our lack of a concern for others. If there is love and compassion for each other, then motivation and active engagements to alleviate suffering will naturally follow. One of my main practices is altruism; this sense of concern for others brings immense inner peace and satisfaction to me. Whenever I meet people, I relate to them as my human brothers and sisters. This desire to create a loving environment may be another reason why I laugh so much.

I enjoy the company of people. I always want to meet new people and make new friends. I love smiles and wish to see more smiles — real smiles — and consider it important to smile at others. I really feel happy when I see photographs of small children smiling at one another. There are different kinds of smiles — genuine, sarcastic, artificial and diplomatic. If we want genuine smiles, we must create the conditions that make them appear.

The Indian police protect me night and day. In addition to their protection, I also appreciate their warmth and smiles. Whenever I ask people if they prefer seeing the Dalai Lama with a serious face, or a Dalai Lama with a cheerful and warm smile, they tell me they like it when I smile. We all feel good when seeing others smiling at us.

My cheerfulness also comes from my family. I come from a small village in Tibet, and our way of life is more jovial. We were always amusing ourselves, teasing each other and often joking. It's our habit. Tibetans are generally optimistic and happy by nature. Laughing is a characteristic of the Tibetans.

I have been confronted with many difficulties throughout my life. Presently, Tibet is going through a critical period. But I laugh often, and my laughter is contagious. When people ask me how I find the strength to laugh at such a difficult time, I reply that I am a professional laugher. The life of exile is an unfortunate life. However, I have always tried to cultivate a happy state of mind by appreciating the opportunities being a refugee has offered me.

My approach to life is a realistic one. Of course, problems exist. But thinking only of the negative aspect doesn't help us find solutions and it destroys our peace of mind. Everything is relative. We can see the positive side of even the worst tragedies if we adopt a broader perspective. Take the loss of our country: we are a stateless people. In addition, we are confronted with many painful circumstances in Tibet. Nevertheless, such experiences also bring many benefits. I've been stateless for more than sixty-one years. As a result, I have become a global citizen. If I had remained at the Potala, I don't think I would have had the chance to meet so many people and leaders, spiritual leaders, scientists, economists, artists, politicians, educators, to name a few. If we take the negative as absolute and definitive, we only increase our worries and anxiety. But by looking at problems from a broader perspective, we can learn to accept it as a part of life. I find this attitude very helpful.

When you get angry, do you express it?

Nowadays, I hardly get angry. In instances that normally may trigger anger, compassion arises in me instead. Generally, if we develop a healthy mental attitude, we will have a calm state of mind. Then when negative emotions arise, these will only last for a short period and will remain at the surface without disturbing the deeper state of mind.

What does strength look like to you?

If we have a sense of caring for others, we will manifest inner strength in spite of our own difficult situations and problems. With this inner strength, our problems will appear insignificant. A sense of caring for others is based on the belief that one's own wellbeing is dependent on other people's happiness.

A selfish attitude is one that remains insensitive to other people's experience of pain and pleasure. A selfish attitude will not bring about a genuine sense of contentment: a compassionate mindset will. Compassion when combined with wisdom brings about honesty, which in turn increases self-confidence. This is how we win people's trust and affection.

Another thing that is clear to me is that when we think only of ourselves, the focus of our mind narrows. As a result of this narrow focus, uncomfortable things appear huge and intensify our fear and discomfort. However, when we think of others with a sense of caring, our minds broaden. When we have a broader perspective, our problems appear less insurmountable. Having a positive mindset, where our sense of concern extends beyond our own, can really make a difference.

What does vulnerability mean to you?

There is a lot of suffering in the world today, particularly for those with limited means of livelihood. Even in this modern age, when science and technology are highly advanced, many still face starvation. It is extremely important to support vulnerable people who are facing

hardship and difficulties. It would be regretful if we fail to show compassion and empathy. Likewise, when you yourself are going through a difficult time, it would be unfortunate if you fail to use your human intelligence wisely.

One of the greatest gifts that we have as humans is our human intelligence. In addition, we have basic human values such as kindness, love, affection, patience and other qualities. When we live our lives using our human intelligence and basic human values, our lives will become truly meaningful.

Unfortunately, we are often swayed by our negative emotions. When negative emotions arise, we need to exert effort to counteract them. In the face of difficulties, we must use our human intelligence and basic human nature to prevent ourselves from succumbing to the force of destructive emotions. In short, despite our desire to be happy, we will not be able to find happiness when we are in a disturbed state of mind.

What role does love play in life?

Ultimately, the reason why love and compassion bring the greatest happiness is simply that our nature cherishes them above all else. The need for love lies at the very foundation of human existence. It results from the profound interdependence we all share with one another. However capable and skillful an individual may be, left alone, he or she will not survive. However vigorous and independent one may feel during the most prosperous periods of life, when one is sick or very young or very old, one must depend on the support of others.

Interdependence, of course, is a fundamental law of nature. Not only higher forms of life but also many of the smallest insects are social beings who, without any religion, law or education, survive by mutual cooperation based on an innate recognition of their interconnectedness. The subtlest level of material phenomena is also governed by interdependence. All phenomena from the planet we inhabit to the oceans, clouds, forests and flowers that surround us, arise in dependence upon subtle patterns of energy. Without their proper interaction, they dissolve and decay.

It is because our own human existence is so dependent on the help of others that our need for love lies at the very foundation of our existence. Therefore, we need a genuine sense of responsibility and a sincere concern for the welfare of others.

We have to consider what we human beings really are. We are not like machine-made objects. If we are merely mechanical entities, then machines themselves could alleviate all of our sufferings and fulfil our needs.

However, since we are not solely material creatures, it is a mistake to place all our hopes for happiness on external development alone. Instead, we should consider our origins and nature to discover what we require.

Leaving aside the complex question of the creation and evolution of our universe, we can at least agree that each of us is the product of our own parents. In general, our conception took place not just in the context of sexual desire but from our parents' decision to have a child. Such decisions are founded on responsibility and altruism - the parents' compassionate commitment to care of their child until it is able to take care of itself. Thus, from the very moment of our conception, our parents' love is directly in our creation.

Moreover, we are completely dependent upon our mothers' care from the earliest stages of our growth. According to some scientists, a pregnant woman's mental state, be it calm or agitated, has a direct physical effect on her unborn child.

The expression of love is also very important at the time of birth. Since the very first thing we do is suck milk from our mothers' breast, we naturally feel close to her, and she must feel love for us in order to feed us properly; if she feels anger or resentment her milk may not flow freely.

Then there is the critical period of brain development from the time of birth up to at least the age of three or four, during which time loving physical contact is the single most important factor for the normal growth of the child. If the child is not held, hugged, cuddled, or loved, its development will be impaired, and its brain will not mature properly.

Since a child cannot survive without the care of others, love is its most important nourishment. The happiness of childhood, the allaying of the child's many fears and the healthy development of its self-confidence all depend directly upon love.

Nowadays, many children grow up in unhappy homes. If they do not receive proper affection, in later life they will rarely love their parents and, not infrequently, will find it hard to love others. This is very sad.

As children grow older and enter school, their teachers must meet their need for support. If a teacher not only imparts academic education but also assumes responsibility for preparing students for life, his or her pupils will feel trust and respect and what has been taught will leave an indelible impression on their minds. On the other hand, subjects taught by a teacher who does not show true concern for his or her students' overall well-being will be regarded as temporary and not retained for long.

Similarly, if one is sick and being treated in hospital by a doctor who evinces a warm human feeling, one feels at ease and the doctors' desire to give the best possible care is itself curative, irrespective of the degree of his or her technical skill. On the other hand, if one's doctor lacks human feeling and displays an unfriendly expression, impatience or casual disregard, one will feel anxious, even if he or she is the most highly qualified doctor, and the disease has been correctly diagnosed and the right medication prescribed. Inevitably, patients' feelings make a difference to the quality and completeness of their recovery.

Even when we engage in ordinary conversation in everyday life, if someone speaks with human feeling we enjoy listening, and respond; accordingly, the whole conversation becomes interesting, however unimportant the topic may be. On the other hand, if a person speaks coldly or harshly, we feel uneasy and wish for a quick end to the interaction. From the least to the most important event, the affection and respect of others are vital for our happiness.

During one of my meetings with a group of scientists in America they said that the rate of mental illness in their country was quite high-around, twelve percent of the population. It became clear during our discussion that the main cause of depression was not a lack of material necessities but a deprivation of the affection of the others.

So, as you can see from everything I have written so far, one thing seems clear to me: whether or not we are consciously aware of it, from the day we are born, the need for human affection is in our very blood. Even if the affection comes from an animal or someone we would normally consider an enemy, both children and adults will naturally gravitate towards it. I believe that no one is born free from the need for love. And this demonstrates that, although some modern schools of thought seek to do so, human beings cannot be defined as solely physical. No material object, however beautiful or valuable, can make us feel loved, because our deeper identity and true character lie in the subjective nature of the mind.

OVERCOMING CHALLENGES

During the course of your life, what have been your greatest personal lessons and internal challenges?

I have great respect for the late Ling Rinpoche, one of my main tutors, whose presence was like solid bedrock for me to lean on in difficult times. When he left this world, although I missed him, I felt that I had to stand on my own. This experience of losing such a great teacher fueled my own determination to become stronger instead of losing hope.

Throughout my life, I have been confronted with many challenges. When confronted with a difficult situation, I first analyze the difficulty to see if it can be overcome. If I can find a solution, I resolve the problem.

If, however, the situation is beyond my control, then what is the use of being unhappy and worrying about it? This is my attitude towards challenges.

COMMANDER CHRIS HADFIELD

ASTRONAUT, TEST PILOT, SPACE STATION COMMANDER

 @colchrishadfield   @cmdr_hadfield

Commander Chris Hadfield (OC OOnt MSC CD) is a Canadian retired astronaut, engineer, and former Royal Canadian Air Force fighter pilot.

The first Canadian to walk in space, Chris has flown two Space Shuttle missions and served as commander of the International Space Station.

On July 20, 1969, after watching the Apollo 11 moon landing, Chris quietly began his mission towards becoming an astronaut – when the gap between being a young boy on an Ontario corn farm and the first Canadian to walk in space seemed unbridgeable.

Canada had no astronaut program, nor would it for the foreseeable future, but Chris stuck to it. He spent his time at home learning mechanics on the tractors and old cars, flying with his father and brothers every chance he could. Enrolling in air cadets, he worked his way up through the RCAF, becoming an experimental test pilot and flying over 70 types of aircraft. He made certain that when the opportunity arose, he would be prepared for it.

In 1995, Chris Hadfield rode his first rocket. He flew again in 2001, installing Canadarm2. He served as Chief of Robotics, CapCom, and NASA's operation in Russia, eventually going on to pilot a Russian Soyuz. During the course of his life, Chris has flown around the world 2700 times, giving him a unique perspective on life.

Do you have a favorite quote or philosophy you live by?

My philosophy is that life is limited, and you are given a certain number of skills and opportunities, and you are the result of hundreds of thousands of years of people who have had similar opportunities and similar skills in the past who have made the most of them. Your life will be most productive and most satisfying if you make the most of the skills and opportunities that you have.

This is kind of how I view life, and also that life can be unforgivingly short so don't wait for some undetermined time in the future to do something that's important to you or to celebrate the things that you have done.

What is one personal quality that you are most proud of?

I'm proud of the unlikely things that I have accomplished because they were the result of my characteristics and the choices of what I did with them. I have done some things that virtually no one has done that were extremely unlikely but also dangerous and complex.

I'm very proud of my three children who are in their 30s who are healthy and happy and productive and none of those things happen automatically.

I'm proud of being with the same woman for over 40 years. So those are the results of the daily choices that I have made and that the people around me have made.

I'm proud of those because they have taken a continuous, careful amount of work.

Having travelled around the world around 2700 times, and seeing the world from an incredible perspective, what are some of the issues that you are passionate about?

I'm passionate about people not squandering the history that brought us to where we are and not learning from it.

I'm also passionate about people having a realistic assessment of the world, not just a 'Chicken Little' assessment of the world.

The reason Chicken Little said the sky was falling was it because it made Chicken Little feel self-important, as if there has never been a major problem in the past, but now there is a serious one - so it effortlessly tends to give one's life purpose if there is tremendous drama.

That's not at all to belittle the problems that we are facing today, they are serious and complex and life-threatening, but it has always been that way, we just tend to over-exaggerate and over-emphasize the problems that we face currently.

You don't have to look very far back in history to see, of course, the horrific problems that people in the past had to face, nor do you have to do very much research to realize just how good we have it right now.

The quality of life, the number of people who are well fed, the expectation of a full life span and the probability that all our children will make it to adulthood, the opportunity for education and self-actualization.

To me, it's never been better as a human being and that's the result of thousands of years of hard work and steady progress in the human condition, in medicine, in power generation, in scientific understanding and so, I'm very passionate about people understanding how we got to where we are.

To me, that's the focus of what I am interested in. I think it's trying to share the incredibly rare and real global perspective that an astronaut gets from the window of a spaceship.

Who inspires you?

I think I had different inspirations and awareness of other people when I was 5 or 10 to what I do now that I'm in my 60s.

Some of them are very famous like, in my case, Neil Armstrong - the first person to walk on the moon. Doing something that has overwhelming complexity and risk and yet doing it well and not just doing it but finding a way to do it that was accessible and thus inspirational, and that inspired me.

I'm a fairly well-known public figure, not as known as some of the people interviewed for this book, and in some parts of the world I have no privacy at all and that's fine.

But as an example, I developed a standard coping mechanism and that is if I sit down next to someone on an airplane, I try to steer the conversation to them for as long as possible because as soon someone realizes that I have flown a spaceship then all normal conversation will cease, and everything will be just about my own personal experiences from that point on.

What I have learned and maybe everyone else knew this intuitively, is that every single person that I have ever spoken to, every one of them, knows things that I don't know and has done things that I have never done or maybe I will never have a chance to do and virtually every one of them has done something heroic, you just have to dig down and find out what it is.

They are fighting some particular battle or are taking care of some particular problem.

What does "being a man" mean to you?

I think it changes depending on the circumstances you are in.

In a primitive societal setting, some of us have to be 100% or mostly committed to child-rearing and some of us have to contend with everything else such as the gathering of food and the dangers of other carnivores and other predators.

For the first almost 300,000 years of our existence, our technology was low enough that anthropomorphism was necessary and it's what kept us alive.

With improving technology, that changes. Women are now vastly freed up to not just be in the business of child-bearing and rearing and that's a huge boon for our species.

We can take advantage of the real strength that we have which is intellect from 50 percent of our population that we haven't really been able to up until now because of the labor saving and life saving devices that we have come up with.

And so, I think the role of a man has changed and it has changed somewhat recently and in some parts of the world it's still changing quite rapidly but we still carry the inertia of the traditions that brought us here either because of societal norms or because of the threats, like in a lot of the less developed parts of the world, we still have to stick with what got us this far but for much of the world that's no longer true and so it makes me rethink the role of a man.

Obviously, you are counted on for your larger size and greater strength in some circumstances but very seldom in my life have those been the distinguishing characteristics. Almost always they have been, how can my wife and I work together as a team in order to accomplish things that, otherwise, we could not.

There was a lot of hoopla recently raised because two American women did a spacewalk at the same time, and to me, that's great, it's just sort of natural.

The most experienced astronaut in American history is a woman who has flown in space for 665 days, commanded the Space Station twice, done 10 space walks and has a PhD in Biochemistry and to ignore that or to think that that is an anomaly or to not somehow incorporate that into how I define myself as a man, is to stick my head in the sand.

It's important to recognize the strength of the other gender and therefore to choose my own path based on that, and if you don't acknowledge that I think you are perpetuating problems that are going to manifest themselves as odd behaviors throughout your life.

I think the role of a man is to make the most of yourself and to look at your particular attributes, your strengths, your weaknesses and balance those versus your passions, your loves, your desires and your hopes and then look for how to change who you are in order to approach the things that you value in life.

Obviously, as a man - none of us are ever going to bear children, we are never pregnant, we never have that biological nurturing role, nor do we have the toughness and understand the incredible agony of childbirth.

And so, to recognize that there are fundamental differences but there are also tremendous strengths on both sides

and to make the most of our own selves, not to over-exaggerate or under-estimate but to make the most of our part in the society that we belong to.

I'm always tinkering and fine-tuning this, especially growing up in a very traditional family where men do the work and women keep house.

I think part of the reason there is a lack of definition for young men right now is that balance is not nearly as necessarily clear as it used to be.

OVERCOMING CHALLENGES

Have there been any key challenges that you have had to face in your life? How have you faced them?

I think, perhaps to put it into perspective, I deliberately and irreversibly chose to be an astronaut when I was 9 years old, in a country that had no astronaut program, so I set my personal goals to do something that was impossible... so that's a challenge to overcome.

It wasn't hard, it wasn't unlikely, it wasn't difficult...it was impossible!

So, I think that's an intriguing way to look at life. To say either, "Someday I hope to be a dentist," or saying, "I am going to be a dentist."

In truth, my goal when I was 9 years old was to walk on the moon. That was my absolute measure of what I wanted to do in life and I still haven't walked on the moon - so by definition, I'm a failure!

I did not do the one thing I have set out to do - however I still may be able to if the technology gets radically better, but I'm not at all disappointed or saddened with myself.

Being inspired by something right on the edge of impossible and then using that to shape the choices of jobs and the things I have done during my life has created a fascinating life and allowed me to all sorts of things that I would never have attempted otherwise.

It has given me great things to be satisfied by - so I think that's been how I have conducted my life - to be relentlessly dissatisfied with my own level of competence and pursuing the things that are important to me, but also to celebrate all of the small joys that have come along the way...you can do both and I think it's a good way to conduct life actually.

I think we tend to honor the imitation of competence, and I think that's sort of grown in society.

As our life gets easier, then the trappings of success become very hard to distinguish from actual success.

I don't think there's much actual pride in just simulating doing something complex.

It's like going to race car driving camp for a day and coming away feeling like you're a race car driver. Or going for a ride in an airplane, and considering yourself to be a pilot, or like having someone carry you to the top of a mountain and calling yourself a mountaineer.

There is maybe a transient Instagram satisfaction in it, but you know better than anyone that you are an imposter and the real joy in life is in the reality of changing who you are instead, not pretending to change who you are.

So, I really respect and try to emulate the people who are truly working to change who they are to be closer to their ideals and not just trying to get the t-shirt!

EMOTIONS

What makes you truly happy? What lights up your soul?

Seeing joy in other people and sharing joy with other people, it can be very small such as doing something with someone or creating something together with other people or by myself.

I play music with lots of people, and the great joy and soul illumination in the creation of art especially when it's shared with other people. I love playing in a band and creating music in an original way. Obviously, I'm not the best musician in the world, that's one person and I'm not the worst musician in the world, that's one other person, I'm somewhere in the middle like everybody else.

I don't worry when I'm playing guitar that I'm not Steve Vai, Santana or Eric Clapton, that's okay. I'm a person playing guitar and creating art, and I love how that feels.

Or to do something as a team that otherwise would be impossible. I was inspired when Neil and Buzz and Mike were the first team of people that managed to walk on the moon and there are similarly amazing individual and collective human accomplishments going on all around the world all of the time... those light up my soul.

I love it when I, or the group of people around me or some team around the world, visualizes perhaps something that doesn't exist yet, like a new piece of music and then works together having to develop skills and capabilities and then accomplish something in a new way that is then illuminating or inspiring for other people. To me, that's the most wonderful thing.

How do you express anger? What do you do to release frustration?

Someone pointed out to me a while ago that if you run into one angry person who's acting like an asshole, then that's okay - but if you run into assholes all day, then you are the asshole - and I found that that was a very good mirror to hold at myself.

Some days, every single person I meet is nice. Then there's some days where every single person I meet seems to have a problem and the odds are, that's just a reflection of how angry I am that day, or short tempered or non-charitable.

So, I think a large part is not to give into transient emotions because it's easy, you can have tremendous emotional highs and lows if that's your nature or if that's your choice.

When I get angry, it's normally a frustration of things not being the way that I want them to be, whether it's my steak is too well done or there is an injustice in the world. I think it's really important to temper your own anger to the severity of the cause or the severity of the issue and to have a little control over your own anger.

But very few things get done in the world without someone being dissatisfied with the way things are and that's just another form of anger.

I think you are well-served to treat your anger like any other state you might be in like tiredness, or rest, or strength or weakness. It's just a transient state of your own self so try and dig to the cause of why, and then not just succumb to your most base and easy actions that fall from it but in fact to temper yourself.

There's nothing wrong with anger, it's how you act that matters.

If you find yourself constantly angry, it's probably not everybody else, it's probably you and therefore, address it, and think about it; "Why am I angry, what am I angry at?"

There's a pretty good chance I'm angry at myself and so why would you be angry with yourself? Probably because you're doing something that you shouldn't or you're not doing something that you should.

You should start thinking about how you need to change the external influences that are in your life or change who you are to be able to more closely get to what it is you want to do.

> *"If you find yourself constantly angry, it's probably not everybody else, it's probably you and therefore, address it, and think about it, "Why am I angry, what am I angry at?"*

What does vulnerability mean to you?

We are all extremely vulnerable - try shutting off the power to the internet for a week!

The veneer of civilization that allows us to pursue our simplest interests is extremely thin and requires a tremendous amount of cooperation so to think you are invulnerable is delusional.

I think you need to have some humility and some thanks. When someone describes themselves as a self-made man, it makes me laugh!

You didn't bear yourself, you didn't give birth to yourself, you didn't suckle yourself, you didn't build the education system, you didn't knit the clothes, you didn't build the power system, you didn't build the society...you are the lucky recipient of all those things.

You may have been able to create something being given all of these great advantages, that's good, that's what you ought to do. But the notion of a self-made man is pompous, and a balloon easily pricked.

So, I think vulnerability is really just another way of saying thankfulness and self-awareness. You need to put it into your own perspective, you don't want to be overwhelmed by your own limitations, everybody has their own weaknesses and their own imperfections and that's normal, just accept that.

As an internationally known astronaut I've got to meet lots of people, figurehead people, famous people. I've spent a night at Windsor Castle with the Queen and Prince Phillip, I've met rock stars and Presidents, Prime Ministers and actors and such and the conclusion I have drawn is that everybody is having troubles, they're having personal troubles and family troubles and friend troubles - and all of those are just forms of vulnerability.

I saw an interview with Paul McCartney – and he's such a measure of individual and musical success - and he said he often feels insecure and insignificant and I thought, "Wow, if Paul McCartney feels that way, then everybody feels that way." That's immensely heartening to hear that.

Vulnerability is necessary and its part of who we are but don't let vulnerability dominate your decision-making, just recognize it's normal.

Despite your lack of abilities or your passing weaknesses, you still are living your own life, no one is going to live it for you. Accept it, there's great strength in it, there's a humility that comes with vulnerability and a recognition that you need the help of others, that's normal, everybody does.

Don't let it be your defining characteristic but don't pretend it doesn't exist.

RELIGION AND SPIRITUALITY

Do you have a spiritual practice and is this something you did in space?

Your time in space is scheduled every five minutes for the entire six months that you are up there. There is mission control in Houston, in Montreal, Munich, Moscow and in Tokyo and they all work 24/7 in order to schedule your time down to five-minute increments for the whole six months that you are on the spaceship.

It's funny... the weird David Bowie Space Oddity, thinking space is lonely and desperate, and Elton John using it as a metaphor for loneliness in Rocket Man for a gay public figure in the 1970s, and the way they recently did First Man with Ryan Gosling portraying Neil Armstrong and how space flight is so sad...it's not sad at all!

It is joyful, it is beautiful, and spectacular, and passionate, and busy, and productive and one of the great life experiences.

It's kind of funny that people broadcast their own biases onto other things inaccurately.

However, we do talk of faith on the space station over dinner, which is the time for conversation. About two or three times a week we would have enough time to actually eat all together and that's a great time to talk about what brought us there and what stirs each of our souls, and it's a very honest place.

Everybody there had some set of soulful guidelines or spirituality, whether it's a regular named religion or whether it's just the way they conduct their own lives and find peace within themselves, everybody has some great strength to be there otherwise we could never have persevered through the decades of unanswered work that got you there.

With the incredible stimulus of the entire world going by the window every 92 minutes, of seeing the whole world in 90 minutes. Recognizing the undeniable smallness of our planet. If you can go around it in 90 minutes, it is not very big.

So, it puts aside our human imagined differences - as if there is some vast difference between a person in Botswana and a person in Boston, when what they need and what they desire in life is virtually identical.

They were just maybe raised with a different faith and a different set of opportunities, but everybody wants the same thing.

That is a self-evident truth outside the window the entire time you're on the ship, but if you never leave Botswana or never leave Boston, it's a lot easier to convince yourself that you are somehow unique or special, or that other people are somehow less than you.

The humility that comes with the reality of seeing the world helps to color those conversations of personal faith and strength.

RELATIONSHIPS AND FAMILY

In what ways have the women in your life influenced the man you have become?

The woman who has had the biggest influence in my life is my wife, Helene, just because I have spent more time with her than anyone else.

Women and men are different obviously and that's great, we need it of course, and the various ways they deal with life is different. I have a much different maternal instinct than my wife and it wasn't me that bore our children and such.

Rather though than saying how a woman has influenced me, it's more "How have you listened to people who are different to you and how have you incorporated their difference into your own decision-making?"

The fact that I'm with the same woman for over four decades just means that I have had close daily interactions with a person who is biologically different than me and therefore has a different perspective on the world and it's made me a much better person.

Listening to her different views, seeing how she values things, and helping her through her demanding parts of life and vice versa.

I also think, it doesn't have to be a woman, it can be two gay men...I think you can find exactly the same lessons and values in that someone just has a different vantage point or viewpoint than you. You shouldn't dismiss someone because they are different from you.

I don't want to just say it's necessarily my wife or a specific woman - but life alone, where you are choosing to be alone, I think is less interesting.

As an example, I toured Europe as a 17-year-old with a friend and I realized at the time that where if I couldn't grab his sleeve and go "LOOK AT THAT!" it would have been an emptier experience.

To be able to share the wonders of life and the wonders of the world and the magnificence of difference with somebody else, especially with someone else who's different than you are, so that they notice stuff that you didn't notice, and they can point out to you when you're being an idiot...it's easy to convince yourself of some very strange things when you're on your own.

I count myself very lucky to have been with the same woman for all that time. The two of us have created a very interesting and successful life, based on love and mutual respect and mutual learning, and also recognizing that we are not the teenagers that we started out as.

So, try and find a partner in life that you are passionate for and that you respect and who thinks differently than you do and then build yourself and continue to create yourself, with the guidance of that person. Look for ways to support them and don't define yourself by the attributes of your partner, instead allow the attributes of your partner to improve the overall whole of the two of yourselves.

My wife would never define herself as an 'Astronaut's wife' and I would never define myself as my wife's profession with an apostrophe 's' husband... I'm not a 'Chef's husband'.

Finding different, beloved people to be next to you, in order to help explain life to yourself and to help to improve your ability to deal with life, is hugely important.

JOCKO WILLINK

FORMER U.S. NAVY SEAL OFFICER; CEO, ECHELON FRONT

 @jockowillink   @jockowillink   Jocko Podcast

Jocko Willink is a retired U.S. Navy SEAL officer, co-author of the #1 New York Times bestseller *Extreme Ownership: How U.S. Navy SEALs Lead and Win*, *Dichotomy of Leadership*, host of the top-rated Jocko Podcast, and co-founder of Echelon Front, where he serves as Chief Executive Officer, leadership instructor, speaker and strategic advisor. Jocko spent 20 years in the SEAL Teams, starting as an enlisted SEAL and rising through the ranks to become a SEAL officer. As commander of SEAL Team Three's Task Unit Bruiser during the battle of Ramadi, he orchestrated SEAL operations that helped the "Ready First" Brigade of the U.S. Army's First Armored Division bring stability to the violent, war-torn city. Task Unit Bruiser became the most highly decorated Special Operations Unit of the Iraq War.

Jocko returned from Iraq to serve as Officer-in-Charge of training for all West Coast SEAL Teams. There, he spearheaded the development of leadership training and personally instructed and mentored the next generation of SEAL leaders who have continued to perform with great success on the battlefield. Jocko is the recipient of the Silver Star, the Bronze Star, and numerous other personal and unit awards.

Upon retiring from the Navy, Jocko co-founded Echelon Front, a premier leadership consulting company, where he teaches the leadership principles he learned on the battlefield to help others lead and win. Jocko also authored the *Discipline Equals Freedom Field Manual*, a New York Times Bestseller, and the best-selling *Way of the Warrior Kid* children's book series.

Do you have a favorite philosophy or quote you live by?

My favorite quote, and the one I live by, is "Discipline equals freedom."

I'm not a very complicated person to figure out. Someone just asked me, "If you were dying and on your deathbed, and none of your books or podcasts were left and everything is going to be gone, what would be the three statements from you from what you've learned in life, what would you say?"

I said, "Take extreme ownership of what's going on in your world; discipline equals freedom; and there is a dichotomy in life that you have to stay balanced on."

Those are the books I've written – *Extreme Ownership*, *Discipline Equals Freedom: Field Manual*, and the *Dichotomy of Leadership*.

Those are the things I operate on and believe in.

There is always a dichotomy in life – you need to keep your ego in check, but if you completely subdue your ego, guess what? Now you're not driven to be successful, or win, and that's not good.

If you control your emotions to a point where you're not showing them anymore, well now you're not connecting with anyone and no-one's going to follow you because you're a robot and human beings don't follow robots.

Even with discipline, if you impose so much discipline in your life that you start to stifle your creativity, well guess what? That is a problem.

Even those have to be balanced, and that's why the dichotomy of leadership and the balance of life is so important.

What drives you and the work you do?

I am just trying to convey some of the lessons I've learnt in my life so that other people didn't have to learn the same lessons the hard way.

People make the same mistakes all the time – human nature drives them in the same direction. A lot of mistakes people make are driven by their ego, clearly that comes out a lot. A lot of people make the mistake of letting their ego drive their decision-making process which is not a good plan, and I would say finally – people have a tendency to behave or react in extreme ways when balance is required.

People have a problem with maintaining discipline in their life – and if you have a problem with that, it's going to lead to a lot more problems in other aspects of your life.

If you have neo-control over your emotions, if you can maintain balance and discipline in your life, you will be on a much better path.

What is one personal quality that you are most proud of?

To exhibit pride in some quality of myself would indicate that I don't think I have room for improvement, which would not be true. I don't look at myself with any high level of pride.

Something I'm grateful for is that I am a hard worker. Whether I enjoy it or not, I'm still going to get it done.

I think I just lacked a high level of natural talent in many categories and the only way I could make up for that was just by working hard.

Who has been the most important role model in your life? Has there been someone who has led by example?

I don't really go to anyone for advice, but there are a few people I look up to.

One of them is Colonel David Hackworth, who was one of the most highly decorated soldiers in the army. He came in at the tail end of World War II and then he fought in Korea and he was a Battalion Commander in Vietnam. He was highly respected by everyone around him, up and down the chain of command.

He wrote a couple of books, including *About Face*, which is the best book I've read about leadership and I read it all the time. I take a lot of lessons away from that.

The other books that I read which inspire me are usually about soldiers, marines, sailors, airmen who have fought, and made great sacrifices and overcome great challenges.

"You have to have strength to keep your emotions in check, you have to have strength to keep your ego in check, you have to have the strength not to behave in extreme ways when you may feel that. It takes strength to maintain discipline on a day-to-day basis."

The themes of everything I talk about are embedded in all these historical books and documents, and the themes are recurring over and over again for thousands of years. That's the way it is.

As Miyamoto Musashi said, "If you see the way broadly, you see it in everything."

When you start to understand the principles that I talk about, you see them everywhere and when you see people doing well, doing right and winning, you will see that they follow those principles.

When you see people losing and falling apart, you will see that they are not following these fundamental principles.

EMOTIONS

What makes you truly happy?

Being alive is good! Helping other people, that makes me feel good, because you get to see people do something they thought they couldn't do or move in a direction they didn't think they could move or achieve something they didn't think they could achieve. That's satisfying.

What does strength look like to you?

You have to have strength to keep your emotions in check, you have to have strength to keep your ego in check, you have to have the strength not to behave in extreme ways when you may feel that. It takes strength to maintain discipline on a day-to-day basis.

There's physical strength, which is being actually strong; having the strength of character to persevere through problem areas; and then moral strength to stand up when something's going on that you don't think is right.

What does vulnerability mean to you?

Part of the ideal and principle of extreme ownership is taking ownership when things go wrong – that means when you mess something up, you say, "Hey, I messed this up." It also means that when you're facing a situation that you don't think you can handle, you say, "Hey, look – I'm in over my head here, I need some support."

This is called humility – and yes you have to have that. How do you cultivate that? You cultivate that by acting that way.

If the people on my team see me say, "Hey guys, I'm not in a good situation, I don't know what to do right now. Can you give me some suggestions?" If you do that, the next time they're in a situation that they don't understand or they need help with, they will raise their hand. So, if you model that behavior, that behavior becomes part of the culture of the team.

LIFE PURPOSE AND SUCCESS

How do you define success?

Obviously, you've got short-term success that you might be looking at – for me, what I define success as is helping as many people as I can.

Trying to teach people the lessons I've learnt the hard way and trying to get them to learn them the easy way. If I can pull that off on a broad scale, that's great.

On a daily basis, when I talk to people or companies or communicate with others and I can give them a piece of information that they may not have had, that's being successful as far as I'm concerned.

What are some of the life lessons that you have had to learn the hard way?

Everything from extreme ownership, to mission clarity, acting decisively, cover and move, decentralized command, keeping your ego in check, prioritize and executive, discipline equals freedom – all those things are things that didn't get taught to me, I had to learn them.

How do you best determine balance in your team and in your leadership?

You absolutely have to take feedback, and you have to pay attention, because you're not always going to have people who verbalize feedback to you.

You have to be able to observe and identify what's happening to see if you're getting out of balance with your team, out of balance with your family, or getting out of balance at some point in your life.

You have to always pay attention. The feedback doesn't always announce itself – it's not always going to be an email in your inbox. You need to pay attention, read and react to what's going on and modulate the various parts of your life so that they become balanced.

And by the way, you'll balance one part of your life today and tomorrow it will be off-balance again and you'll constantly have to make adjustments. It's not like you can reach a steady state.

I can tell you to do something right now, and the next day the advice will be different, because the battlefield has changed. It's not going to work the same way. So yes, you have to apply thought to your life.

Yes, be stoic; yes, be aggressive; yes, be dominant – but if you take those too far, you'll put yourself in a bad situation. So, you have to be balanced, and it applies to both men and women. It's part of being human, that's the way it is.

RELATIONSHIPS AND FAMILY

How do you maintain balance in your life between work and family?

What I tell people is that if they focus too much on their work and providing for their family, they'll look up and not have a family anymore. If they focus so much on their family that they don't focus on their work, they'll look up and not have a job anymore.

So, you have to find a balance between the two – and that's something you have to modulate on a daily basis. You know what? You're not going to be able to go to every dance recital, or every ball game for your kids and that's the way it is.

I was deployed over and over again in a big giant swathe of my children's life, and I'm not the first person to ever do that and that's been going on with men for thousands of years.

People know how to deal with that, kids know how to deal with that, families know how to deal with that – it's not easy but it's normal. For me, when you're doing your job you focus on it and do the best you can, and when you have time and you're with your family, you give the focus to them.

Everyone asks how you balance it. You just balance it, that's what you do. Just like being on any team, you explain what you're doing and why, and then you invite feedback.

When I was in the military, and I was gone all the time and I was focused much more on my job than I was on my family, I just had to explain to my wife, "Hey listen, right now my biggest focus absolutely has to be this SEAL team or this SEAL task unit. We're going to war and I'm responsible for these guys, and the best thing I can do for them and their families and for me and our family is to focus on being prepared for war."

When you met your now wife, how and when did you know she was the one? What are the values behind your relationship?

We met in a pub, and I knew I was interested in her because she was this stunningly beautiful woman and I saw her across the room and went up and talked to her and it turns out she was actually nice as well, which was a pleasant surprise! Yes, I knew immediately that if I could convince her to be my wife, I would do my best to do that.

She cooked a prime rib recently, and it was amazing – she knocked it out of the park, and I wanted to renew our vows!

My wife has a great understanding of my personality and she does her best to provide the support needed to allow the personality to move at the pace it wants to move at.

We don't really have conflict – I don't get emotional, I de-escalate situations quickly, I take ownership if something's wrong. It's pretty straight forward.

DR DEEPAK CHOPRA

AUTHOR AND CLINICAL PROFESSOR OF FAMILY MEDICINE AND PUBLIC HEALTH, UNIVERSITY OF CALIFORNIA

 @deepakchopra   @deepakchopra

Deepak Chopra MD, FACP, founder of The Chopra Foundation, a non-profit entity for research on well-being and humanitarianism, and Chopra Global, a modern-day health company at the intersection of science and spirituality, is a world-renowned pioneer in integrative medicine and personal transformation. Dr. Chopra is a Clinical Professor of Family Medicine and Public Health at the University of California, San Diego and serves as a senior scientist with Gallup Organization. He is the author of over 89 books translated into over forty-three languages, including numerous New York Times bestsellers. His 90th book and national bestseller, *Metahuman: Unleashing Your Infinite Potential* (Harmony Books), unlocks the secrets to moving beyond our present limitations to access a field of infinite possibilities. TIME magazine has described Dr. Chopra as "one of the top 100 heroes and icons of the century."

Do you have a favorite quote or philosophy you live by?

Love in action!

Love without action is meaningless, action without love is irrelevant but when you practice love in action, you can accomplish the impossible.

What are the issues - whether social, environmental, political or economic - that you feel are most pressing and for which you feel the greatest personal concern and responsibility?

Generally speaking, I don't worry about anything at all. I have no self-concern because I know that existence takes care of itself and existence is not just human existence, it's all existence.

So right now, climate change, social injustice, economic injustice, war, terrorism and climate change, health, wellbeing and happiness are all entangled, they are all inseparable. They are not separate entities.

We have a distressed ecosystem and worrying about it is not going to do anything and having hope also is not going to do anything. We need creative solutions and creative solutions come when there is emergence, when you have maximum diversity of talent, of training and opinion and maximum diversity of background.

Like humanitarians, social workers, scientists, technologists, neuroscientists, geneticists, environmentalists, poets, story tellers, entertainers and educators. When they all come together, we can create an emergent ecosystem of shared vision complementing each other's strengths and having a problem that they can find a solution together then we can actually create a more peaceful justice. Otherwise, we are ready for extinction and as far as the universe is concerned, humans may be the cancer.

It might be good for the planet if humans disappear, but I think if humans don't disappear and become part of the web of life which we are ultimately an expression of nature, then we can reverse everything including climate change and bring about a sustainable planet, a healthy planet and a joyful planet. We need to have shared vision and complement each other's strengths and also connect emotionally and spiritually. Today we can do this through technology and create online and offline communities of support and that is what I am doing with a project right now www.neveralone.love. It is exactly what I am talking to you about.

"Love is more than a sentiment or emotion. Love is the ultimate truth at the heart of the universe which means that we are the same spirit in different manifestations. When we experience that we fall in love with ourselves and our world. Because the world is our own manifestation."

Who inspires you?

Today, no one.

In the past there has been Buddha, Jesus Christ, Nelson Mandela, Mother Theresa, Mahatma Gandhi and many other people who are not famous.

Actually, today I could say to some extent President Barack Obama, but otherwise I can say only in the past.

LIFE PURPOSE AND SUCCESS

What do you ultimately strive for? What is your mission in life?

I would like to see a critical mass of awakened beings that can help us achieve a more just, peaceful, sustainable, healthier and joyful world.

OVERCOMING CHALLENGES

Have there been any key challenges that you have had to face in your life? How have you faced them?

In the beginning I thought there was because everybody was very critical, almost hostile to my worldview. I realized after a while that if I was going to be affected by criticism then I wouldn't be able to do anything, so I decided not to be personally affected and sought to be open to feedback. The moment I made that decision there was no challenge internally.

Can you articulate this worldview that other people were critical of?

The worldview that other people are critical of comes from ancient non-dual wisdom traditions which regard consciousness as fundamental reality and the physical material world as a perceived reality that is essentially a projection of consciousness. The two worldviews have been in conflict for thousands of years. For example, Plato was an idealist, and his student Aristotle was a physicalist. Today, this conflict is referred to as the "mind body problem" or the "hard problem of consciousness".

How has failure, or apparent failure, set you up for later success? Do you have a "favorite failure" of yours?

Yes, I was trained with some great academics and I didn't agree with them, so I actually had to leave my academic training for a while and that was very challenging. I didn't have any money and had to work in an emergency room just to pay my bills. It was a very good lesson for me to say, "Stick to my truth and ultimately everything would be fine."

If I had stayed in my fellowship of endocrinology that year, I would still be in a lab looking at rats, that's not a very attractive life to me.

I'm glad I did have the academic training, ultimately, I got my thoughts in internal medicine and endocrinology so I could use that knowledge and training to do what I do now. I'm very glad that I was part of academia and also glad that I didn't stay there as I would have failed that and now, I am successful because I had the guts to walk out.

EMOTIONS

You outlined earlier that 'Love without action is meaningless, action without love is irrelevant but when you practice love in action, you can accomplish the impossible.' Can you define what love means to you?

Love is more than a sentiment or emotion. Love is the ultimate truth at the heart of the universe which means that we are the same spirit in different manifestations. When we experience that we fall in love with ourselves and our world. Because the world is our own manifestation.

What makes you truly happy?

Gratitude for existence and the fact that I have a loving family and loving relationship with the world.

How do you express anger? What do you do to release frustration?

Every emotion has a biological response, and every emotion is actually necessary and that includes anger.

Anger is the animal response to threat so when a primate is threatened it goes into a fight or flight response which is a survival response so anger is built into our system as is fear. Fear makes the animal take refuge through flight; anger readies the animal for combat. Every emotion has a biological function.

Right now, anger is turning the world to hostility which is a very different thing. Hostility is the desire for vengeance, which is very toxic, anger can be a good release.

Anger is remembered pain, fear is the anticipation of pain in the future, guilt is the direction of pain at yourself, and depression is the depletion of energy as the result of these toxic diversions.

The process is always to feel your body to not judge what you are experiencing, just replace it and express it with yourself, share it with someone who is intimate, do a ritual for release and then let it go. I have been doing that now for the last forty years, so I don't experience anger.

I do experience impatience but not anger.

What does strength look like to you?

Strength is self-esteem. The progressive realization of worthy goals. The ability to love and have compassion, vulnerability and the power to manifest your dreams. It also takes initiative, calculated risks and willingness to step into the unknown.

What does vulnerability mean to you?

Vulnerability simply means strength and power. It means asking yourself, 'What am I observing, what am I feeling, what do I need, how can I be vulnerable and request the fulfilment of this need in every relationship?'

In my view vulnerability is power.

"Anger is remembered pain, fear is the anticipation of pain in the future, guilt is the direction of pain at yourself, and depression is the depletion of energy as the result of these toxic diversions."

What makes you laugh?

The ignorance of the world.

We have a world that is ready for extinction and people are behaving as though life is normal. If they are ready for extinction, they should go to the bar and get drunk.

Everything that are known issues today are solvable so that makes me frustrated, but it also makes me laugh. How come as human beings we are not even in our adolescence? We are still infants. I laugh because that's the way it is, we can't do anything.

SPIRITUALITY AND MINDFULNESS

You are known for your insights and teachings of mindfulness and meditation. What do you do to relax and connect with your inner self?

I am always relaxed and connected with my inner self. I currently do nothing. As a practice I am grounded in Being. However, after saying that, I enjoy three hours of meditation, yoga and pranayama everyday including diving deep into the nature of my physical death.

What role does meditation have in your life in managing stress?

I do not manage stress because I do not have stress. Meditation allows me to get in touch with my soul, infinite possibilities, spontaneous evolution.

How has gratitude impacted your life?

I have lived with gratitude all of my life. It allows me to live without hostility.

BEING A MAN

Has your concept of masculinity changed and evolved over time?

I never had the masculine identity which is so popular in the west. I grew up in an environment where all of us, boys and girls, embraced both our masculine and divine archetypes.

What advice would you give to your 14-year-old self?

None. My 14-year-old self was a 14-year-old self and would have behaved exactly as he was. Giving advice to your younger self is an oxymoron. The younger self would not like to listen to self anyway.

RELATIONSHIPS AND FAMILY

In what ways have the women in your life influenced the man you have become?

My mother and my aunts had a very important role in my life, they made me understand that we have both the divine feminine and the divine masculine in our own self. The divine feminine nurtures beauty, nutrition, affection, tenderness and creativity and the divine masculine brings action and responsibility. I have always embraced both the divine feminine and masculine in my own life.

What qualities are most important for you in being a father?

I have been spending a lot more time with my family but also, I have a very special relationship in that we don't engage in political or ideological arguments, we allow each other to express ourselves and that we also have immense emotional bonding and we do not impose ourselves on each other.

My wife has always taken care of the children and grandchildren. I have been involved, of course, but I am much more involved now and yet in a way I realize that each person, child, or grandchild has their own life to live and their own purpose and unique expression.

In our family the relationships are always to allow everyone to do exactly what their passion is, and that has worked very well for all of us.

LAIRD HAMILTON

BIG-WAVE SURFER AND PHILANTHROPIST

 @lairdhamiltonsurf   @lairdlife

Laird Hamilton is best known as an American big-wave surfer and pioneer in the world of action water sports. In addition to his affinity for the water, Laird is labeled as an inventor, author, stunt man, model, producer, TV host, fitness and nutrition expert, husband, father and adrenaline junkie.

Laird has appeared in a number of feature films and surfing documentaries including *Radical Attitude* (1992), *Wake Up Call* (1996), *Step into Liquid* (2003) and *Riding Giants* (2004) where he also served as executive producer. He also performed as a stunt man and surfer in *The Descendants* (2014), *Water World* (1995), *Die Another Day* (2002) and *Point Break* (2015).

In addition to his film work, Laird has appeared on numerous television shows such as Oprah's Master Class, Charlie Rose, 60 Minutes, Chelsea Handler, Conan O'Brien, Steven Colbert and The Ellen DeGeneres Show.

When he is not busy surfing the biggest waves in the world, inventing new water toys and appearing in Hollywood features, Laird is a philanthropist. He has always had a great passion for helping others live a happy, healthy life, as exhibited through his work with non-profit organizations such as the Surfrider Foundation, Race Across America, Pipeline for a Cure for Cystic Fibrosis, Rain Catcher, Muscular Dystrophy and City of Hope.

Do you have a favorite quote or philosophy you live by?

I live by a lot of them, and first of all quotes and parables is a great way to learn and to teach and apply. Mom said to me, "If you can't be true to yourself, you can't be true to anyone."

There's so many but if I had to pick one, that would be the one. It has to start there. It has to start with you and your ability to be honest with yourself and that's where the growth comes from. Then you can go outside that and use the adage of "Straighten up your own yard first before you go help somebody else."

What are the issues - whether social, environmental, political or economic - that you feel are most pressing and for which you feel the greatest personal concern and responsibility?

I think for me it's values. What are our values and what's important to us?

The reprioritization of values - where are we putting our energy?

The Dalai Lama has a great quote when they asked him what his thoughts were on humanity, and he said it's interesting you know, "Men will give up their health to get wealth and then they have to give up all their wealth to get health."

How we go about the pursuit of accumulation and get more stuff and then we are stripped away like we are in the situation right now with the coronavirus and this probably magnifies it right now more than it ever has.

Then we go, "Wait a second, health, family, people I care about, community, I want my friends close by, a good meal, a good night's sleep." The irony is we then look at nature and we see nature really thriving, the animals are feeding and breeding and it's all good, they're not affected by this, nature doesn't need any more.

It is probably why religion has been so dominant in human history, it's all about values and if you ask, "What are your values, what's important to you, what do you care about?" If you want to make a shift, you need to lead by example.

Of course, I always care about the planet, I'm really connected to nature and she's not happy right now, she's not stoked. I'm a consumer like everyone and I'm at fault as much as anyone, but I think there is a big disconnect.

It comes back to the values, what's important to you. If you say nature is important, the earth's important, well then you might conduct yourself differently. But if you dump the trash in the ocean and then fish it out and think it's all going to be okay; it doesn't work.

We need to take care of where we are, it's a pretty cool spot.

Who inspires you?

I don't think I put that burden on any one person, I look to try to find truth and it comes out of all kinds of places that you might not expect. You know what they say, "From the mouths of babes."

I think it's about being open to and looking for truths.

I've followed quite a bit of Jordan Peterson's work of recent times and again, I find it coming from all places and then that becomes the interesting thing and not putting the burden on any one person. We are all falling short, we are all incapable of the responsibility of somehow being a prophet or something like that, we know that doesn't work, it's more like where can I find things that I relate to.

We have so much access right now, more than we ever have had in the history of the world. The amazing thing is we have the most access sitting in our hands, yet we choose to use it for the things that are the lowest attribute...we have this amazing technology, but we go and watch dumb, crappy, stupid stuff that makes no sense.

We have this tool that lets you access all knowledge!

LIFE PURPOSE AND SUCCESS

What do you ultimately strive for? What is your mission in life?

Firstly, I would like to be a good man, a good father, a good husband, a good friend and I would hope that I have the opportunity to be able to maybe teach people they can do things they didn't think they could.

I have always enjoyed helping people and I think that is my higher calling, that's something I can do.

Whether I have done this through athletic pursuits or ideas and innovation. Somebody from the outside could look at this differently but it's never been from a selfish position, it's always been about sharing.

Someone asked me recently about getting older and honestly, when I was little, I saw myself being old and having young men come to find me to seek ideas. I like that the young and the hungry come to me to search for knowledge or insights.

I've had this in me for a long time and it seems like that there is an aspect of that, that has come to fruition and I realized

that it's probably my highest calling.

I think we have lost that a little bit these days, the respect for the elders, the old wise men...I'm not going to say I'm wise or anything but the dynamic of looking up to the elders has gone.

I had that in my life with Don Wildman who was 30 years to my senior. I looked to him and respected and admired a lot of his traits. I have many older guys that I look to and, suddenly, one day you are in that position. One minute you're looking up to a guy and then you turn back and there are guys looking up at you. It's pretty interesting and that transition is undetectable.

I remember one time I was with a group of monks meditating and we were in a position and I looked over at the monk and asked if there was ever a time when this is not uncomfortable, like how much time does it take until it's not uncomfortable?

The monk said to me, "Never!" I was like, "What do you mean never?" He goes, "It's always uncomfortable, it's supposed to be, so you are in the present."

How important is collaboration and teamwork to achieving success?

Well first of all, humans are communal creatures, we operate best in communal or team settings, that's where we excel.

In the past we were great hunters, and we could take prey down, but with multiple people you can take on bigger prey and with multiple people you can really build a village. The saying that two people working together does the work of three individuals.

One thing for sure is that loneliness is death and if everything you ever did was not seen by anyone or no one was with you when you experienced it, it greatly diminishes your experience. If you are alone and going, "Wow, that was amazing, I'm glad I did that or glad I survived that," it's a different experience.

When you go through experiences together, you bond in a way that you can't really do any other way, you can't make a bond without experience no matter how you feel about them.

It's built into the human psyche that we need the human bond, it helps us survive.

As someone who has done things individually and in partnerships, the level of what you can accomplish together is amazing.

When you are doing something by yourself, after a while, you kind of need to get affirmation. Maybe I'm out of my mind and what I'm doing isn't that great. Then you have someone come along and go, "That is amazing, that's incredible!"

We need that affirmation and support.

If you're an innovator or whatever it is you do, the confirmation is that you have people join you, it's like religion, everyone believes what you believe and that confirms that what we feel is special.

Even people doing individual things need support. A solo climber, for example - they still need people to support them and when they finish, everyone gives him the affirmation that is part of the human desire and is a mechanism for our own survival.

OVERCOMING CHALLENGES

How has failure, or apparent failure, set you up for later success? Do you have a "favorite failure" of yours?

I have had a few and they usually resulted

in the thought of dying, the belief that I'm going to die.

The result of that has definitely made me change the way I have approached things.

I've been lost at sea, I've had plenty of times in the ocean where I thought I was going to die, I grew up getting taken out to sea in rip currents and thought I was going to die every time.

I have had so many moments and I think that that is the story of my life, these failures are what has made me.

I had a big fall last year and the guy that was with me said, "Oh my god, you fell, you never fall!" I was like, "Let me get something straight, I have had more falls and wrecks than most people's successes and maybe some of the most horrific crashes, and some of the most horrific failures in surfing."

The result of these has also provided the opportunity for the successes; there's not one without the other.

There is no success without failure, that's the marriage! If every time you did something you were successful, you wouldn't appreciate it.

That's the danger we run into when we create situations where everyone's a winner, no one is a loser...hang on, that's going to be a problem.

One of the teaching methods we use is failure, and my failure list is long. It has absolutely enabled me to do the things I've done and the methodical approach that I've taken, the planning and training and having these major injuries has led me to push myself. Like a broken leg, the equipment broke so we've got to make it stronger, we've got to make it better and able to survive.

I think there is something to be said in never giving something too much value.

The ability to fail and ignore it is a good trait. Fail, ignore, get up, don't indulge yourself in it. That can stop you, it can limit your success and I think that people run into that and when they fail, the fear of doing that again can hold you back.

I have a concept that I have been talking about for a long time, called *Crashing*. It's about the skill of failing, and it's a skill, if you can get good at it, you wipe yourself off and get back to it, get your brain clear, and start again. There's an art to that. It's the unrewarded art of failing that you don't get rewarded for, people don't say, "Hey that was a great failure!" but without that ability to fail you don't succeed.

Everybody who is good at anything knows how to fail at it - unless the failure killed them.

They can take things from the failure that they can use next time to help them and it could be one little nugget each time but over the years these build into instruments that allow you to avoid those bad situations in the future.

America loves this concept, we like to bring them up and then knock them back down, we love the Cinderella story and rising from the trash and bringing them up again until they fall again, they keep coming up and coming back stronger. America loves this!

EMOTIONS

How do you express anger? What do you do to release frustration?

One thing I know for sure for me personally, I need to be worn out, I need to be tired and then I need to be well rested with proper nutrition and I have a lot of good techniques for wearing myself out and it makes all the difference in the world for me.

I run and when I run, I'm very cooperative – and I know it. I'm fortunate and blessed that with my lifestyle I can wear myself out every day.

And then – reacting slowly. I react slowly to situations and being fatigued may help that! Moving slowly and pulling back and not being reactionary, not reacting to emotion in the moment. If I can just take a couple of breaths and think about it, I completely change my response.

Believe me, the thing rears its head daily and sometimes I react in a way that I don't admire or respect about myself. It's an ongoing effort but I have a couple of tools that help me with it, and I think when I realize its fear-based, then I'm like, "Okay, now what are we talking about?"

If it's fear-based, what am I scared about? If I'm not scared, maybe I'm not angry?

My daughters can still poke me in a spot that I'm not ready for, and these are ever evolving processes we need to learn. I think when you're really good at it, you're done here – you're complete.

What does vulnerability mean to you?

It's obviously some sort of reward that I seek, there's reward from vulnerability and it feels good to be vulnerable because it's honest.

The truth is we are all vulnerable always. To pretend we're not, well then, you're lying to yourself and we're back to the saying, "You can't be true to anyone if you can't be true to yourself."

Being vulnerable I think is the most honest thing. You don't have to look over your shoulder – you're not having to look around, because you're open. There's a reward to that.

Look at history, I mean Jesus would tell you that. You can drive nails into my hands and poke me with your spear, you don't get to be much more vulnerable than that.

There is something about vulnerability that brings joy and a certain happiness to you because of the honesty – you almost feel like you've been cleansed. There's an aspect to having yourself out there and saying, "Here I am!"

It could be in front of a giant wave and then you survive it and you're like, "Wow, that wasn't as bad as I thought it might have been," and sometimes our vulnerabilities are created – and the situation may not have been as bad as what we thought it might have been.

Do you talk with anyone or have a group of friends you can talk to about how you feel when things are happening in your life, or do you keep these thoughts internalized?

I have a core group of friends and people that are around and I'm pretty open about stuff, I don't hold it back, I don't close it down, I get rid of it consistently, there's not a lot of build-up and I've done that forever.

My wife, Gabby, always laughs about it. I talk about the pressure cooker a lot - if you just keep letting the pressure off it doesn't build up but if you don't, then the thing blows the lid off. So, there's something to be said about letting stuff out on a regular basis so it doesn't happen without some control.

I think a lot of it can also be connected to faith. If you don't believe that it's going to be okay or you doubt if you are going to get through, if you don't believe that stuff - it's going to build up on you.

I'm an optimist, I have a tendency to believe, I have faith that I'm going to make it and that keeps stress at a certain level.

SPIRITUALITY AND MINDFULNESS

Do you have a practice that you use to put your mind and body into a peak state?

It's not something really obvious, I think my mindfulness comes from my discipline and the way I conduct my life, there is an aspect to my preparation that feeds into my psychology where I don't have regrets, I don't look back and question.

I have eliminated a lot of those insecurities. Firstly, I believe that I can and also the way I approach each challenge. I do a lot of breath work and heat and ice sessions and there's a mindfulness aspect to all of my training.

My mind is the part of me that allows me to challenge myself or not and any stressful situation helps you deal better in another stressful situation. If you are stress tolerant and you practice things that are stressful on a regular basis, I think there's a certain relationship with stress that enables you to not let it affect you.

There's a mindful practice to my life, when I sleep, when I wake, how I eat, all of those aspects. For me the biggest challenge is trying to be a nice parent and that's taking a lot of mindfulness right now.

BEING A MAN

What does "being a man" mean to you?

Well, it's a dirty job!

In my opinion being a man requires you to do the dirty work you know. I hate to use it but when the toilet breaks, you're the guy, you're the one on call and that's a metaphor for life. When things are crappy, when things aren't going great, it's time to man up and you have to be steadfast in that.

The way the world is now, I think we have to have a heightened sensitivity to the complexities of what's going on. Men have been able to hammer their way through and right now that's not working, you have to be a little more aware. I always talk about compassion as part of the solution.

Have your concepts of masculinity/being a man changed over time? Is it significantly different from when you were a teen?

I think it's a little bit like searching for the truth, seeing what works. I'm reading a book right now about a bunch of different admirals and there's something that I say all the time and the guy says it in a little different language, "Sometimes the example of how not to be is better than the example of how to be."

You have one idea when you're younger on what it is to be a man - they have certain attributes.

There are certain attributes amongst all of them that are the ones you are attracted to and as you start to understand different men, you really see that a lot of behaviors are based on fear and being scared.

I think as a man, you say masculinity is tough, but there's so many different faces of toughness.

Again, I go back to compassion, being compassionate and having that sensitivity and all the physically toughest guys that I've met, are usually the sweetest, the nicest and the gentlest. They almost go the other way before they would go to the physical side and you realize that toughness is a state of mind and that there's guys that aren't physically threatening, but they are so mentally strong.

There's a military saying that I always liked that I often quote, "Slow and smooth is fast."

It's like Napoleon and people say what a brutal guy he was, but he had a trait where he used to get mail. He wouldn't open it; he would put it away for a while and open it later. He would react differently, in a calmer way, reacting after time.

As I have got older, I've evolved. You start off when you are young, and it can be scary. You haven't made a place for yourself, you don't have a wife and a house, you haven't hunted, and you haven't caught prey as an example of being able to provide. You're scared, you can be aggressive and angry and then you need to use that as a driving force, harness that fear and that anger to drive you.

As you age, you may have success in whatever it is you're pursuing, you get a family and all of a sudden there is change. You need to decide that aggression is not sustainable - first of all, it's not good for you. Being angry, which basically means being scared, is not sustainable.

Then you need to think about contentment, "Maybe I'm being content with what I have and I'm okay."

If there was a single piece of advice that you could give every young man in this world, what would it be?

Oh man, that would be a long conversation!

It probably sounds like a cliché, but the fact is I would say, "Be patient." When you're young, it can't happen fast enough and I still have to remind myself now of that.

I think the ocean has trained me to be patient like when you are relying on the weather to bring you something special.

If you can build patience into your life, you won't have the disappointments that you didn't get the things you thought you were supposed to.

I would also say, don't drink. Whatever you do, don't drink.

RELATIONSHIPS AND FAMILY

Who has been the most important role model in your life? Has there been someone who has led by example?

My mom, she's the one. She passed away some time ago.

"There's a mindful practice to my life, when I sleep, when I wake, how I eat, all of those aspects. For me the biggest challenge is trying to be a nice parent and that's taking a lot of mindfulness right now."

You have a tendency to get disappointed in life when you put too much pressure on people and you look at somebody and go okay, "You're a role model" but then they do something and stuff up and you don't totally respect that.

For me personally I've cherry-picked things that I have admired in people, like being honest and respectful...these attributes that I've picked but maybe because I didn't have someone who was in the position of being a role model. It was an ambiguous thing, there were a couple of people - but they weren't role models, so I am going to try to become the thing that I think is a role model, given what I know.

Maybe I haven't seen what I would like to be. I've seen things in people that I admire but I never saw it all in any one person, which makes sense to me because we are all individuals.

I would like to be the man that I believe would be someone that I would admire and respect, let's just say that.

I don't want to put a burden on anyone and possibly be disappointed. No expectations, no disappointments.

What are some of the values that underpin your relationships with women?

I can say one of the traits that I admire - and it started with my mother and then with Gabby, and I see it in my daughters and it's starting to show more in my girls as they grow - it's their work ethic.

Guys think they work hard! I'm like, you can work hard breaking a rock for eight hours but I'm talking about the consistency of the details and the volumes of life and the relentlessness of their compassion.

The depth of their empathy, the volume of details, and the ability to organize and get things done and that they can love us...it's pretty cool.

I look at Gabby and think, "Wow, it's amazing - you can put up with me almost better than I can!"

Has fatherhood changed you?

There is no doubt that fatherhood has changed me as a man in more ways than I think, and in ways I don't even understand.

I describe being a father as like making a Samurai sword, you take steel, you heat it, you beat it with a hammer then you stick it in ice. You do that over and over and over.

Your kids take you; they heat you up and then they stick you in a bucket of ice. There's a tempering that occurs and a patience and tolerance develops that you didn't even know existed in you.

A willingness to just serve that you didn't know existed. I need to serve my girls in ways that I'm confused by. The level in which you need to serve is to the point you would throw yourself in front of a bus for them and serve them at the highest level.

One thing I wanted to say too, I've been pretty consistent in talking about it in the past when people say, "You have kids, and you do these things that are dangerous."

I've seen it in other people who say, "I used to do this stuff, I used to be daring but now I don't." Well, that's wrong, you can't put that onto your kids, they didn't ask you to have them, they are your choices.

It's important for your children to see you doing something that you have spent your entire life becoming skilled at and what that does to you, I think that's very important.

PATTY MILLS

NBA PLAYER, SAN ANTONIO SPURS

 @balapat   @patty_mills

Patty was born on August 11, 1988 in Canberra, Australia. His father Benny is from the Torres Strait Islands, and his mother Yvonne is an Australian Aboriginal originally from the Kokatha people in South Australia.

Patty plays with the San Antonio Spurs in the NBA and is the only Indigenous Australian to win an NBA Championship (2013/14 season). He is also a triple Olympian (Beijing '08, London '12, Rio de Janeiro '16) and currently represents the Australian Boomers.

Patty has founded the Team Mills Foundation to support women and underprivileged families, culture, diversity and enact change in the environment.

Do you have a favorite quote or philosophy you live by?

I didn't have this quote growing up as a kid, it came later to me in my career and it's by Bob Marley and he says, "My life nah important to me, but other people life important. My life is only important if me can help plenty people. If my life is just for me and my own security then me no want it. My life is for people. That's way me is."

It was something that I felt so connected to because of the position I have gotten to in my career as well as understanding all the people that I can possibly inspire and positively impact their lives as well. It's a very special piece for me.

What is one personal quality that you are most proud of?

If I was to say one thing, it would be the act of staying true to who I am and never being ashamed of who I am.

Coming from experience, I realized you don't have to change who you are to think that you can succeed. I think that's what a lot of people with my background believe. There are so many barriers and walls up that they feel like they have to change, like they are only going to be accepted if they change.

It's not true at all and that's something that I would like to pass on.

You seem driven by helping people, where does that come from?

That just comes from my culture to be honest. Coming from a place with such rich traditions and cultures and then growing up in an environment outside of that and also knowing that not many people from our culture have been able to get to a certain point. I have just always seen myself as a role model for my people and in its simplest form, it's the understanding of community and what you need to do to play your part to help the community thrive. My sense of community is where it really comes from.

What are the issues - whether social, environmental, political or economic - that you feel are most pressing and for which you feel the greatest personal concern and responsibility?

When we talk about issues and the ones that concern me the most are social equality and sustainability. Class, gender, race and culture. When I think about this, I relate it back to my culture as well and everything that affects. Then there's sustainability and the environment and how to look after the lands so we don't continue to have wildfires throughout our countries. When I talk about the oceans and how to look after the reefs, everything leads back to caring.

I see it everyday living in Texas with the oil and gas and when I look at it through my culture and everything that we do where we live off the land and how important the land and the ocean is to us because we need our source of food and everything including life comes from that, so when you see it being torn up for other reasons its heart-wrenching.

Who inspires you?

Professionally speaking, Cathy Freeman from a cultural, professional and athletic standpoint and how she fused all of it together.

Mom and Dad with their experiences growing up and their ability to make such an impact on communities through their work.

Also, Eddie Mabo and Martin Luther King, these types of men that have preached their entire life and their messages are still felt today. At the end of the day, it's almost like I'm just another part of pushing their messages.

Indigenous culture is so deeply rooted in discussion and storytelling, how do you feel the western world compares?

That yarn, the sit-down storytelling about culture does not happen enough anymore. There is a real lack of ability just to sit and listen and acknowledge and understand – and that's something within our culture where it plays such a big part. It helps you to calm down to sit and listen which at the end of the day is a great skill. Storytelling has played a big part of my life growing up.

BEING A MAN

What does "being a man" mean to you?

I like this question.

With my background of culture, family and sport I think what being a man means to me is diversifying the qualities of being a man. I believe you can only do this if you have enough respect for yourself to acknowledge and understand that there are different qualities needed for different environments.

The thing I would relate this to is on the basketball court or in a sporting environment, where the quality of being a man is one thing, but you can't bring all that energy home and have it the same way with your family. There's a different set of qualities of being a man when you walk in the house and you have a family. I think it's acknowledging this and understanding it first that you do have to diversify and have qualities in different buckets, if you like.

Have your concepts of masculinity changed over time?

I think this has developed and continues to develop.

I moved to the other side of the world at around 18 or 19 years old which gave me a perspective that's so different from what my culture is and what I was brought up with. I continued to see what being a man means in different environments.

It continues to develop, and it will continue to grow when I'm a parent.

If you could have a conversation with your younger self, what advice would you give yourself?

I think the first thing would be, "Grab a seat, little one, and buckle in, this isn't going to be short. Have some patience, we are going to talk story and have a good yarn."

The main message for me has always been the ability to respect yourself so you know how to respect everyone else around you.

This applies in so many different situations on a daily basis and if you can't get that down at an early age, you might not ever

get it. Respect is huge in our culture, both Aboriginal culture and the Torres Strait Islander culture and it starts with respecting yourself, so you know how to respect others.

LIFE PURPOSE AND SUCCESS

What do you ultimately strive for? What is your mission in life?

To be honest I don't think I have found it and I'm not necessarily out there looking for it at the moment. As I go about my career and find myself in situations to be able to help inspire others, I guess you could say that's the closest thing to it. I get so much fulfilment out of helping people and it has a reverse effect where it inspires me to keep doing what I have been doing and do it better. That might be my mission, I don't know yet.

I think of our people and where I come from and to now be in a position where I can give back in ways that can make a meaningful impact.

Both Mom and Dad have unbelievable histories, and Dad sacrificed so many things to the point that he brought education back to Torres Strait because there wasn't a great system there. So, I guess it's always been in our family to give.

How do you define success? At what point did you identify as being "successful"?

I think my story is still being written, so when it's all said and done, and I don't mean just basketball - that's when I'll be able to really look at this question.

I set my goals and then try to accomplish those, whether it's sports or other parts of my life, so maybe some goals; yes, I have achieved those. But to answer the question, I don't think that I know what success is yet, I'm still working on that by going out and working it out, but it's still being written.

OVERCOMING CHALLENGES

Have there been any key challenges that you have had to face in your life? How have you faced them?

Whether it's been injuries, racism or cultural challenges - I think I have had a lot of adversity, but they have all helped me get to where I am right now. Getting injured in a sporting environment is inevitable. Adversity is something that you have to take on and enjoy that process of overcoming that adversity.

Would I wish that all upon someone younger? No, I think there's probably other ways to get where I am now.

How has failure, or apparent failure, set you up for later success? Do you have a "favorite failure" of yours?

I'm not sure if this is a failure but as an only child, to dream of achieving greatness in sport and in basketball and to sacrifice so much that is completely opposite to my culture and my traditions.

It was tough to remove myself from my sense of belonging to my homeland to pursue this dream, and in my heart of hearts I knew that if I could do this and achieve something and chase my dream and get there, I could inspire others to chase their dreams.

I had an inkling of this at a young age which kept me determined but I could always see from friends and other families that - although they didn't say it - I was

moving away and I wasn't following the normal path.

I felt they may have thought, "He's gone, we've lost him, he won't know who we are if and when he makes it." However, I realized you can go and chase your dreams and still understand who you are and never forget where you have come from.

That's the best advice I can give to someone - you might be in a small community dreaming of something big, it can still get done without you losing your identity of who you are and where you are from and your accomplishment can inspire so many other people.

I get this from my role models that I've mentioned. Eddie Mabo is an example when you talk about land rights, his fight for land rights was because a western society of people from another culture was trying to tell him the rules of his own land.

"There is a real lack of ability just to sit and listen and acknowledge and understand – and that's something within our culture where it plays such a big part. It helps you to calm down to sit and listen which, at the end of the day, is a great skill. Storytelling has played a big part of my life growing up."

EMOTIONS

What makes you truly happy?

Being able to inspire people and help people that are in less fortunate situations than I am. It's the ability to help that truly makes me happy and the joy that I get from seeing the impact that has. Whether it's a big impact or a small impact, if I'm able to help in some way shape or form, that means a lot and it goes a long way in terms of self-fulfillment.

I created the Team Mills Foundation to make a positive impact on communities worldwide. We have a great sense of community and the Foundation is based on the values that have been passed down from generation to generation.

How do you express anger? What do you do to release frustration?

Being from essentially a calm culture, it's almost a meditation, I don't mean going into a Zen space, it's more the ability to take deep breaths and walk away from a situation and really being able to calm yourself down.

Sometimes I feel I do it better and I shorten that fuse of time and am able to calm quicker by doing this.

Sport has definitely helped me as has my culture. Growing up with racism has actually helped by being able to walk away from very heated moments and take the high road. It's helped me to be able to walk away when anger is present, or I feel that coming on.

What does strength look like to you?

I say mental toughness, and I say that knowing that mental health is a big part of a lot of men. Again, it's one of those qualities that means different things depending on the environment, but I feel strength comes from mental strength more so than anything physical. It's the strength to have the qualities of being a man, whether it's respect, empathy, appropriate fear and back to acknowledging and understanding having strength to be vulnerable in certain situations.

What does vulnerability mean to you?

You have to first accept vulnerability and recognize that you are in that position. At times I think people try to defend themselves or ignore the fact that they might be in that situation.

That's the first step for me, recognizing and understanding it. Being able to truly let go in those situations and not have your guard up, not bottle everything up... doing that doesn't make you any more of a man.

Truly being able to let go in vulnerable situations is needed and if it ends in tears, then so be it, it's part of the process.

SPIRITUALITY AND MINDFULNESS

What role does religion or spirituality play for you?

A big part of Aboriginal and Torres Strait Island culture is spiritual in a sense; your connection to the land, the sky, the sea and the stars is everything and it's something that I still feel very connected to every day. Even being on the other side of the world, that connection is stronger than ever. I can sit here today as a 32 year old, living on the other side of the world and can say that I still practice culture and everything that comes with that on a daily basis. I was brought up with story-telling, so when things aren't going great for me, I can turn back to my culture for guidance and sense of purpose.

What pastime or practice enables you to relax and connect with your inner self?

Meditation is something that is big in sports and in my process of getting ready for a game it's something I do. A lot of my meditation comes to me through song and dance.

I do a lot of traditional dancing and the songs and hymns that are sung in my culture are all spoken in language. There's a part that when I am listening to these songs being sung by family, I get into a deep mode and all the feelings and emotions come out of me when I'm dancing or even singing in the car on the way to a game.

It's how you connect these things and relate it to what you do on a daily basis and I really feel the power of it.

A simple connection for me is my jersey number in the NBA is #8.

One of the reasons that I'm number 8 is Malo is the god of Meriam which is Murray Island in the Torres Strait which is where my family is. My grandmother is from there and Malo comes in the shape of an octopus. An octopus has 8 tentacles that also represents the 8 tribes that are now on Murray Island and one of those tribes is my tribe, Dauer Meriam.

So, when things aren't going great, I can go back to this and know who's back there and connect with the stars and the sea and then I go, "Alright, I'm ready to go again, let's get this thing done!"

RELATIONSHIPS AND FAMILY

Who has been the most important role model in your life? Has there been someone who has led by example?

Mom and Dad, without a question. Both of their stories are so intense and deep and meaningful and educational - without a doubt, they are the two who have made me who I am today. I have idolized everything that they have done in their own lives and then how they have tried to guide and help me navigate through my life as well.

Every now and then I look into how they would have dealt with certain situations and I'm sure I will continue to do that. I guess that's a fortunate thing about being an Indigenous Australian and having an Aboriginal mother and a Torres Strait Islander father, you get the best of both worlds!

"Coming from experience, I realized you don't have to change who you are to think that you can succeed. I think that's what a lot of people with my background believe. There are so many barriers and walls up that they feel like they have to change, like they are only going to be accepted if they change."

In what ways have the women in your life influenced the man you have become?

The role of strength, all of my strength is from my mom, and knowing what she has been through in her life.

Mom is from the Stolen Generation and how she was brought up is incredible and nothing that I have gone through in my basketball career or life outside compares and I assume that these are challenges or adversities, but nothing that I will go through will be in any way shape or form as hard as what Mom went through.

Other people who are from the Stolen Generation, especially mothers on both ends of the fence whether it was the child that was taken away from her mother or the mother who lost her children and had to find strength.

Looking at what happens in today's society and today's world, it's still affected and has an impact because of what happened to these women, it's still very traumatic.

How do you maintain the right balance between your career and your family?

I have no family over in America, they are all still in Australia. In San Antonio it's just my wife Alyssa and our little pup Harvey and the balance that I find is knowing that I can go to work, play basketball and leave it on the court and come home and be who I am.

The sheer commitment of who we are in understanding our cultures and being able to continue with that helps me stay connected to back home.

WIM HOF
EXTREME ATHLETE

 @iceman_hof   @iceman_hof

Over the years "Iceman" Wim Hof has put a number of extraordinary achievements to his name, including 21 Guinness World Records. Extensive training enables him to control his breathing, heart rate, and blood circulation and to withstand extreme temperatures. Here are some of his most memorable achievements:

- Running a half marathon above the Arctic Circle, barefoot only wearing shorts
- Swimming underneath ice for 66 meters
- Hanging on one finger at an altitude of 2,000 meters
- Climbing the highest mountains in the world while wearing shorts
- Running a full marathon in the Namib Desert without drinking
- Standing in a container while covered in ice cubes for extended periods of time

Wim's motto is: "What I am capable of, everybody can learn". With his Wim Hof Method, he teaches people from all over the world, including celebrities and professional athletes, to control their bodies and achieve extraordinary things.

MY LIFE

My oldest child is 37 years old and my youngest is 3 – it's amazing! It gives me all colors and all levels of perspectives.

I am much more conscious and I'm much more experienced, but, let me tell you – you get a baby at my age and you've forgotten about it all! It's all new! It's amazing how the miracle of life displays itself. To me, it's a daily journey – I love it!

I had my first relationship with a woman who left me after 15 years through a suicide – she was schizophrenic, and she jumped off a building that was eight stories high. She was the mother of my four children.

That happened in 1995, and of course, I was heartbroken. Psychiatry could not help her – all the injections and medicines and pills could not help her. It happened over many years, going into darker and darker places. I was helpless and I had to continue with four children alone, with very little money.

My discipline in what I'm doing got me completely through.

Cold water makes you still in the mind and the breathing exercises change your chemistry. I learnt to do that every morning at 4am, before the children got up, and every day I was present and completely there for them.

We created, slowly but surely, a new life. We've done really well, and right now they all work with me and we have a business that is spreading the news of a great method all over the world. It's growing, growing, growing and we have a very powerful bond together, rooted in the loss of my wife and their mother. It has bound us and brought us together.

We got out of this and I found a new relationship, and I was not pre-meditating having another child, it just fitted, and there it was and here I am.

The method is spreading all over the world, and we are helping so many people and we are fundamentally changing science, as it is. That's because what we have found was not in the books and now it's changing the books. That's all from major challenge - the body and mind coming from a very dark place from the loss of a mother – emotion, emotion, emotion. You can't grasp emotion – only time you can learn to come out and deal with this deep grief.

Iced water is really making your mind still, and when it becomes still you change the patterns of everyday grief. You learn how to survive and to purely "just be."

With four children, you see the purpose of life – you've got to be there! You can't be depressed, you can't be emotionally

suppressed or captivated in your mind – you've got to go, you've got to be, you've got to feel!

You've got to answer them, you've got to be on top of everything – and that's what, ultimately, has got us to be able to demonstrate what science is not showing – and that is emotion. Emotion is the biggest one – if you talk about "real men" – I talk about "real emotion".

That's what children want to know, that's what the new generation wants to know. Emotion is deep nature, and for deep nature you have to go deep outside in nature, to learn how to control.

When you get divorced, or there's a suicide, or a mother loses her son or daughter, when we have not learnt how to deal with our emotions from deep in our physiology – our breath, body, and of the unseen – then we are lost.

We are lost when something is too big for our normal control.

When I lost my wife, I actually gained something from the universe through the love for my children to rise like a phoenix from the unknown to now, knowing.

We are going now to a deeper place, neurologically, transcending physical, mental, religious, and cultural differences, and people need to come together in love – it's the way we are built! Life is to be loved.

When you're in love with someone, you don't think – you fly! Learn to love life and you will fly!

For example, if a tree expels what we need, and we expel what a tree needs, we are one with nature. All this gibberish in the mind should shut-up and we should go deeper and understand oneness.

A book like *Men: Real Conversations* is good – it shows an absolute direction for the world and how to become one with it all, and how to gain absolute confidence and power, by getting back to core values – which is happiness, strength and love.

You will be driven from the inside – and that makes a real man. And those real men will be able to pass on a heritage for the new generation and the world.

Do you have a favorite quote or philosophy you live by?

"Get high on your own supply!"

"Shut up your mind"

"Breathe motherf*cker!"

Really get deep into yourself, become a man, control yourself, get into your chemistry. In nature, there is plenty for everyone - it's the inner power, but we live too much in our comfort zone.

We have the ability to f*ck up the whole world, but we cannot find our own happiness, strength and health.

We have no control over nature because we ARE nature. We should come back into harmony with nature. After building big buildings, bridges and shooting rockets to the moon, now it's time to come back to the beauty of this paradise that's called earth, in harmony with nature.

It's not simple to become simple, but do it.

"When you're in love with someone, you don't think – you fly! Learn to love life and you will fly!"

Who inspires you?

I have a lot of heroes – Mandela, Gandhi, Socrates – he loved the cold!

What would we be though if we were always looking up to someone? I'm not looking down – but I'm also not looking up to nobody. I see the best in everybody. That's what you and me are doing in this book – it's giving absolute direction on where to go. We are the future for those to come. We present the love of life.

If there was a single piece of advice that you could give every young person in this world, what would it be?

Just be happy, strong and healthy – the rest is bullshit!!!

EMOTIONS

How do you express anger? What do you do to release frustration?

If you go into cold water, anger has no place. If you go into cold water, conflict has no place. If you go into cold water, the residue of the rest of the world is washed away.

If you do that regularly, not just once – I do it every day in my icy swimming pool, and I love it – all these worldly things are washed away.

Together with these breathing techniques, which evolved from the cold water – you learn to breath deep – and breathing deeply changes your chemistry. I've learned how to do that.

When my wife passed away through suicide – I really had to be in the here and the now and get into the depths of myself every day. That is what I did with military discipline every morning at 4am with the breathing and ice water, and it made me a happy man, a cleansed man – still with the grief – but I was cleansed. I could function for my children; I could function emotionally free from the burden of a broken heart.

We have to go back to innocence. Back past any difference and into the moment. When that is there, everything becomes righteous, you radiate like the sun, and its good energy.

But when it is blocked and twisted in the mind, and conflict is there, you will be burnt and become unhappy and the chemistry and the immune system will be deregulated.

The breathing techniques and the ice water is amazing, but in the end, you need the belief. The belief that we are actually real men and real women. Real men make real women. Real women make real men. When they come together, there is no conflict. There is oneness.

LIFE PURPOSE AND SUCCESS

What do you ultimately strive for? What is your mission in life?

I am into changing the knowledge of accessing the depths of the brain, how to change the mapping of the human will related to DNA, the building-blocks of our life.

A man on a mission never sleeps! He is always on the go, he is driven. We will pave the way for those to come.

Everyone has a purpose and mission to go past conflict and to go past dualism. The mind keeps on thinking gibberish through politics, indifference and separateness.

Real men go past their fears, their inhibitions, their blockages, their differences and they create peace. Peace within and from peace within, you create peace out there, and people will be drawn to that peace.

It's like being like the sun – once there is peace, there is no drainage through the mind of energy – you just animate energy.

That's me – I'm not into money, I'm not into business – I've never been. For that, my son is doing excellent work. I had 12 managers before my son became my manager – and he is a lot better! I had no money when I was with these other managers, and suddenly my own son is bringing me financial freedom, but I don't care – I am still the same.

Fifteen years ago, I earned €7 an hour doing truck driving because I had to work – with all my beliefs and practices, people thought I was strange.

Belief makes a real man.

How do you define success?

The principle of success is to do something together. If you go and do it alone, you do it fast, but if you do it with a group, you go far. We are social beings. We are built to be in love with each other. When a group develops, consciousness grows.

What do you think was your main quality that led you to your success?

You feel a deep sense of injustice and that is your trigger to do something. You don't know at that moment which direction to take or what to do, but you will find it on the way. You just cling to that gut-feeling that something is wrong, and something needs to be done.

You face your anxiety, you face your conditioning, you face your fear while growing. Just try and just do it. You go one way, it doesn't work; you go that way, it doesn't work – but the third way will work! From there, you build stepping stones, you become stronger, you learn how to tackle fear, you become more confident and you get a hold of yourself. That makes a real man. And then the journey only begins.

The journey becomes incredible – because you are transcending differences and to transcend what makes you full of anxiety or always thinking that you are helpless or that you don't know your purpose.

If you don't, you submit yourself to the daily conditioning of 9 – 5 like everybody else. How boring is that! You are built to be not boring, and to be going for it every day, and to feel that you are alive!

Just start to live – I'm not afraid to die, I'm afraid not to live.

I make sure – every day - I'm alive! I go into swimming pools – and the cold always cuts like knives through you, and then you get through this, and suddenly the cold is no longer there, and the adversary is no longer there, and the stress is no longer there. You have become one within.

OVERCOMING CHALLENGES

Have there been any key challenges that you have had to face in your life? How did you maintain the energy to keep going?

That's an interesting question – many failures and much oppression and suppression I have suffered and experienced. Frustration can go as far as you let it, and you can face it and turn the table.

I lost my wife, I have got no certificate, no diploma, no degree, nothing whatsoever. I ain't got nothing. There I was, always trying to bind things together. It's hard working in a system that is dependent on certificates and diplomas and degrees.

There I was – I've learned the power of the cold – and the cold teaches you how to deal with deep stress. The cold is really merciless and righteous. It taught me everything I need to know, into physiology and the mind, and it let me tackle it all and to endure all these so-called frustrations, limitations, blockages and grief.

RELATIONSHIPS AND FAMILY

You have raised a strong, happy family – what's the key to your communication with them?

Communication comes from self-confidence. Children have to learn to stand on their own. What I show them is that true communication is every day in uninhibited love for life and making jokes - stupid jokes - to crush the mind that wants to become complicated with some blockage or some dilemma, and which consumes too much energy.

I make stupid dad jokes that open up any communication! People begin to laugh – and when they laugh, it's all open again! That's the foundation of communication.

I've got the love for my woman, I've got the love for my life, and we are sharing that!

You've got to laugh every day, and you've got to love every day.

ANDREW KURKA

PARALYMPIC AND WORLD CHAMPION ALPINE SKIER

 @andrewkurka   @Andrew_Kurka

Growing up, Andrew Kurka wanted to be an Olympic wrestler.

But an ATV accident he had when he was 13 years old derailed those plans.

The accident, which happened in 2005, broke his back and left him paralyzed. A couple of years later. a physical therapist introduced him to skiing.

Andrew started alpine racing when he was 17, and now competes in the slalom, giant slalom, super G, downhill and super-combined events.

As a World Champion medal winning para-alpine skier, Andrew qualified to represent the U.S. Paralympic team at the 2014 Winter Paralympics in Sochi for his debut Paralympics.

On March 10, 2018, Andrew won the downhill at the 2018 Winter Paralympics in Pyeongchang, South Korea, his first Paralympic medal.

Do you have a favorite quote or philosophy you live by?

I adopted it when I was young and just started skiing. It's "Life's short, live it fast." It epitomizes, to me, what it means to keep pursuing perfection in every little thing. It's essentially "Life's short, never stop pursuing."

What is one personal quality that you are most proud of?

My fortitude and grit, even when things seemed hopeless in life - from the loss of my leg function to concussions, where I forgot my name. The one thing I always had was grit, I was able to tough it out, to find a perspective and new way of looking at things that helped me to keep pushing forward.

What are the issues – whether social, environmental, political or economic – that you feel are most pressing and for which you feel the greatest personal concern and responsibility?

Simplifying life is something I have always been guilty of. I feel people constantly complicate it, whether it's to find reasons to dislike another or to even dislike themselves. I think the one thing this world needs more of is for people to work at caring. To work at helping others, to work at helping our planet, to work at helping themselves. Changes for good don't happen by sitting idly by.

BEING A MAN

What does "being a man" mean to you?

Being a man, to me, means being the best version of myself. Someone that the rest of the world, whether it's men, women or children, can look up to.

Have your concepts of masculinity/being a man changed over time? Is it significantly different from when you were a teen?

With age masculinity seems to change for all men personally. Whether gay, straight, trans, bi-sexual. Young, old or somewhere in the middle. To me, being masculine is simply a man who chooses to be the best version of himself, no matter what he chooses to be. When I was younger, I thought it was lifting heavy weights, being the fastest runner, having the toughest chin. Now I still respect all those attributes equally, but I've come to realize some of the most masculine men in this world lead with their heart and with a pen.

What qualities are most important to you as a man? Why are they important?

Integrity, to me, is a personal battle we all fight. It is the epitome of your true character. Who are you when no one is watching?

How have you trained your heart and brain to respond to scenarios? Do you choose to do the right thing instead of the popular thing?

These questions are just a few questions that define integrity. Integrity envelopes the rest of the moral structures and questions, which is why I think it is the most important.

If there was a single piece of advice that you could give every young person in this world, what would it be?

My one node of advice to every young person would be to do your best, at whatever it may be. Find the thing that best defines you and work at it. Never stop working, whether it be on the thing you love or working on yourself, never stop and you will never have a regret.

EMOTIONS

What makes you truly happy?

Happiness for me has always been in the simple things. The small goals. I try to set some every day so I may move forward and achieve every day. I can go on to conquer the world, in my own way. This way I can never look back in despair or disgust. Because I have achieved – whether it be a little or a lot – I have still achieved.

How do you express anger? What do you do to release frustration?

Emotions have always been difficult for me, a weakness – a constant struggle. It's taken a lot of work, asking others how they deal with it and seeing how others handle themselves has really helped.

My weakness has always been the lack of emotion. In my mind I have learned to analyze the situation from almost a third-person perspective. Even when it comes to fear, I lack fear in the presence of logic.

I see things for what they are, and for what I need to do, to make the best of that situation. I explain that, so that maybe if you have the opposite issue, you might be able to use logic to assess it better and control your emotions.

What does strength look like to you?

Strength to me is epitomized by a quote from Christopher Reeves, "A hero is someone who has overcome, in spite of overwhelming obstacles." Whether it's a single father or single mother that has to work nonstop to supply for their family, an Olympic athlete that overcame the worst possible scenario, or a man that simply never gave up despite every failure. Strength to me is perseverance in the face of everything that could ever go wrong.

What does vulnerability mean to you?

Vulnerability, to me, is being able to put pride behind you or beside you for the betterment of others and the situation being faced.

Sometimes your pride is afraid that others will see you as weak. Sometimes your pride is afraid that honesty won't work out in your favor.

One of the hardest things I have ever had to face consistently in life is putting my pride beside me so others may walk in front.

What steps have you taken during times when you have felt stressed or down? Do you talk with anyone about how you feel when things are happening in your life, or do you keep these thoughts internalized?

Whenever I feel stressed or down, I use that negative emotion and try to make a positive action out of it. I take that emotion and drive it into something positive as I try to find a solution. When I find multiple different options, I present it to my friends and family or present them to the problem I'm facing, to try to work through a solution.

OVERCOMING CHALLENGES

Have there been any key challenges that you have had to face in your life? How have you faced them?

Key challenges in my life have consisted purely of painful failure. In some instances, embarrassing failures. From crashing in my first Paralympics and breaking my spine for the third time, to breaking my femur or crashing in a completely inconsequential, unchallenging portion of a racecourse. Then there was failing to find the funds to keep pursuing my dream. The one thing I did in all these situations that helped me to accomplish and to achieve victory was I faced the failure, I faced the challenge, and I faced the embarrassment.

I learned from it and focused on being a better version of myself so I would never have to face that again, or if I did, I would know how to handle it.

How has failure, or apparent failure, set you up for later success? Do you have a "favorite failure" of yours?

My entire life is filled with failure, filled with loss, filled with regret, filled with pain. It's those things that remind us we are alive. It's those things that make us better versions of ourselves. Without that catalyst in life, we would never become truly better.

LIFE PURPOSE AND SUCCESS

What do you ultimately strive for? What is your mission in life?

My mission in life, to put it simply, is to accomplish my goals and dreams and to help others in the process with what I love and how I love it.

How do you define success? At what point did you identify as being 'successful'?

Success to me is defined by accomplishing a goal you've been striving for. It could be simple, it could be complicated, it could be a dream. A lifelong obsession or something you've been working towards. The moment I achieved true success was when I achieved the Gold Medal at the Paralympic Games – the moment I became the best downhiller in the world. Something I had failed at many, many times and strived for my entire life. There's plenty of other things in life I haven't achieved yet, and many more successes to come.

What makes you feel fulfilled and energized?

I am energized by the thought of success, and the the work I know it would take to achieve it. I am energized by the thought of knowing there's someone out there working harder. That there is someone out there who was born more talented. That there was someone out there that was pushing hard to achieve the same success I strive for. That feeds my energy.

RELIGION AND SPIRITUALITY

What role does religion or spirituality play for you?

Spirituality is a large part of perfecting yourself. To me it is extremely important because, in many many instances, the problems in life come from within.

If you prepare internally and analyze yourself, you can often have solutions no one else could see. That comes from looking inside your own soul, your own mind, and analyzing yourself to seek perfection.

Is meditation a regular practice for you? If so, please describe the role it has in your life.

Yes, meditation is a key part of success. For me it's just a few minutes of quiet before bed. Or even driving on the road with the radio off. I find myself looking inside my own head and finding solutions to problems I may never face.

I find myself visualizing success and thinking about the next step I need to take. Or sometimes when I take that moment to slow down and reflect, I realize I need exactly that, to take a moment to take a break so that I can return stronger. Without that meditation or sense of focus, I find it becomes easier to be overwhelmed.

What pastime or practice enables you time to relax and connect with your inner self?

For me, connecting with my inner self is finding something I love and reflecting

with it or reflecting on it. In my life it's fishing - it's quiet and it's with nature. I still have to work at achieving a goal and try different things. But it's nice to let my mind wander a little while fishing.

RELATIONSHIPS AND FAMILY

Who has been the most important role model in your life? Has there been someone who has led by example?

Growing up, my wrestling coach and my mother played a large role in my life. My mother was a single mom, who worked hard to supply for her two boys. The hard work showed me a clear example of what it takes to overcome. My wrestling coach gave me that outlet, to take what my mother had taught me, and apply it directly to life and the wrestling mat. I'll never forget the moment I won my first state championship, I walked off the mat and my coach didn't hug me, didn't give me a high five, and he hardly smiled. He looked me in the eyes and said, "Remember in this moment, there is somebody better out there."

The fire of success in my life was planted that spark when I was just a boy.

In what ways have the women in your life influenced the man you have become?

Women naturally have the strength of love and compassion where most men lack it. My mother, my grandmother, did things most women wouldn't fathom. They worked harder than most men and achieved things most couldn't. All the while being loving, emotionally caring, and going out of their way to be kind.

That on its own is inspiring.

BRAD KESELOWSKI

NASCAR CHAMPION

 bradkeselowski   @keselowski

NASCAR champion and Rochester Hills, Michigan-native Brad Keselowski is recognized as one of the most prolific drivers in all of NASCAR. Brad competes full-time in NASCAR's premier division, the NASCAR Cup Series, driving the iconic No. 2 Ford Mustang for the legendary Team Penske.

Brad also competes in select NASCAR XFINITY Series races behind the wheel of Team Penske's No. 22 Ford Mustang. Since joining Team Penske in 2010, Brad has earned the NASCAR Cup Series championship, the NASCAR XFINITY Series championship, and has played a major role in Team Penske's four (4) NASCAR XFINITY Series owners' championships. He also scored the 400th and 500th wins in Penske's storied history. As of the end of the 2020 race season he has scored a remarkable 74 total race wins across all three NASCAR's major series.

Brad founded the Checkered Flag Foundation in 2010, a charitable organization which honors and assists those who have sacrificed greatly for the United States – this includes military veterans, first responders and their families. Brad resides in Mooresville, North Carolina with his wife Paige and their young daughters Scarlett and Autumn.

Do you have a favorite quote or philosophy you live by?

Vince Lombardi has this quote on excellence that I really like. "We can't achieve perfection, but just maybe if we chase it, we'll catch excellence."

What is one personal quality that you are most proud of?

This one is going to be kind of funny in a way. My answer is stubbornness. I'm proud of stubbornness and I think I have to give a reason behind it – it is because stubborn people will fail and will keep trying.

What are the issues - whether social, environmental, political or economic - that you feel are most pressing and for which you feel the greatest personal concern and responsibility?

My greatest personal concern? I think it's my children and their ability to be good Christian kids. That concerns me the most.

Who inspires you?

Elon Musk and Roger Penske. Elon Musk because he's not afraid to fail and he dreams big. Roger Penske because he is a perfect example of excellence in the way he is relentless with his pursuit of chasing perfection.

LIFE PURPOSE AND SUCCESS

What do you ultimately strive for? What is your mission in life?

I strive to be successful which blends into the second question regarding mission. To me, success feeds my mission in life of being able to be blessed to be a blessing. You can't be a blessing to others if you're a mess yourself.

How do you define success? At what point did you identify as being "successful"?

Generally speaking, growth is success. At what point did I identify as being successful? There is not just one point. Success comes each day in one form or another. So, I define success as growth and that growth could come in a number of ways – it could be financial, it could be professional, it could be spiritual. That, to me, is what success looks like. Looking back, I can identify being successful many times in my life; certainly, in my

career when I first became a professional race car driver. That personal success came first when I was able to live on my own and didn't need my parents. Next is when I was able to get married and, beyond that, it's when I'm able to raise my children and see them be and do and become great things.

What do you think was your main quality that led you to your success?

Again, my stubbornness, hands down. It was easy to pack up and quit multiple times. I was just too stubborn. Oh boy, it's hard to pick one example of stubbornness. If I was to give you one example of that, it was probably when my family's business (my father's own racing team) went under and I had to decide what to do with my career and my life. Even though I could have easily done so and pursued another career at that point, I chose instead not to give up on racing. I didn't give on racing just because my Dad's team didn't make it.

With respect to my manufacturing business, Keselowski Advanced Manufacturing ("KAM") of which I am so proud, it was about starting a business that no one else really believed in with a technology that's unproven and trying to make it work. Every day, there was a setback but in the face of these, we just kept on going.

What makes you feel fulfilled and energized?

Certainly, being a top race car driver in NASCAR does! To me, I love the pure competition of it and there are two things that make it special to me. One is that every race that we run I know where I stand. There's a clear measuring stick and the thrill in that is that I know every week where I rank. The other is the excitement of it - just having that opportunity to be able to prove yourself each and every week.

How important is collaboration and teamwork to achieving success?

A simple motto is "Life is a team sport". As much as we all want to believe that we control our own destiny, I never have.

OVERCOMING CHALLENGES

Have there been any key challenges that you have had to face in your life? How have you faced them?

Yes, multiple challenges. Probably the biggest challenge is also one of my biggest measurements of success. It was when I started with Team Penske and tried to do all I could to help the team win their first NASCAR championship which they had not yet achieved. What part did I play in helping them to achieve that? By pulling everybody up and building a team - building a team that is cohesive and talented. I'm super proud of the fact that, from my very beginning with Team Penske, I was able to help the team focus on and face key challenges collaboratively.

The results were extraordinary! Our team not only won races and Championships but, along the way, I became the most winningest race car driver in Team Penske history!

How has failure, or apparent failure, set you up for later success? Do you have a "favorite failure" of yours?

Yes, for sure. When my family's racing team business was forced to discontinue operations, I suddenly was on my own to find another race team to drive for. This difficult circumstance forced me out on

my own to become a race car driver that would have to learn to compete on the highest-level stage. Prior to that time, my goals and aspirations were to be a racer on the lower stages.

It took my family's business to fail for me to get the opportunity or to even have the vision that I was capable of doing more. In a roundabout way, it forced me to broaden my expectations and goals. My goal before that was just to continue my family's business. After, however, it opened me up to a vision of success at a higher level. Once I started to achieve success at a higher level, I just kept raising the bar further and further for myself to build future successes.

EMOTIONS

What makes you truly happy?

What makes me truly happy is seeing other people I work with or live with in my life be successful.

How do you express anger? What do you do to release frustration?

Besides staying up really late?? Like my wife, Paige, will tell you, I don't sleep when I'm angry. That's probably a strange way of expressing it, but the reason why I don't sleep is because I try to digest its source and it takes me a long time to digest it and to cope with it and understand it. So, how do I release it? Basically, I sit and think about it until I can rationalize it. It isn't my style to throw fits or stomp around anymore although I did struggle with that somewhat in my teenage years and younger – fortunately, I just kind of grew out of that. Over time, I just started to realize that it wasn't helpful.

I have frequently talked about one principle by which I try to practice each day – living with truth and grace. The truth/grace principle is very simple. It's the belief that if you want to be like Christ, that you live your life full of truth and grace. And that's how it's described in multiple biblical writings. The two are very important to go together because they cannot exist independently of each other.

If you tell the truth to someone without grace, they won't hear you. It becomes the bear in the woods or the tree in the woods, however you want to look at it, because if they don't hear you, then it didn't exist, so it denies the truth and vice versa. If you tell a lie with grace, it's really not grace, it's self-serving. So, I believe that in order to live a Christ-like life full of integrity, you must at all times have truth and grace.

What does strength look like to you?

To me, strength looks like the ability to accept life's hardships and to not lose your cool physically or emotionally in spite of it.

What does vulnerability mean to you?

Transparency.

How do you deal with conflict and diffusing difficult situations?

I try to put myself in the other person's shoes. If I would feel the same way in that person's shoes, then I would try to have empathy. If I would not feel the same way in that person's shoes, then I try to use truth and grace to explain to them my position and hope they'll understand.

"What makes me truly happy is seeing other people I work with or live with in my life be successful."

Do you talk with anyone, or have a group of friends you can talk to, about how you feel when things are happening in your life, or do you keep these thoughts internalized?

I certainly talk to my wife and that's one of the beauties of being in a marriage.

SPIRITUALITY AND MINDFULNESS

What role does religion or spirituality play for you?

It's the moral cornerstone of my life.

What pastime or practice enables you to relax and connect with your inner self?

No doubt, it's going to church.

RELATIONSHIPS AND FAMILY

In what ways have the women in your life influenced the man you have become?

I have two daughters, a wife, a Mom, three sisters (I was the youngest sibling) and a female dog! Wow, we're adding up pretty quick here! All of them, in their own ways, have given me perspective that does not come naturally to me. And, at times, this has been incredibly useful.

How do you maintain balance in your life between work and family?

It's an everyday challenge especially in my profession. The biggest way I found to help to maintain balance is to wake up early. I didn't understand that for a long time until I was married and had kids. It was then that I started to understand why you wake up early. It is because the time in the morning is generally less valuable than the time in the afternoons spent together with your family and with that in mind, one of the best things that I have been able to do is to wake up earlier, go to work earlier, and return earlier.

In addition, as my profession is stacked with travel, I try to travel with my family when possible so we can be together.

Is being a father an important part of your sense of manhood?

I think so. Being a father in a lot of ways is being a provider and I think, whether we want to admit it or not, more times than not we define ourselves by those abilities. I would say that fatherhood has changed me in the sense that I have much more empathy than I used to have. Patience, patience, patience is an important quality for me.

MICK FANNING

SURFING CHAMPION

 @mfanno   @mick_fanning

Mick Fanning burst onto the ASP World Championship Tour in 2002, when he finished in the top five in his rookie season. A complete hamstring tear in 2004 delayed progress, and he could only get back in the water after major surgery and six months of intense rehab.

Mick returned in 2007, and won the ASP World Championship, also winning the Championship in 2009 and 2013.

The J-Bay Open in July 2015 will always be remembered for Mick's encounter with a Great White, but it didn't keep him out of the water for long and he finished second behind 2015 world champ Adriano de Souza.

In February 2018, Mick took the big decision to step away from WSL Championship Tour surfing completely and announced his retirement after his beloved Rip Curl Pro Bells Beach event.

Do you have a favourite quote or philosophy you live by?

When we were growing up, we had a picture on the fridge of a stork eating a frog, and the frog is grabbing the stork by the throat, and it says, "Never give up."

That was something I saw every day – even if you are on the verge of the end, don't give up.

That's been something that has helped me out a lot.

What is one personal quality that you are most proud of?

It's always a hard one – judging yourself is a scary thing. You try to be humble and level-headed a lot of the time. I guess, for me, always trying to be honest and loyal to the people who did the same to me. I got brought up that way by my parents. Even if things didn't go right with some people, have the courage to speak the truth and own that, and then be able to accept when you've got failures as well.

Honesty is a two-way street – and I heard the saying of "Be nice to the people on the way up, because you'll meet them on the way down." A lot of the crew I have worked with and been friends with are the same way. You might go in and out of each other's lives but whenever you need something or they need something if you're there for them, there's a role reversal when you need them. The circle of life just keeps rolling.

One of the poignant things in J-Bay after the shark incident was when all your mates arrived when you came back in. That collaboration in such a singular sport seems really strong.

When you come from nothing – we never had a whole lot of money – I found that friendships and camaraderie, particularly in surfing, to be really important.

Even though, as you said, it's a singular sport, the camaraderie in surfing is really, really deep. If something happens, or someone gets hurt, everyone's there to help out. Even though we are selfish when the best wave of the day comes through - because we are dealing with Mother Nature all the time, when it comes to caring for each, we're able to switch off and make sure this person is okay.

Even if you don't know the person – there have been many times where the most important thing is to get that person back to the beach safely or make sure they're okay.

That's the beauty of surfing.

You mention Mother Nature at its wildest – is there a fear of the ocean at times?

Oh definitely, I just said this to someone the other day. We pretty much went from

hero to zero in one wave. The wave before, my mate got one of the waves of his life and the next one he got absolutely beat down. That's just how quick Mother Nature can change, and that's why it's so humbling.

There's a difference between crippling fear, where you just can't go there, to a respectable fear where you respect everything that can and may happen. That's something we have to live with.

I think that's why when people watch surfing, and they want to see surfers talk smack to each other like boxers or UFC fighters who just talk absolute trash to each other because they're so confident. Even though you might be confident against that person, Mother Nature can just humble you so quickly, so you have to pump the brakes a little bit and keep those thoughts to yourself.

Can you explain the buzz and exhilaration of surfing?

Surfing is one of those things – even though we do it for work, we do it for a lifestyle as well. I think that's why it's so different to every other sport – once most sportspeople are retired, they're retired, they're never running onto that field again. We still get to go out and surf. It puts you in the moment all the time. If you're on a wave and thinking about something else, then you miss things and you make mistakes.

In a wave, you can do things that totally shock yourself – like falling out of a tree and landing on your feet, where other times it's like the perfect ballet dance, where you think, "Wow, I just nailed that." It might not be a perfect 10 in the judges' eyes, but to you, you know that "I couldn't have done that any better."

That sense of pride is something that runs

through a lot of surfers – from beginners right through to professionals. I guess the closest thing you can compare it to is hitting the perfect golf shot. You might hit a million shit ones and then, all of a sudden, you've got the perfect one and that's the one that makes you go back the next day.

What are the issues - whether social, environmental, political or economic - that you feel are most pressing and which you want to fight for?

I think it's the earth as a whole. As humans, we are doing so much damage to the earth, the oceans, the animals – but also to each other. As humans, it's not going to be a flick of a light switch to change the world, but I think we all need to take a step back and ask ourselves "What can I do to help this world?" One thing I kept playing over in my mind before conceiving a child, it's like with all this bad shit we see in the news, do I really want to bring a child into this world?

But then I think, if I can help show this child all the good things – maybe they might go and be the change something needs. It's about humans helping out, I think.

Who inspires you?

There's been so many – I look at so many different people. There's obviously a whole bunch of sports stars that you look at from the outside and you try to take little things, here and there, from them.

My family have taught me so much, my friends have shaped me to be the person I am. Even just people walking down the street, or people you accidentally run into, and you see how happy and free they are.

I've got my group of close friends that I confide in, and I have a really great support network in that realm. It's a bit of everyone, I think.

EMOTIONS

What makes you truly happy? What lights up your soul?

Ever since I was a little kid, it was all about "How do I win a World Title? How do I win events to get to that World Title? How do I become better?"

All of a sudden, I got to this point where I had won world titles and I looked in the mirror and said, "Is this exactly what's making me happy?"

My goalposts had changed. Now my goal in surfing is to be able to create art with friends and create something where you're working together to create the perfect image or create the perfect sequence of film. So that's where my head is at, at the moment. I could easily sit on the couch and get really fat, but I still feel like I have this urge for my own personal legacy to go and create. I don't care if people don't like it or if they love it, but for me I can look at it and say, "Everything came together in that one moment."

What lights up my soul? It's all kinds of things – experiences with your mates, or your loved ones. The thing that fills my soul is when you're in this moment and you take this second or a minute to soak it all in. I think with how fast-paced life is, we skip over that.

Everyone's different – but for me, I like to take a moment and say, "Okay, I've got a picture of this in my brain and I can revisit that later."

To be able to stop in those moments, it gives clarity.

Even when I was competing, I have these pictures I remember clearly.

That's how I fill my cup of tea.

You're known as a world-famous world champion surfer, who punches sharks in J-Bay. Is this art that you've mentioned the legacy you want to leave?

The fame was never high on my priority list – I just wanted to prove to myself that I could do it. I didn't need the person down the street to come and give me a high-five. Fame is definitely not anywhere on my priority list – if anything I wish I could get rid of it!

The personal pride and sense of fulfilment is something that I have always looked to, and bettering myself each and every day in the sense of "Okay, I could tweak this or tweak that."

Especially with Mother Nature, if you're not ready, it's going to pass you and you're going to regret that forever. It's always, "Am I prepared if that perfect moment comes?"

The legacy part of it is more for me, particularly where I am now trying to create art. It's about me looking back when I'm old, fat, grey and bald and saying, "I did that, and I remember that feeling." I don't need someone to write about it, I just want to remind myself when I'm old.

What does vulnerability mean to you?

Vulnerability is really hard. I seriously think it's the most courageous thing a person can do to look in the mirror and look at the flaws that we have, personally. It is, for the lack of a better word, f*cking scary!

If you don't look at these things, then it just starts spiralling and it gets worse and worse. It's like a tree growing, and the roots get longer and longer, and it starts building and building. If you can nip that bad root as soon as possible, that's important. Sometimes we don't have the strength or the courage to deal with it at that certain time, but let's face this when we have the courage and personal strength to deal with it and be open and honest, not only with ourselves but with people we're getting help from.

The story where it all came from was when I lost my brother when I was 17. When you're so young, you're so impressionable from other people. At that time, everyone was sitting there and saying to me, "Be strong, be strong." So, I thought "be strong" was to show no emotion, bottle that shit up and never show anyone where it is.

I absolutely hate when people say that. I put these walls up that I didn't even know. People would come to me, crying, and I would be pan-faced, thinking, "It doesn't bother me" but it would play on my mind when I went home.

It wasn't until I went and saw a psychologist and in the first 10 minutes I figured out I had this wall that I couldn't break through and next thing, I'm just bawling in this office. It really showed me that I have to work on this – it's taken me many years to build this wall up, I can't just bulldoze it down in one session. I need to take it down, brick by brick.

That's been something I still work on today, and it's something I find even from a day-to-day and you start thinking, "F*ck, am I dealing with this right?" and as soon as you voice it to someone, it's actually not that big of a deal. It's scary to get to that point. People get to a point where because they open up and talk to someone, they go the other way and think, "Am I being a burden, pouring this shit onto you?" So, it can work both ways.

"What lights up my soul? It's all kinds of things – experiences with your mates, or your loved ones. The thing that fills my soul is when you're in this moment and you take this second or a minute to soak it all in. I think with how fast-paced life is, we skip over that."

You've got to be able to work on yourself – you can voice what's going on to other people and get advice but until you do the work internally and personally, it's never going to heal itself.

You've experienced great loss from such a young age, and I appreciate your bravery in talking about it. You've lost two brothers. Even though they're not here anymore – they're still part of who you are. What role do they play in your life?

It's funny you say that. I was close to them and I'm still close to them. I feel like they're with me. I feel like their energy is still in the universe and it comes back and forth, and I see it at different times. I feel that they're with me at different times.

My brother, Sean, who passed away, every time he's with me, I feel like I've got heaps of energy, but I've got too much energy, so it makes me want to be almost naughty.

Then, my other brother, Peter, who most recently passed away – he was more naughty, but when I feel like he's with me, I feel really calm and really clear in my thoughts, and go in this flow.

I can still talk to them in that sense. You've still got to celebrate those times and acknowledge them. They show up at times where I need extra strength or power to do the things that I'm doing, the extra confidence. I'm still very aware of when they're here and asking them for guidance from time-to-time.

The rest of my family – my mom has taught me so much, my dad has taught me so much, my sister and my other brother. I've learnt so much from different things and I take little things from them and mash it all into who I am. I've learnt from observing them and being with them.

How do you express anger? What do you do to release frustration?

It's such a powerful feeling – sometimes it just takes over.

A lot of the time, if I find myself in that situation, it's like, "Take a step back. Is this really worth all the commotion that I am carrying on with right now?"

If it's something that keeps bubbling up with a person or with yourself, go and deal with it and talk it out, or talk to someone to get the feelings out.

A lot of time, we manifest so much in our heads that we make a situation way worse than it actually is. You just get lost sometimes in your own brain. Everyone does it, everyone.

I'm sure even the Dalai Lama's gotten angry sometimes in his life.

Everyone deals with it differently – probably the scariest thing when it comes to the feeling of anger is looking in the mirror and asking, "Am I creating this, or is this from someone else?" And a lot of the time, we can say, "Maybe I'm creating this." So maybe give yourself a slap on the cheek and get on with it.

LIFE PURPOSE AND SUCCESS

How do you define success? At what point did you identify as being "successful"?

I am the son of two immigrants who moved to Australia and we didn't have much growing up. Now I'm lucky enough to live in a big, beautiful house on the beach. That's successful. I've got a beautiful fiancée and a son. If that's not success, then I'm being a bit of a dickhead – or maybe a real dickhead!

Success comes from hard work. It's doing the things when you don't want to do it. It's putting your hand up when everyone else is putting theirs down. Everyone looks at these 'quick-fixes' to become successful. But there's no magic trick, it's just straight-up hard work.

OVERCOMING CHALLENGES

How has failure, or apparent failure, set you up for later success? Do you have a "favourite failure" of yours?

Oh man, I do that every day. Probably the one you learn the most from is when you hurt someone's feelings and you think, "Oh I've really f*cked up now. How do I not do that again?" In competition, we fail every time, and that's why succeeding is so good. In everyday life, you're learning as you go. It's not something I like to dwell on. It's like, "Alright, I messed up. How do I not do that again?" and move on.

That's the biggest thing – acceptance.

Touching on the shark incident at J-Bay – it was pretty harrowing. How hard was it to step back into the water?

Not hard at all. I've seen hundreds of sharks. The reason I say it's not hard at all is because the ocean is where I do all my healing. From the outside, looking in, people might think, "If I came across a shark, I am never jumping in the water again." But if you ask those same people, have you nearly been hit by a car walking across the road? And how many times have you walked across since?

For me, it's just what I do. I had a few days out and definitely had to collect my thoughts and definitely had to see what was real and not real. It made me listen to my inner instinct a bit more. As surfers, sometimes we think we're being a bit of a wuss thinking there's a shark out there, but now – if I think that and I don't feel right, I'll just go into the beach. I don't need to be a hero.

Even the first time I did go surfing, I saw a shark and I was like, "Okay, I guess they're marking me at the moment!" It wasn't a hard decision; it was just something I had to work through.

It was something I had to talk through with my loved ones and people who care for me, who were questioning me going back in the water. They thought I would, but probably not as quick. They were conversations I had to have and have the strength to tell them that I'm going to be okay and I'll make smart decisions.

The healing side of the ocean was so much more powerful than just that incident, so I had to go back.

What's one of the hardest decisions you've faced?

That's a tough one. Probably the one that I was most unprepared for was deciding to jump in a car when I found out my brother, Sean, had been killed in a car accident. To have an undercover car pull up when I was walking home, and being so scared because I didn't want to jump into the car to find out what was going on – we didn't know anything at this stage. It was like, "Do I? Don't I? Do I? Don't I?"

I was the first to know – so I had to tell the whole family, and that was something that I wasn't prepared for. How do you tell someone that? That was the toughest decision.

SPIRITUALITY AND MINDFULNESS

What role does religion or spirituality play for you?

I'm not religious – even though we got brought up as Catholics. I was never that person who could go to Church. The world we live in is the spiritual part, going in the ocean every day and getting out in nature – I think that's the spiritual realm.

Whoever or whatever created earth has put it here for us to enjoy, and I learn so much from Mother Nature. That's my way of going to Church each day. I guess I am a bit spiritual! It could get really weird, but I'll try to keep it level-headed - I learn from surroundings.

BEING A MAN

What does "being a man" mean to you?

I think it's so many things – being a helping hand when people need it, it's having the courage to be vulnerable, it's being that piggy-back when your friends and family need help, it's being a sounding board.

On top of that, it's about having fun. There are so many amazing things to enjoy in this world. There are lots of things we feel we need to change, but there are also so many other things we don't need to change, we just have to keep pristine or we just need to admire. I think that's where we get lost by focusing on the negatives – let's focus on the positives and see the amazing things that we can do in this world and enjoy what we have.

I don't want to be one of those grumpy old dudes sitting at the BBQ on the beach, telling people to piss off.

Have the concepts of masculinity changed throughout your life?

It definitely has – I think it's changing not only for me personally, but it's changing globally. When I was growing up, it was about 'show no emotion', 'you can't cry in front of your mates', or 'you can't show you're weak.' That was a big thing. Even in just the last ten years, or even less, it's changed to "We're humans too and we can be vulnerable. We can show signs of weakness."

That's where I see the courage and strength – to be able to show that takes a lot of courage but if you're surrounded by the right people and the right support network, you can get through those moments.

If there was a single piece of advice that you could give your younger self, what would it be?

That's really hard. The speedbumps you hit, the corners that you take, the forks in the road, all these different things. These are the things that shape you to who you are today. If you are given a cheat-code, you might miss these moments, and not appreciate them for what they are.

It's a really hard one for me – write a letter to your 16 year-old-self – well he's not going to read it anyway, because he's being a little maniac! At 16, I'm going to make mistakes and figure out how to get through it!

ANDREW SEALY

YOGA ARTIST

 @andrew7sealy   @andrew7sealy

Andrew Sealy is a connection catalyst, a Yoga artist, and a movement creator. His days are spent traveling to find adventure, practicing to cultivate growth, and constantly absorbing wisdom to create new experiences that he shares with love to his friends around the world. He finds joy in interviewing Yogis from all walks of life to share their inspiring stories on the Yoga Revealed Podcast.

From a young boy exploring the beaches of Barbados, Andrew has always had a profound connection with nature and its healing properties. With his profound curiosity of body-mechanics and human potential he set on a path to build his temple through the devout practice of Yoga.

When you ask Andrew why Yoga? He answers with a smile; "Yoga is a complete science of self-discovery that is not a competitive sport or mere challenge of wit. Yoga is the only practice I have found that truly challenges me to embody positive change while integrating all aspects of self-discipline to bring forth harmony within the body, mind, and soul."

Do you have a favorite quote or philosophy you live by?

I would say my philosophy that I live by is definitely that I stay true to my heart. I feel that the philosophy of staying true to your heart means that you only hold to be evident truth that comes through experience and really understanding the intuition you bring forth into your world is what creates your reality.

It's all a matter of doing your best that the perceptions that you see are through a clean lens, so that the actions that you lead comes from a place of truth that comes from your heart.

The clarity you have, did you find that through yoga or is it something that you had already?

I would say it's a combination. Yoga has definitely been a huge catalyst to me finding that clarity faster, but I feel that everyone has it, and is born with it.

Throughout life, with society, parents, schooling, all of that tends to cloud what our truest expression of self is. In practicing things like yoga, meditation, Zen Buddhism, all these things bring us back to the realization that the truest expression of self is understanding that we are all one.

That deep connection of understanding we are all one brings us back to the realization that all we must be is true to who we are. When you're born as a baby, your existence is joy. If you look at a baby, they're usually pretty happy!

We are mostly happy, we are mostly content, we want to be. We desire that place of feeling loved, wanted and valued. The opportunity to get back to that place is getting rid of all the frivolous thoughts and impressions that have been made by others that are not ourselves.

What is one personal quality that you are most proud of?

The characteristic I'm most proud of is my compassion for myself and others. Really learning to love yourself unconditionally is the key to being vibrant, healthy and happy and really bringing that really good energy into your existence and your communities, your relationships, your children and your family. I think that really comes from a place of self-love because the only way I can give something is if I truly embody it myself.

"You've got to do your best, that's all you've got to do. If you give your best, you get an A, because it's your best. Don't care about the test score, if you give your best, that's all that matters. That true dedication to bettering yourself."

So, I feel that when we truly embody that deep sense of love for our self, then that love becomes effervescent and spills over.

I really do love myself – I experience myself on the daily. I take a nice shower, I do my meditation, and when I look in the mirror I smile because I feel really blessed to be in this existence. It's not just my work that got me here – it's my parents, it's my grandparents, it's my teachers, it's all the people who helped push me to become the best version of myself, and to give me a clear reflection to say, "This is who you're showing up as right now, who do you want to become?"

In those opportunities, that's really what catalyzed me to understand that having love for myself means also being my number one critic as well.

My primary school motto was, "Never settle for less than your best." So as a young man, that was instilled in me. Don't compare yourself to the kid next to you, or your brother or sister or what your dad did in the past. You've got to do your best, that's all you've got to do. If you give your best, you get an A, because it's your best. Don't care about the test score, if you give your best, that's all that matters. That true dedication to bettering yourself.

What are the issues - whether social, environmental, political or economic - that you feel are most pressing and for which you feel the greatest personal concern and responsibility?

I would say that the biggest conundrum is how we as humans claim to be free and sovereign, yet we concurrently live in a state where our rights to be free are completely and utterly being infringed on. The number one thing that has been very disappointing is how many of our leaders are completely skewed by money – they don't have our best interests in mind.

The fact of the matter is that if anyone is to lead us, we give our power to someone who is supposed to create a world that is beneficial to the majority of people, we have to be very mindful as to the powers that we give them. I feel now, more than ever, it's really time to look at how we can create more communal power. More small communities that are built on a deeper sense of empowering the regular, everyday person – and really coming back to what it means to be in a community, knowing what it means to "know thy neighbor" and what it means to be honorable to your own family.

We are only as strong as our weakest link. It really brings me back to the thought process that as a human race, right now we are failing.

I feel very dissatisfied by the amount of people who are oblivious to how they can empower themselves by what they eat, the types of channels that they subscribe to, the types of books that they read, the

way they spend their time. I practice Karma yoga, and it is really deeply instilled in how we treat each other.

I feel a lot of people are not treating themselves with common sense, that sense of resilience, that sense of self-study that really brings a deeper sense of understanding another.

That's what we are constantly faced with is this separation – its "Us against them" or "They did this" or "I don't have any power because that person holds the power." No, we have the power. We, together as a community, as a nation, as a world. I feel now, more than ever, it's time for us to realize that or we will continue on this path of self-destruction.

I am also a firm believer that those who believe in the power of "we" and the power of unity will bring forth a deeper resonance in how to progress forward with that wisdom and transcend that crisis.

Who inspires you?

I feel that it's not just one person – it has to be a unified collection of like-minded people. Although I say "like-minded" it doesn't mean that their experiences have to be alike. It just means that they have to be open to hearing new perspectives. I feel that open-minded leadership is what creates a deeper sense of resonance that brings forth positive progress.

Think of how many people signed the Declaration of Independence? Think of how many people it took to create the United Nations? All of these things were created by a collection of really intelligent people who came together.

That really intelligent group of people needs to be balanced with feminine energy – I feel that is really the problem and the recurring fault that has occurred in the hands of man, we have forgotten about wo-man. The other balancing energy is the feminine energy – you don't just have day, you also have night. We have to understand it's a balance that creates a deeper synergy of harmony that is able to bring us into a space where we can progress.

In what ways have the women in your life influenced the man you have become?

I would say that the most valuable relationship that I have had thus far in my life is my relationship with my mother. Time and time again, I am reminded of the power, the grace, the strength, benevolence, the nobility of women – simply because my mom raised me until the age of 7 as a single mom.

Up until that time, I had this perspective of my mom as my provider and also being so kind and resilient, and making sure I was fed in times where there was barely enough for us both to eat.

Even in those rough times, her resilience, her happiness, her kindness was there. That, I feel, has been a big impact on my life and how I respect and honor women as a whole.

I witnessed my mom give birth to my two little sisters at the age of 7 and 10. That, I will say, was a huge, mind-blowing experience. That – for a young boy – was a rite of passage. A lot of men have not witnessed that, nor do they feel as though it would be something valuable in their life. I feel it brought so much more understanding to, not only the pain that it takes to bring life into existence, but also how important and how precious life is.

So, from that early stage in life, I realized how vital it is to be cognizant and mindful – especially when you're with a woman and it becomes a sexual relationship. My experiences really brought a deeper appreciation to how I treat women and how I showed up as a man to women, because I understood, "This is how it looks to take care of a woman, this is how it looks to be a man who is there for their significant other."

I witnessed my step-dad step into the picture and take care of my little sisters and take care of my mom – they're still together to this day. I had the duality of witnessing my dad and how he treated the situation, and then how my step-dad treated the situation and that gave me a deeper understanding of how I can present myself as a man.

Has your concept of masculinity changed since you were a teen?

Certainly – my concept of masculinity was deeply shaped by my father, my step-father, but mostly by my grandfather. Throughout my mom's pregnancy with my little sisters, my grandfather was the most admirable male figure in my life. He brought my family from Barbados, and I am deeply, deeply grateful for his leadership, his resilience and for showing up for the whole family.

He does it in such a unique way – he's a fire-eater, he eats fire, and walks on glass and he had a really incredible dance troupe called the Caribbean Heat in Barbados. He is known as Basil the Magnificent and he dances with earth, wind and fire. He danced with Michael Jackson and is in music videos from the 80s.

My grandfather led a very adventurous, wild life but he was so grounded and so kind. He would say to me, "Be kind to thy mother and thy father and your life would be pleasant in the land." He was always saying be kind to people, treat people as you wish to be treated. He would give me deep conversations about how important it was to do my best, because there's no reservations or regrets. The past is just the past – then we can be present and move into the future.

My grandfather is awesome – he's definitely the man who shaped my masculinity.

LIFE PURPOSE AND SUCCESS

What do you ultimately strive for? What is your mission in life?

I would say, ultimately, I strive for harmony. Harmony in my existence with all existence. Finding that deep preservation of energy that is effort and ease. The simplicity of bringing forth the action without any attachment. The truest offering of my heart to this world is to be service to all humanity through the harmonious nature of existence.

OVERCOMING CHALLENGES

Have there been any key challenges that you have had to face in your life? How have you faced them?

When I was young, I was sexually abused by a family member. It was one of those experiences where early on, you recognize something as being wrong. You know that it's wrong but because it's someone who is close to you, and someone who is respected, you don't know what to do.

I had a deep intuition that what was going on was wrong – because it was also being experienced by a cousin of mine as well,

she was getting the brunt of it. I told my mom about it and I remember her saying, "You can tell me anything, don't worry." She always told me never to be afraid to speak up.

This instance of being molested happened on multiple occasions and it got to a point where I realized that if I didn't speak up then not only would it happen to me even worse each time, but it would also happen to my little cousin even worse. I witnessed what was happening and I knew I couldn't let it happen again.

I told my mom, and I just remember the feeling of the weight lifting off my shoulders when she just held me and when she held me, and I was able to realize that the pain that I was going through and my cousin was going through didn't have to happen. All it took was speaking up.

I think that was the huge milestone for my existence because I feel that a lot of people don't speak up for the discomfort that they've had, for the wrong that has been done to them, for the trauma that they've experienced.

Vocalizing is one of the first ways to heal trauma. That vocalization of letting go of that tension, that energy – that has to happen. If it doesn't happen, it gets bottled up inside, and the more we bottle up tension, the more that the tension and stress wears on our emotional body which is deeply connected to our spiritual body.

I would say the practice of yoga has helped me reverse that tension that got so bottled up – the times where I wanted to punch someone, those times that I felt so beaten down where I couldn't get up, the times where I was so pushed into a space of stress, I could feel my stomach turning because I was so angry and wanted to explode energy.

All of that energy gets held in the physical body, whether it's in your hips, your shoulders, your lower back – wherever it is. All of our bodies hold tension and energy differently and it gets wound up as knots, ulcers, tumors, and as far as cancer.

We realize time and time again that when we let out a sound – even just a deep breath or a sigh – it lets out so much tension. That's why I am so dedicated to giving people the steps that they need to be able to release the tension that has been built up over years.

If I can give people the tools to get through that tension, then I feel that my existence is being fulfilled. I feel everyone is here to share their best gifts, and the only way we can do that is if we are clear and we can share from a place of happiness, a place of joy, a place of love, a place of existence.

EMOTIONS

How do you express anger? What do you do to release frustration?

I would say that I definitely have been angry before – as I continue to age, my anger meter is drastically lowered. I remember in my early 20s, I had fraternity friends who would anger me by doing adolescent, male stuff. Like being in the locker room and being whipped by a towel or having someone play a prank on you. I realized early that the more angry I would become, the more I reacted, the more they would continue to do it.

So, I realized I don't have to give anyone a reaction. Just let it be what it is - I don't have to throw a tantrum, I don't have to throw a fit. I don't have to expend more energy than I have to.

Energy is vital and that's what I've come to realize – the energy that we expend when someone puts us past our phase of comfort is energy that can either go towards coming back to that space of comfort which is then literally harnessing that energy, or it can be energy that is expended and exhausted.

What does vulnerability mean to you?

I feel vulnerability is very similar to anger in that it's putting it out of your comfort zone. When you're able to be out of your comfort zone and to receive – that's true vulnerability. One of the best ways we can be vulnerable is by receiving feedback and constructive criticism. It's receiving words that aren't easy to receive but will make you a better person.

I think that's one of the highest accolades – to be someone who receives constructive criticism with grace. When you're at that stage, that's when you're able to transform energy, and that's when we become a true leader.

"I would say that the most valuable relationship that I have had thus far in my life is my relationship with my mother. Time and time again, I am reminded of the power, the grace, the strength, benevolence, the nobility of women – simply because my mom raised me until the age of 7 as a single mom."

A leader is someone who can take that energy and use it to empower both themselves and others and lead the way. Others can see, "Wow he didn't get upset, he didn't yell at the other person, he just took it as an opportunity to grow."

My grandpa would always say, "You have two ears and one mouth" meaning you should listen twice as much as you speak.

Poetry is one of the things you do to release yourself. Is the poetry just for you or do you share it with others?

Poetry has been one of the most relieving ways of processing experience. Oftentimes, whether it's been a good experience or a bad experience, I will write a poem. Especially if it's an experience that is thought-provoking – whether it's a breakup with a girlfriend, whether it's a promotion at a job.

I write poetry every single day.

I think the first poem I ever wrote was when I was 13 and I tried to commit suicide. I wrote this poem that was so simple but so profound because all these emotions that had brought me to wanting to commit suicide were there, and I was literally writing a suicide letter.

Then, I tried to commit suicide. I had filled up a bathtub with water and put cinder blocks on my chest and my parents were not home. At the time, I was babysitting my little sisters, and I got into the tub and the water was overflowing and I turned off the water, put the cinder block on my chest and then waited till I couldn't breathe anymore. I remember getting to the point where there was a ringing in my ears and I was blacking out, and I heard my little sister crying. And my first thought was, "Who is going to get her?

Who is going to pick her up and rock her back to sleep? I can't leave her."

So, I got back up out of the tub – I had enough strength to get out of the tub – and dried myself off and went and rocked my little sister back to sleep. That was a very profound moment for me. It brought me to this space where I realized *I'm not just living for myself*. I think that's the truth of human existence, we're not just here for ourselves. This is a unity, a conscious collective, and everyone is a unique part of this magical existence that we call life. The more that we realize that the more we can live in harmony.

Here is one of my poems:

When you have nothing to prove you have nothing to lose.

Harmony at mind. A reality you choose.

Create your destiny. Actions light the fuse.

Bring light to this world as Nature's favorite Muse.

All you got to do, keep Shining and Aligning.

Can't rush Collective Consciousness...

It's all perfect timing.

Here is one from when I was pretty frustrated, in response to a person who was basically saying that because I was so happy and go-lucky, staying in Costa Rica during the COVID crisis, they felt that I was being vain.

For us to survive, we have to change our behavior

To change our behavior, we must change our beliefs

Enhance your awareness, awaken your perception

Focus your intention and choose your direction

Fear or love

Self-proven results above all illusion

Don't get lost in emotions, they only create confusion

Unshakeable faith and natural harmony

You can't taint the source of light in we

Love me or hate me, I swear it won't make me or break me

I'm going wherever source chooses to take me, and your words won't sway me

We are in dire race between crisis and education

Humanity at stake, only love can cure separation

Let's honor our differences and unite for greater purpose

Individuality is temporal, we rise in unity, you already know this

I haven't published any of my poetry yet – I really plan on creating a poetry book at some point of time. That's one of my dreams – to create a poetry book with incredible pictures as well, where you can read the poetry and see the postures and bring yourself into a great space. I always do photos of yoga in nature – humans are a piece of nature and the more we see ourselves as such, the more we have a deeper connection to nature.

Yoga is about grounding to nature – what energy do you take from the earth when you connect with it in such a raw way?

I would say the energy I would take from the earth is the energy that gives us birth – it's the prana, it's the life force. It's the pure essence of vibration that comes from the nurturing of a mother, as Mother Earth is all of our mothers.

She is the resilient, magical, absolutely abundant life force that has given us all life. That means every vegetable, every seed, every fruit, every bird, all life forms come from the earth. The more we as humans connect to the earth, the more powerful we become in a harmonious way.

When we are connected to the earth with our feet and grounded in nature, yet at the same time, connected to the heavens with our minds, our consciousness, and our opportunity to create. We almost become gods in our own reality – that is the truth of our existence is how we find the balance of becoming as close to the heavens as possible while still being rooted in the earth.

I love doing handstands – I feel like when your hands are on the earth, you can really feel the resonance of the earth because your hands are intrinsically connected to your heart, whereas your feet are connected to your spine so when well-grounded with your feet on the earth, you feel a really grounded sensation but when you turn it upside down, you're almost giving back to the earth.

What piece of advice would you give a young person these days?

The deepest piece of advice I could give a young person today would be, "Have faith in your existence and have faith in your purpose because having faith in your purpose really does allow you to progress into a positive realization of humanity."

I really feel we need more faith in our purpose. Our number one priority should be to find that purpose and to bring that purpose to light within our existence.

I feel that a lot of humans have been distracted by material wealth, by all these things that separate us by comparison, and really put us together rather than bring us together. Time and time again, when we really dig deep into what our purpose is, most people's purpose is to be of service, not only to themselves, but to their families, their neighbors, and to humanity.

When we tap back into that attunement and that unification of understanding that human existence is to be of service to one another because we are all in this together, then we can truly align to our purpose and have faith in our future.

JEB CORLISS

PROFESSIONAL SKYDIVER AND BASE JUMPER

 @jebcorliss   @jebcorliss   Jebcorliss

For as long as he can remember, Jeb Corliss has dreamed of flying. One of his earliest memories came when he was 6 and sitting in the back of his aunt's car watching birds jump from telephone poles, opening their wings and soaring. "When I get older, I'm going to do that," he said. His aunt explained that when he got older he would realize that humans can't fly. "Maybe you can't," he replied, "but I'm going to."

Sure enough, Jeb has dedicated his life to human flight, and in so doing often makes the seemingly impossible a reality. He is one of the world's foremost and best-known BASE-jumpers and wingsuit pilots.

He was first drawn to BASE jumping after seeing it on TV when he was a depressed and suicidal teenager. "It was this concept of wow, very few people in the world are willing to do that. And if I do it, well then, I've done something that very few people would ever be willing to do. And if I failed, well then, I got what I wanted."

Jeb has made more than 2,000 jumps, from the likes of the Eiffel Tower, Golden Gate Bridge, Angel Falls in Venezuela, the Petronas Towers in Kuala Lumpur, Malaysia, and into a half-mile deep cave in China.

Do you have a favorite quote or philosophy you live by?

"My time on this world is limited, but what I can do with that time is not."

What is one personal quality that you are most proud of?

When I say I am going to do something, I do it.

What are the issues - whether social, environmental, political, economic - that you feel are most pressing and for which you feel the greatest personal concern and responsibility?

The excessive over-population of the human species which has become the root cause of all issues this planet faces.

BEING A MAN

What does "being a man" mean to you?

For me I don't think of things in these terms. I see strong people and weak people. They can be either men or women and most of it has to do with mental toughness. Has a person spent the time learning about themselves? Have they figured out their purpose on this planet?

If they have discovered their purpose, do they have the courage to follow through with whatever it takes to live that purpose?

Is this person willing to sacrifice personal comfort, relationships with people they love, maybe their lives?

If they have found their purpose and are willing to sacrifice, then I would call them a "man" even if they are a woman. In this context being a man seems to refer to being strong.

Have your concepts of masculinity/being a man changed over time? Is it significantly different from when you were a teen?

I have never thought about this. Not when I was in my teens nor now. The idea of being a man has always been irrelevant.

Being strong is what has mattered, and you don't need to be a man to be strong.

When I was young being strong meant sacrificing everything to turn dreams into realities. It meant controlling fear and facing death. It meant understanding my mortality and accepting the inevitable fact I am going to die.

This acceptance of death inadvertently gave me the ability to shed my fear of it and allowed me to operate in extreme high stress situations. Once you accept death as the inevitable outcome of any given situation it allows you to calm your mind and helps you to focus on the task at hand, giving you a better chance for success.

But my approach as an adult has changed a bit. I no longer feel the need to put myself in such life-threatening situations anymore. I have calmed with age and am capable of finding joy in more simple endeavors. Family and friends play a more important role in my life now. To be strong now means to care more about the relationships in my life and I am no longer willing to sacrifice them. Death is no longer such a large focal point for me.

So, the short answer is yes, things have changed significantly from my teen years to my 40s.

What qualities are most important to you as a man?

Seeing all these questions are focused on being a man I will go ahead and play along. Being a man is about being strong. It's about doing what you say you will do. It's about having the courage to be true to yourself and follow your passions wherever they may lead you. But this applies to all humans, not just men.

If there was a single piece of advice that you could give every young man in this world, what would it be?

Be kind and try not to be a dick.

EMOTIONS

What makes you truly happy?

Turning dreams into realities has always been my path to happiness. The more people think something is impossible the more satisfaction I have gotten from actually doing it.

How do you express anger? What do you do to release frustration?

I have found confronting fear has been one of the most cathartic experiences of my life. Facing the things that bring me dread have helped me channel negative emotions like rage and aggression into a more positive direction.

What does strength look like to you?

Strength is accepting reality for what it is and not trying to distort it into what you wish it to be. Drugs, drinking, pain killers, these are all attempts at distorting reality. A strong person listens to their pain, they don't try to hide from it. Pain is a signal telling you there is a bigger underlying issue. You must work on solving that issue, don't just take a pill that covers up a symptom, fix the problem. It takes strength to feel your pain and listen to what it's telling you.

What does vulnerability mean to you?

Being vulnerable doesn't compute. I do not think in these terms. My entire life is about training mental toughness and vulnerability is the very thing I am working to eradicate.

What steps have you taken during times when you have felt stressed or down? Do you talk with anyone about how you feel when things are happening in your life, or do you keep these thoughts internalized?

I work through my issues with extreme risk taking. It has helped me to focus on big ideas in times of depression.

Most of my best creative ideas have come from dark moments in my life. When things get dark for me, I tend to pull away from those around me and lock myself away. It becomes a downward spiral that I have to consciously focus on in order to pull myself out. That is when I begin daydreaming about what I would do if death was no longer a concern. These ideas quickly become a roadmap to my next project, and it has always seemed to help pull me out of despair.

OVERCOMING CHALLENGES

Have there been any key challenges that you have had to face in your life? How have you faced them?

My biggest challenge has always been my own mind. Fear, self-doubt and in many cases not understanding why I do the things I do have all wreaked havoc in my life.

Keeping a clear vision of where I want to go in the future has been challenging. What I do is dangerous, and I have been seriously injured over the years. I have watched some of my closest friends die and I have been covered in their blood.

These experiences have had an impact on my mind and trying to justify why I continue is not always an easy task. There is a paradox I am constantly dealing with.

These activities give my life purpose and make me happy, yet they will most likely kill me in the end. These opposing forces are difficult to come to terms with and it's a constant work in progress.

How has failure, or apparent failure, set you up for later success? Do you have a "favorite failure" of yours?

The concept of failing is complex. I personally do not feel failure is real. It's a construct of one's own mind. Usually when a person feels they have failed it really is just them giving up on whatever the given task is.

If you never give up on whatever the task is then you are just in the process of making whatever it is happen. Some tasks can take years or even decades to realize. Some people just don't understand how long some things can take to make happen.

I don't feel I have ever failed at anything. I have hit roadblocks. I have had things placed between me and the things I have wanted to do.

Sometimes it was financial, sometimes it was people telling me it wasn't possible, sometimes it was me telling myself I couldn't do it.

But if it was truly important to me then I would keep putting in the effort for as long as it took to make it happen. There are things I am still working on. You only truly fail if you decide to give up. That is a choice you make and sometimes it's the correct choice. If it wasn't important to you then by all means give up on it.

But in that case, I don't really see it as a failure either, it was just something that didn't really matter to you in the first place.

LIFE PURPOSE AND SUCCESS

What do you ultimately strive for? What is your mission in life?

This has changed over time. When I was young the mission in life was to see how much I could take before I would break. After a few decades of testing and breaking myself, I have learned a lot about who I am and what I am capable of. I no longer feel the need to keep testing myself. Now I am a more peaceful person.

The meaning of life for me now is just experiencing reality for the little time I get to exist. I am just trying to experience everything in the most unfiltered way possible.

No drugs to distort my senses. Just being present and using my senses that have developed over billions of years of evolution to feel everything as deeply as possible.

How do you define success? At what point did you identify as being "successful"?

There was a quote I heard when I was young that I love. I am not sure who said it first, but it goes like this, "The key to happiness is having dreams and the key to success is fulfilling those dreams."

I started feeling successful the instant I started focusing on turning my dreams into realities.

What makes you feel fulfilled and energized?

Waking up in the morning is all it takes these days to make me feel this way. Every second I get to exist is magical now.

SPIRITUALITY AND MINDFULNESS

How important is religion or spirituality in your life?

I am agnostic/atheist, so religion/spirituality means nothing to me.

What pastime or practice enables you time to connect with your inner self?

Standing on the edge of a dangerous cliff knowing that in the next second I will need to do something very specific or I will die brings me to a special place. It isn't something you can fake; you have to really know that death is clinging to your back just waiting for you to make a mistake. This moment connects you to the universe in a way that words cannot express. All your senses are heightened to their absolute optimal performance.

You feel the air against your skin. You hear the insects crawling in the grass. You can see in the dark. The Zen call it the now and that is where I can always find my center.

What do you do to relax?

I dive with sharks to relax. There is something magical about spending time with the last of the dinosaurs.

RELATIONSHIPS AND FAMILY

Who has been the most important role model in your life? Has there been someone who has led by example?

I have never really looked up to anyone. I was always far too focused on trying to kill the demons that were ripping away at my mind through life.

In what ways have the women in your life influenced the man you have become?

I was raised by my mother and two sisters. My mother is stronger than any man I have ever met. That is the main reason I see men and women as equals in dealing with what's important. Being strong comes from facing fear and pain and my mother has done that better than anyone I have ever met...

91

ANTHONY TRUCKS

FORMER NFL PLAYER AND ENTREPRENEUR

 @anthonytrucks   @anthonytrucks

Anthony Trucks is a former NFL player for the Buccaneers, Redskins and Steelers, American Ninja Warrior, coach, consultant, author, speaker, husband, and father of three incredible kids.

Anthony is an entrepreneur who rose to have one superpower - the power to operate at his highest level by navigating life shifts and shifting his identity right along with them to reach his full potential. Anthony created Identity Shift, a company that teaches people how to upgrade how they operate to close their "Identity Gaps" and level up their life and business.

He didn't choose this path however - it chose him when he was given away at three years old into the foster care system, and experienced beatings, starvation, and forms of torture all before the age of six. It then turned into eight more years in foster care before being adopted into a poor white family as the only black person.

Anthony has spent the majority of his life fighting to find out who he is and what he's meant to do while he's here.

Do you have a favorite quote or philosophy you live by?

Own Your Shift – 'Own' that there's work to be done; 'Your' – it's your work to do, you can't hire someone to fix your life, it's your work to do; and 'Shift', once I know that there is wrought to be done and I have to do it, the shift work is to shift perspective, shift actions, shift reactions to make my life changes, so I can own my shift and get stuff done.

I came to this accidentally – I broke my life, man. We either break our lives and figure out how to fix it or we figure out how to tape it together and leave it broken.

For me, a lot of it went through my childhood, being in foster care and craziness, and then running through a decent place in life. I played in the NFL, I met my father, I got to a good tier.

I'd gone through a lot of headaches in the foster care system, lots of abuse and different stuff, and growing up in an all-white family. So, identity has always been that thing that I've been navigating.

So, I got to this point where everything was great, being in the NFL, having a kid, life's good... then all of a sudden it broke. I lost my career in football to an injury, so I lost that part of my identity, had two more kids with my high school sweetheart who was my wife at the time, and when I got done with football, I tried to find this thing that made me 'me' again.

How could I become special like I did with the NFL? So, I opened a gym, and I gave too much to it. I was there all day, I was never home, I neglected my wife and my three kids. So, I ended up getting to the point where I broke that. My wife had an affair, so that broke the marriage; I wasn't a present dad, so I broke those relationships. The business was 9 months in, and almost bankrupt, and my body was out of shape.

I got to the point at the bottom where I was kind of like, "I don't want to be here anymore, if this is what happens post-NFL."

When you've reached a peak like that, you start to think, "There may not be a peak like that again." That realization is heavy, especially when everything is on your chest and there's no-where to go.

I got to rock bottom and at one point wanted to end my life, and then I climbed out of it through some great mentors, some good friends, some good perspectives and finding something I could latch onto, which was, "There's gotta be something, for all the crap that's happened in my life, man, there's gotta be some reason it all happened."

I had this amazing foster mom, who adopted me, and she taught me unconditional love, that I had never seen before, so I kind of wanted to carry on her message.

When she passed from MS after 17 years in 2014, it was like this wake-up call to find a way to give back to the world that unconditional love. She had allowed me to reach a higher level of potential than was supposed to be done for a foster kid. It also allowed me to make something of the craziness by teaching other people how to do what I had done, accidentally. I'd navigated the shifts of divorce, of my childhood and abuse as a kid. For many people, one of those things shuts them down for life, but for me I had taken the licking and kept on ticking.

So, I went back and looked at the psychology of it, the neuroscience of it, and the stories of my life, and turned it into a process to teach people how to shift. So "Own Your Shift" is something I've always been doing, I just teach people how to do it myself now, more proactively.

The ability to have that insight, and to reflect on your life relatively early in life – where did that come from?

I think it came from me getting to the point of realizing that I was the common denominator in all the problems. Cause when we have problems, we don't like the idea that "Oh, it might be me" – we don't do that at first!

It's like, "No, it's her. It's her fault that the marriage was bad, and she had an affair. She ruined it." Or "It's the economy's fault that the business won't grow" or "I have to focus on the business, and the kids don't get it that I can't be present and play games with them" or "I'm always busy at work, I don't have time to work-out."

All these things, you start creating these stories for and then you realize you're just kind of covering up dog crap. It still stinks, but you just can't see it.

So, the world thought everything was great for me, and inside I was like "I'm not happy." I was not doing something that brought me joy anymore. My mom passing away woke me up. I thought, "This woman had no capabilities of physically fulfilling her full potential, and I'm over here going through the motions, this can't be."

I ended up at one point – real honest – I had been doing the single life, the playboy thing. I'm a man of faith, and I was steering clear of my faith and it didn't feel good. I had gone to Russia and had this interaction with a woman who didn't even speak English, but I flew her over to the States cause, you know, 'Playboy guy gets the foreign girl'.

I just remember I woke up one day, no kids and just her and I couldn't even talk to her, and I just had this awful feeling of "If my kids saw me, I'd be disgusted. This is not what I want them to aspire to. I'd be embarrassed for them to see me living this lifestyle."

So, it was just time to shut-off. I removed myself from distracting situations and started asking myself some really hard questions. Like, "All these things happened - and you were always present in them – what was your fault?"

Like, the marriage – I had to own up to the fact that, yes, she did what she did, and it was horrible. I take nothing from that, that's on her. However, there were two people that took us to a position where she even felt she had to make a choice in the first place to seek out things that fulfilled her needs.

The business – I had this ego like, "I'm a former NFL guy, everyone's gonna work with me!" But I had to realize, I don't know anything about business, man. That's why my business is failing.

Or health-wise, quit making excuses, and work out with my clients.

Or – be a father – what does it take, an extra hour or two? Stop taking more clients on - I was spending more time with other people's kids than my own!

So, there was just these realizations, that "Okay, I've gotta work on fixing these relationships." The insight came through a lot of really hard conversations with myself and other people.

What are the issues - whether social, environmental, political or economic - that you feel are most pressing and for which you feel the greatest personal concern and responsibility?

For me, it's always been human potential. I have a lot of weird perspectives that come from being raised in an all-white family as a black man, I have a lot of perspectives that have to do with society and how we work and what people feel entitled to, I have a problem with how people who deem things that seem small to me to be huge to them, but I also have a sense of great appreciation for humanity and the different levels we are all on, and the different relative situations we've experienced.

I want people to get out of their own way a lot of the time. How can you go to the back-end of your days and have something left in the tank? It irks me.

I also know my potential in the lane I want to be in – I'm in the Season of Dad – I want to be present for my kids, I don't want to be on the road and gone for months. That's not the life I desire. However, I do want to know – in my lane, what can I do? What can that person across the street do? While we may feel separate, you are part of my world. I may not interact with you directly, but I may interact with you within three to four degrees.

What can I do to be a better human, a better dad? Do I need to read more books to get a promotion and show up at the next level of life, to make my kids see that a dream is possible?

What's the next level that people can access now to truly take advantage, seeking a higher level of potential to upgrade on a daily basis to a better life? There's no better time than now – you're given the grace to be creative and figure it out.

It's all about potential.

LIFE PURPOSE AND SUCCESS

What is your mission in life?

My ultimate mission is to have an amazing funeral. I came into this world, given away as a kid, and no-one cared to be around. My mom didn't even want me around. That's kind of a crappy thing to have to experience and live with for the rest of your life. The person who birthed you was like, "Nah, I don't want this thing."

So, for me, when you think about a funeral, people go to a funeral because you've impacted their life, genuinely, in a way that made them feel like you were something special. I don't know that it will be MLK size or JFK size, but a cool, big funeral because people are like, "That was a good dude." That's what I want to do – however it comes to be - so that it's a bigger crowd on the way out than it was on the way in.

How do you define success?

I define my success by my ability to have some kind of control. I have control over two things that matter – one is I have control over myself. I have a really good connection to who I am, what matters most, how to take insight without taking it as an attack. People can talk to me and tell me something they don't like about me, and I'll actually take it in. I have good control of that, therefore I'm not very capricious, I don't go up and down emotionally very often.

The other thing I can control is my time – and because I can control my time, I can control my life. I can control when I wake up, I can control when I go to sleep, I can control what I want to buy, I don't have a feeling of being a leaf in the wind. That's one of the biggest things people struggle with when they don't have control, because they're always bracing for impact.

I don't need billions of dollars to be happy. I need money and I like having the ability to have security with my family, don't get me wrong. But I don't live so far outside of my means that I'm stressing out.

OVERCOMING CHALLENGES

How has failure, or apparent failure, set you up for later success? Do you have a "favorite failure" of yours?

My favorite failure – I like that, it's eloquently stated – is the point at which my marriage fell apart. It's more so because I was in a situation growing up where the female in my life was my mom and I was always seeking her approval. That relationship carries so much weight with me.

When my marriage fell apart – she was my high school sweetheart, my first love. We had three kids, went through college, before the NFL, before I was anything. Then that falls apart.

The guy that I was, up till that point, had not done the things that he needed to do to be able to carry on successfully past that point.

The reason it's my favorite failure is because it snapped me up into a situation where I was forced to look at the things that were going wrong. A lot of us are waiting for that "pivotal moment" and unfortunately I hit it – but I don't think we all need to hit it to make an adjustment. I was forced to have to re-visit myself.

It took me three years to really wake up – I was stuck in that fog for far too long. When I finally got to see the beauty of the moment, I would go through it three times to get where I am now. I got remarried to my ex-wife, we've been together for over four years. It's amazing – I would put my marriage up against any other marriage in the world. I love her. There's so much security and not even an ounce of trust issues. It's different.

I upgraded, I had to do the work.

Parenting – I'm not a perfect parent – but I'm present. I can drop my kids off in the morning, and pick them up, and be at every sports meet. I'm there – the control helped me do that.

Business – because I understood what was wrong in the business, I now always have a coach. Before, the ego was like, "You're too good, you don't need help." Now it's like, "I can see what I'm doing but I need someone to see the field."

Health – because I have energy, and I take care of my body, I show up to my day better, my brain is fueled better, because I have a solid body.

All of these things are dialed into my life now – that moment my marriage fell apart was the seed that I watered to have these moments now.

EMOTIONS

What makes you truly happy?

Family. That's it. A lot of people talk about it, but my wife and kids are just about to go hang out at the track – we're a good unit. That means a lot. When you're a kid, you think living with your best friend would be so cool. I get to live with my best friends. We have fights, we have arguments, but there's never a desire to walk away from it. When we have good times, they're really good times, that gives me a special warmth.

Someone asked me, "What are your favorite moments in life?" and genuinely it's when we are all on our big couch, blankets across, watching a movie. I'm going to miss those days when they're all grown up, and there's all these extra husbands and wives and children.

If you're settled at home – everything else in the rest of the world can be tried and you can fail, and you can get back up, knowing that my wife and kids are going to be there.

When do you feel your strongest?

I feel my strongest when I am my most honest. Usually, when you talk about strength it's about something you can grab and control. I feel very weak in water but very strong under a barbell. When I'm honest with myself, I get more control back.

MEN: REAL CONVERSATIONS

If I'm dishonest, then what happens is whatever I'm thinking can be changed, therefore I feel helpless, and helpless leads to lack of control, which makes you feel weak.

When I go back to a place of being honest and acknowledge that there's something that needs to be worked on and I go and put some time into that, that's strength.

I pride myself on being able to clear through the cloudiness of anger, and to have a logical conversation, faster than most people can. It can take me a few moments to extrapolate what part of this is anger driven, and what part of this makes sense? If I keep having this angry conversation, we will get nowhere, so I just calm it down and go to logic as fast as I can.

What does vulnerability mean to you?

I don't think anyone likes being vulnerable. It's difficult – but I like what it does. If you think about vulnerability in the sense of what it is – I'm going to share things that I typically wouldn't share.

When I go up on stage, I realize I'm not there for Anthony anymore. I'm in front of 3000 people, and I'm taking something from their lives, moments from their life. If I'm taking anything, I have to give back something 10-fold. What I can give you back has to be of benefit, has to be something of value. The only way it's valuable is if I go to the depths, and divulge this to you, because now I can connect with the humanity of you. And now I'm really serving you.

But if I just said, "Oh yeah, it really hurt and it sucked a bit to deal with that," that's different to a conversation that I had to sit with the realization that the woman that I lay next to had laid with another guy. That made me feel like I was a worthless man.

I had to open those parts of me and share them and so other people go, "Oh wow. One, I'm not alone and two, I see how he did that, maybe I can."

There are very few things that make me fearful. The crazy instability we've all faced recently - I've been here before, I was born into the dark, I've been bathed in it since I was three.

SPIRITUALITY AND MINDFULNESS

What role does religion or spirituality play for you?

It's really important – I'm a man of faith definitely. We go to church every Sunday and pray before every meal. We actually live it, it's trying to show up with actions.

I have my days where I cuss, because I'm again not perfect. It's not easy, but it's a thing that we are always trying to be better at. It's been a huge part of what's fixed my marriage, it was a huge part of what kept me from craziness as a kid. Faith has been a humongous anchor, but I don't force it on people. As long as it guides me by my principles and directs me on what I'm

> *"There are very few things that make me fearful. The crazy instability we've all faced recently - I've been here before, I was born into the dark, I've been bathed in it since I was three."*

98

meant to do here, and gives us our north star, I'm cool with that.

What do you do to relax and connect with your inner self?

When it's quiet at 5 or 6 in the morning – the house is quiet, the world is quiet – that's the time Anthony gets to hang out with Anthony, and I get to have a conversation with the quiet guy inside. I have thinking time and I read.

Meditation, I try to shut everything down – I try not to think about who I am and what's going on.

BEING A MAN

You were in foster care at a young age and have had many men in your life. Has there been a man who has been a primary role model for you?

I didn't know my biological father's name until I was 21.

My [foster] dad is only 12 years older than me – I was a foster kid; he was a young guy. I love my dad to death but he's not a very evolved guy. As all of us do, there are things he needs to work on. But emotionally I surpassed him at a certain point in time.

I love the guy more than anything – he would support me, drive me to games, watch me in college, like an 8-hour drive after a 16-hour shift. Dude is nuts, he can fall asleep standing up.

What does "being a man" mean to you?

That's a great question. I'm just going to go with the aspect of a heterosexual, basic male. Being a man, means to me,

showing up in a place of strength and a powerful calm. Because if you think of the characteristics of what people like to be around, it's a powerful calm that's not overbearing or intimidating.

We naturally have perspective and the viewpoint of strength, but I don't want strength that scares me, I want strength that feels calming. There are men that I'm around that are big and muscly, but they're sporadic and odd and always trying to play the alpha. I let some guys be alpha around me because I don't feel like having the alpha battle.

Can you be powerfully calm? Can you be a big, strong, powerful person but also have a calmness about you that makes people around you feel very comfortable, safe and at ease?

What are the guiding principles you use to be the best version of yourself?

There are two aspects I've learnt. One - what is right? And two – what would a good man do? I set intentions of what I can do, and I fight to do it, so that at the end of the day when I look this guy in the eyes, I'm like, "Yeah, you did a good job." And then every day, I try not to let yesterday's guy down.

That's always been the route – what would a good man do? I love this quote we had in college, it was on the side of the football room and it said, "The best kind of pride is that that compels a man to do his best, even when no one is watching."

That's always been a driver for me.

If I find out people have done something that's in the dark, or it's off – I quickly lose respect and cut people off. I've had the same friend group since 4th grade, cause they're solid men. There's a couple I've added along the way, of course, but there are very few and some that have gone in have gone right back out.

They say you're the average of the five people you spend the most time with, but I think you're the average of the expectations of those people. My guys push, man. They're trying to be good fathers, they're trying to be better husbands, trying to take care of themselves. So, it's the expectation that I'm around.

I'm a regular guy with regular problems, having a regular career, and a regular desire to help people.

One of the reasons I got to the dark bottom was that I kept everything inside. Now I get it out. The people I choose don't judge me – they listen, they understand the struggle. The people I invite in I know respect me and I know their hearts. Because I know their heart, I can trust them with mine.

Have your concepts of masculinity/ being a man changed over time? Is it significantly different from when you were a teen?

To an extent. I think there is a nuance that's different for men and women.

Men have to look good to women in terms of being attractive, but then in a man's world you also have the dynamic of the alpha situation.

Masculinity is this weird dynamic of "How do I show up in front of other men?" and then "How do I show up in front of a woman?"

For example, if I'm a guy with a girl, talking privately – the conversation is different than two guys in a room with a woman.

Masculinity – what I've found it to be – is "Are you comfortable with yourself and are you settled inside?" Because when I'm comfortable with myself, I don't care what this guy says. That creates the alpha control – you can't budge me. There is also a peace and a calm when I'm talking. Are you settled? Do you have a grasp of who you are and where you show up? Do you have a sense of self-confidence?

When you're settled, it's a different level of masculinity because you can serve with that masculinity in a positive way.

Being in an NFL locker room with teammates, all performing at a really high level, how did you remain centered?

If you are uncentred and unsettled, they'll feel it. Even if it's centered on one specific emotion, which could be anger or frustration. Some guys don't smile so that they don't show weakness. So, it's interesting to watch the dynamic.

Staying centered at the time – it's not even a focus – it's just staying employed. It's the most unsettling, unstable environment ever. They tell you every day that you have no job tomorrow, and one day it comes true.

So, it's "How do I operate fully?" when no part of my emotion wants me to do so. You start to learn how to manipulate the levers of your emotion, more than you ever need to and that gives you a chance to be more connected, but you're never centered. There's too much stress at all moments.

What would be your advice for your 14-year-old self?

I think it would be "It's not your fault." I was a crazy kid, man. But I had this thought that a lot of what I was experiencing was my fault. Like, I wasn't good enough for my mom to love me, I wasn't good enough for the families I was living with to feed me or not beat me, so for a lot of years I had this thought that "It's your fault."

When you think things are your fault, you have to face the music and climb – and it's a long, tough climb; or you have to be like "that's who you are – you don't deserve anything great."

It took me a lot of time to realize that "Wait, wait – none of that was my fault." Because of the position I was put in, it crafted and shaped who I was, so the 14-year-old guy was because of how the 6-year-old got treated, and that's the thing you have to extrapolate and realize.

I can go back and go, "Hey dude, that's not your fault," which means you have a clean slate to go do some work and create what you want to create.

RELATIONSHIPS AND FAMILY

Who has been the most important role model in your life? Has there been someone who has led by example?

I don't know that there's one single person – but my mom has played a humongous role. My mom taught me through actions how to love. We were poor, so it wasn't like she taught me money or academic skills but she taught me how to show up and be cool with being you. How to be okay with who you are, accept that guy, and to show unconditional love.

She allowed me to crack the shell and let people in. A guy like me, growing up in foster care, it's hard to let people in. Trust is a really difficult thing for kids like us. So, when I grew up, I still had that wall and she taught me how to let it come down.

In what ways have the women in your life influenced the man you have become?

'Softening the edges' is the best way to explain it. I played the highest level in the world in football, playing in one of the most alpha positions being a linebacker. You're rough and tough. The only thing is at that peak you need to come down a little bit to be human. It's easier to be in that environment when that's what you're bred to do. If you go on that field and you don't have that edge, they will smell blood and you will be taken down quickly, it's just the nature of it.

Then because you've been a linebacker, there's an expectation of what you're meant to be like, which is odd because that expectation leads to a lot of suicides and negativity and feeling like I have to live up to this thing that doesn't exist.

The women in my life have allowed me to have different, softer perspectives. It's interesting, I have a pedestal because of sports, because of accomplishments, because of how big I am, because of what I look like physically that I become unsettling to other people. I become like a pattern interrupt.

I open up a different lane of what could be possible – a larger black guy who grew up in a white family, who played professional sports, who is very nice and I'm not intimidating but I have the edge, and the ability to lift people up.

Women in my life gave me the ability to do that, to see that I don't need to be abrasive and rough to get what I want, but quite the opposite.

KANWER SINGH

RAPPER AND AUTHOR

 @humblethepoet   @humblethepoet   Humble the Poet

Kanwer Singh AKA Humble the Poet is a Toronto-bred MC & spoken word artist with an aura that embodies the diversity and resiliency of one of the world's most unique cities. With tattoos, beard, head wrap and a silly smile, Humble commands attention. He stimulates audiences with ideas that challenge conventional wisdom and go against the grain, with dynamic live sets that shake conventions and minds at the same time.

Do you have a favorite quote or philosophy you live by?

I have many! Maybe the newest one, after an experience with Wim Hof, that I borrowed from him is "Breathe, Motherf*cker!" It definitely helps a lot in terms of dealing with stuff, just remembering to breathe.

A good quote that I stick by is, "Life is a tragedy for those who feel, and comedy to those who think." That's one of the ones that sticks with me a lot when dealing with a lot of the circumstances we all deal with. Looking at them objectively definitely helps me a lot more.

A new mantra, after reading Ray Dalio's work, is "There's not 10,000 hours, there's 10,000 trials and errors." I'm really embracing the idea of making mistakes, messing up and failing quick – and learning quicker.

It's an American philosophy – in Canada, we don't have the entrepreneurial spirit as strong as they do in the States. It has to be viewed as trial and error, it can't be viewed as victory and defeat.

From that standpoint, as I spent more time in the States, I really recognized that people were okay if they were starting their 9th business. That's how you get there, that's how you figure it out, versus "What will people say if I fail?"

Who inspires you?

It's an interesting question, because admiring people is something I've been wrapping my head around recently. The more you get to know someone, the more challenging it is to admire them because you see their human side. I was born in the 80s, where there was still a mystique around celebrities and there wasn't a

child of an
immigrant

complete picture. It's okay for exemplary people to be normal and flawed. So, I think a lot of the people I grew up looking up to, seeing where they're at – they may not be those people I look up to anymore.

It's interesting, a lot of the people I look up to are the ones that are no longer alive because they're no longer in a situation to f*ck it up. One of the most impactful ones is Malcolm X. Reading his autobiography was a big shift for me.

Mumia Abu-Jamal, who was on death-row for many years and now serving life in prison, for a crime many people say he didn't commit. He is a prolific writer, and he has written some really cool books and I think that his thought process was super inspiring to me. I was exposed to his story when I was 17 and it was my first taste of activism and that put me on an activist path, which is one of the reasons I became 'Humble the Poet'. My early work was all based on activism before I evolved into writing about the human condition.

Andre-3000, Outkast – getting to know these people through their work, their lyrics and what they share.

When I was exposed to the work of these people, nothing was the same.

Your role models seem to have a focus on injustice – is that something that drives you?

Definitely – my definitions of injustice have changed as I've gotten older and I've probably abandoned the idealisms of it. I am very focused on people living on their own terms – there are places around the world where that's not possible, and then there's people like us who live in much freer societies who build their own cages. I'm trying to get people out of the cages they've built for themselves, at least. That really excites me.

I do consider myself an activist – but I'm more of a sniper now than a guy with a machine-gun. As I've been able to move into different circles and meet people who are CEOs and billionaires, I've been very cognizant about how they impact social change and what they do. A lot of it is very boring, behind the scenes policy changes. A lot of it is not as sexy as Malcolm X or Martin Luther King. I think the weaponry has to change.

I was raised with the idea that we are here to fight injustice, but it has to evolve beyond sticks and stones and soldiers and guns, and it has to involve information warfare, influence, political lobbying and all of that.

I think the African American community has laid a great blueprint for how other under-represented groups can get involved and have a bigger impact. It might take 30 years to see something happen, but something will happen.

EMOTIONS

Talk to me about expressing emotion as a man. Have you found it challenging?

If you're a man who is encouraging vulnerability and you're dealing with a world who is saying, "No, all the men I've ever looked up to are these alpha males and they never cried," you're always going to have a clash and that's definitely been something that I've dealt with on so many different levels.

When I first started, I was very afraid of dealing with racism and showing my face, and having people say mean things about me in the comments.

And I did – I got the Osama Bin Laden comments – but I did not expect that the vast majority of the resistance I would get would be within my community.

People would say, "You look like this, you need to act like this and you're not! You should not be swearing, you should not be sitting with a girl in your video, you should not be talking about sex. You're hanging out with gay people!" And what they're doing is reinforcing any biases they have.

They would say things like, "White people are going to think we're like 'this' if you do 'that'" And I was like, "I'm not PR for white people's beliefs."

I've come across so many people who had no idea what a Sikh was, had no idea what a Punjabi was, who were able to show me nothing but love and respect.

I only lose the fights with people about these issues if I engage with them, and I don't.

People's opinions on my work are much more indicative of who they are, and it's telling their story, not mine.

What makes you truly happy? What lights up your soul?

Eureka moments. Having moments of eureka, like legitimately going "How have I gone my whole life without putting two and two together, how have I never met this person, how have I never come across this idea?"

That means a lot to me. Discovering new places – I've been riding my bike through the city. Me and my buddy treat it like a video game, unlocking new maps. I'm riding in neighborhoods that I've driven past a million times but have never absorbed. I'm riding through parks that I've always known about but have never bothered to go through. That gives me so much happiness – a five-hour bike ride

excites me a lot.

Having new experiences – having one foot in the complete unknown makes me very happy. I want to do as much as possible while I'm here. I'm of the belief that this is not a dress-rehearsal, this is it. Don't save it – if you want to do it, do it now. Spend your life, live your life.

How do you express anger? What do you do to release frustration?

Being alone is very important for me. I don't have dramatic emotional outbursts, but I do have a sharp tongue, so I've found myself in challenging situations, where if I'm around people I do have the potential to make things worse through the things I say, even if it's in a calm demeanor.

Recently, I was working on a deal with a company, and I was going out for drinks with the CEO and COO and we'd been going back and forth for months. They sent the paperwork, and I hired a lawyer to look it over, and while I was doing that, the founder of the company killed the whole division, which killed my deal – leaving me with five figures in legal fees. I never expected that, that wasn't something I thought of – they weren't corrupt people, but there was a chain of command. I wasn't aware of that, so when the CEO gives me a contract and goes, "Let's get to work" I think I'm talking to the boss, but he wasn't.

It was a challenging situation – I wasn't in the situation to feel betrayed because no-one was looking to betray me – so I had a lot of frustration and I didn't know where to put it. That was an interesting experience for me because initially, I was very upset, and I did make them all feel very bad. None of them were trying to run from the situation or trying to hide from it.

I should have taken more time before speaking to them – I have since had conversations with them and they're still trying to get me money for the legal fees and they're trying to make up for it.

I'm still trying to be more cognizant of these situations where if you get some news you didn't want, take a day. Don't react immediately because you may say something you don't believe to be true later on, and you may make things worse. Even the simple fact that you could burn a bridge because you said the wrong thing to the wrong person.

I write this a lot, "Life is going to throw you curveballs, practice your swing." The next curveball I face, I will be more mindful not to handle it too emotionally.

SPIRITUALITY AND MINDFULNESS

What role does religion or spirituality play for you?

It's interesting – growing up, I was given a deeper than normal education on Sikh history and philosophy by my mom, "Here are the rules; don't cut your hair, don't eat this, learn these gurus' names, learn these holy sites."

Then I started learning about kam, krodh, lobh moh, and ahankar which are lust, greed, anger, attachment and ego and how these things take away your peace and I started to realize that there was a real philosophy behind being a Sikh, and it's not an identity, it's a philosophy and a way of life. It mirrors Buddhism and Hinduism – Eastern philosophy all came from the same place.

I think, as I got older, I adopted that a little bit more. In my last book, I had a chapter on my evolving relationship with God. Going from my first memories of praying, and begging God for stuff, to becoming a flaming atheist to probably landing where I am now, which is "Matter cannot be created or destroyed. Everything is one." We are a drop in the ocean.

I am not worried about something above or below judging me, but I do understand that I am a part of the grand algorithm. I'm a part of something. From that standpoint, trying to find more opportunities to be more visceral and primal is important.

Going on safari in Kenya a few years ago showed to me just how primal we really are. We're not Zoom calls and bank accounts, we're more than that. The Zoom call falls out? Who gives a shit? You're doing all this work for what? You're doing it to live. Why don't we just live instead?

I now look at modern religions as the art of being a good person. This is how people figured things out before we had a scientific method. It's not the enemy of science.

I'm experimenting with the simplest form of meditation I can find, which is to sit there and do nothing. Don't chant, don't breathe, don't focus. Do nothing and hopefully the inbox of the brain starts to sort itself out. Have no expectations and do nothing.

Peace is the absence of everything else, love is the absence of everything else. Having less is what's going to give us more.

LIFE PURPOSE AND SUCCESS

What do you ultimately strive for? What is your reason for being?

Selfishly, my reason for being is to experience as much as I can. The way

I fit into the system of things is that my life circumstances and experiences have allowed me to put things into words very well, whether as a rapper, a designer or a writer. I can communicate very well with words and I understand the importance of keeping things light and digestible, which allows those ideas to add value to other people.

In the grand scheme of things, as an artist my job is to bring new ideas to the world and a lot of that comes through scaffolding and simplifying complex ideas that may only be accessible to people who have had resources and education that most people don't have. Everyone deserves to have that access.

My chosen purpose right now is to live, learn and share. I get access to more creative communities and greater minds which then lead to more eureka moments that I seek.

Do you classify yourself as successful?

I think yes – from a superficial, resume standpoint I am extremely fortunate. I can pay my bills, I can pay my parents bills and still have plenty left. I am in control of my day and my schedule. The only people telling me what to do right now are people who I have hired to do that – a personal trainer or someone else I'm working with.

From those standpoints, and from what 6 or 7-year-old me hated about life, I'm in a good situation.

We're always striving for more - I have to remind myself that my competition is yesterday's version of me and that I should continually focus on progress and challenging myself to do harder things to build my self-respect more so than my self-esteem. Outside validation is a potato chip – it's addictive and you'll never get enough.

A couple of years ago I saw a billionaire friend of mine take a cold shower and I was thinking "Why would you do that?" and now I get it – you have to continue to do hard stuff and challenge yourself to feel better about yourself. Being broke used to be the challenge, people not knowing who I was or not knowing my work used to be the challenge, now I have new challenges.

I am definitely more successful than I ever thought I would be, but it only challenges me to dream even bigger. And I've definitely caught myself not dreaming big enough.

OVERCOMING CHALLENGES

How has failure, or apparent failure, set you up for later success? Do you have a "favorite failure" of yours?

Yeah! I quit my job. I was a schoolteacher and I quit my job, thinking I had a record deal that was going to pay me twice the amount of money I was making as a schoolteacher. So, I quit my job. I owned a property that I had rented out, and I kicked my tenant out and moved in there. I took in another musician that I was living with and let him live there for free while he was helping to work in the deal.

Then the deal fell through, he disappeared, and next thing I knew I was drowning in debt. I had $80,000 in debt, no income, no understanding of how creatives achieve income, very little self-worth and I hit what's considered 'rock-bottom'. That was the foundation I really started to build myself up from. It took a long time, it was very slow, but I would never have had the balls to pull the trigger on my dreams. It was only because someone had made an empty promise that I took the leap of faith.

When I fell down and crashed and burned - that's when the story really begins.

That's probably my favorite failure because it was probably the most defining and there's nothing romantic about it – there was no quick turnaround, it took me five years to get out of debt and learn how to make money as an artist. I had to move back home with my parents, I had to make a lot of sacrifices, but it helped me develop my self-awareness, it helped me learn to take personal responsibility. It helped me become more aware of when I was cutting corners and the consequences of all of that, and it forced me to take a look at all the things I was avoiding in terms of my romanticized ideals of the world, my unrealistic expectations of life, my low expectations of myself. Ever since then, it's probably been the most defining moments of my life.

Do you still welcome that vulnerability into your life?

I want to say yes, I want to say nothing can rattle me, but the truth is that nothing will rattle you until something rattles you. I've definitely come across a few more failures, some more intense, some less intense. That experience prepared me for change, and reminded me that I had to be adaptable, I had to be open. I had to spend less time judging a circumstance and more time understanding a circumstance. It taught me a lot and I think now future failures are teaching me to have more empathy for myself because I have the manual on how to deal with tragedy but page one has to be 'Have an emotional reaction, lose your cool, make space for that and then turn to these top tips.'

What has happened with COVID-19, there really wasn't too much impact on me – mentally or physically. I was very quick to try to find the opportunity in the chaos, my mind was already prepared for that and for a downslide in life. I was thinking everything was heading one way in the world and would head in another. I wasn't thinking pandemic, I was thinking a real estate crash or a stock-market crash. That put me in a situation where I was sitting on cash, I was sitting on savings and I was really prepared for a worst-case scenario. I wasn't prepared for the monkey wrench of not leaving the house, and not exposing my parents to anything. It's new learnings.

I've gone through a lot and I think I understand now that challenges will make you stronger, if you're up for the test. It's just the timelines are never the timelines you ask for. I'm cognizant of the unpleasantries of not being in control – I'm not at peace with not being in control, when I'm not in control of the situation, it does make me upset and I can recognize that. It doesn't necessarily change my emotions and make me okay but at least I'm aware of it.

It's a double-edged sword, but at least I'm learning new things which is super important. I haven't welcomed failure yet; I haven't welcomed discomfort completely in the ways I've seen in other people but I'm definitely dramatically better off than I was even a year or two years ago.

I'm not worried about what other people think, but am I worried about making an investment in something that might not pay off? I still worry about that. But I'm not really worried about judgments and approval of other people.

RELATIONSHIPS AND FAMILY

In what ways have the women in your life influenced the man you have become?

I grew up with my mother and my two sisters – Mom is great. She would tell me stories every night and she shared with me everything she learned that day. She got into spirituality and religion after hurting herself at work – she worked at a factory around the corner from our house, and she was so happy but within 18 months she hurt herself, and she and Dad didn't have the tools to deal with it. Spirituality is what helped her get through that.

I've had many different inputs in my relationships with women. "I want a strong man, I want a tough man" but then I've also had "You're not strong enough, you're not tough enough."

You realize that there is no universal way to treat anybody – it's a matter of listening and adjusting accordingly.

That's my advice – listen and be continually open. Your success in life, particularly when it comes to women, is based on how much you're willing to learn. The greatest teacher for young men is the women in their lives, but the women are learning as well, so there's got to be a level of space. Definitions and relationships are always changing.

What was your relationship like with your father?

There definitely weren't any sit-down talks that had an impact – I learnt a lot of things by osmosis. He always viewed life as "You take care of your kids and they'll fly the coop. They'll pay you back by taking care of their kids." He worked long hours – he has a master's degree in economics, but he drove a cab when we moved to Toronto, so he never used his education.

He is very intelligent – he instilled a level of learning, and it's one of the reasons I became a teacher. Neither of my parents are easily impressed – they weren't happy when I became a teacher, they were even less happy when I became an artist. Their benchmarks are very different.

Now that I'm older, I've caught him being vulnerable, I've caught him off-guard, so it's cool.

What does "being a man" mean to you now?

It's recognizing your strengths and not simply posturing strength. There's strength and vulnerability. I may be able to cry in front of you, and you recognize it as strength, but that may not be the same for other people.

I was teaching in a neighborhood where a lot of the kids didn't have father figures or healthy male role models and so we were coached. I remember my principal telling me, "You are going to tell the kids you're afraid of spiders, even if you're not. Because they need to know that men can be afraid, and that's okay." I didn't grow up thinking men could be afraid and that required a lot of unlearning for me.

Is there a piece of advice that you could give your 14-year-old self?

Definitely. I'd say, "You're smart, and from a cognitive standpoint you have benefits that other people may not have, but that's not going to take you very far. Persistence and hard work will take you dramatically further in your life than your brain ever will. But if you can bring your brain along for the journey, you'll be in a magical place."

CHAZ BONO

ACTOR

 @therealchazbono   @chazbono

Chaz Bono is an American character actor and the only child of famed entertainers Sonny and Cher.

An acclaimed author, Chaz has written three books including *Transition*, which was released in 2011. *Transition* is his groundbreaking and candid account of a forty-year struggle to match his gender identity with his physical body and his transformation from female to male.

He has shared his life and experiences in, and produced the three-time Emmy nominated documentary, *Becoming Chaz.*

Chaz has a rich history of advocating for LGBTQI rights, having worked for two national LGBTQI organizations, and as public speaker on college campuses and at events around the world.

In 2012 Chaz decided to pursue his lifelong goal of a career as a working actor. He began doing theater in Los Angeles, and was cast in independent films *Dirty* and *Gods and Secrets*. He is best known for the role of Lot Polk, in *American Horror Story* Roanoke, and Gary K Longstreet in *American Horror Story Cult.*

Do you have a favorite quote or philosophy you live by?

I don't know that I have anything in particular – I just try to be the best person I can be. I try to keep my side of the street clean as much as possible. And also – and I'm trying to say this without sounding corny, but it does sound corny – I really try to give back to people and help out when

I can. It's a nice thing to do and when you put yourself out, others do the same for you and it just is a circle of positivity in your life.

I play and collect yoyos – it's a community – several times in buying something from Facebook (there's a big community of people who buy, sell and trade yoyos from each other) and I'll find myself chatting with someone who struggling with recovery and needs someone to talk to, or somebody struggling with an issue around their sexual orientation, or whatever and in a town where they're having a difficult time and just not expecting to have that discussion. That happens to me all the time. So, reaching out to somebody and asking a question – it opens up a floodgate of them really needing to talk to somebody who is exactly like me.

That happened really recently, connecting with an actress on social media, we started talking about a situation she was going through. She just really needed to talk to someone.

Or when you're on set and make an effort to get to know the new guys – a lot of them were younger and it's important to make these guys feel at home.

You can be someone who has a little bit more experience who can help someone else who is struggling or who doesn't know as much. It might be people coming into acting class who are new and just don't know the business at all.

There was an actress who was in the class – she was really funny and talented. It was a masterclass, so everyone was really good, but she wasn't getting anywhere.

So, I said that I would take the time to have a chat with her and brainstorm a little bit. It turned out she didn't have a tape of herself, and I was like, "In this business, that's the first thing you've got to have – so try to find a student or independent filmmaker where you can get some really great footage of yourself, because until you have that you're going to be banging your head against the wall."

It's just information she didn't have. A lot of people did that for me and continue to do that for me in this business so it's important for me to do that for other people.

It's a matter of not forgetting how difficult life can be, and not forgetting your life experience to help others.

EMOTIONS

Do you know what makes you happy?

Honestly, what makes me the happiest is acting – working.

I got into my first acting class when I was 14 and went to school for that in New York at a performing arts high school. Not knowing exactly why at the time, but I just couldn't play female characters. I got that when I was cast as a male character in a *Midsummer Night's Dream* in my senior year. From 14 to 18, that's all I wanted to do, and it struck me that I wasn't really going to be able to do this, as commercially, at that point when I graduated high school in 1987 there were no opportunities to do anything edgy or out-there.

Then I got back into an acting class after almost 25 years in 2012 and it changed my whole life and got me back into doing this thing I love again. At this point in my life, that's the thing that makes me the happiest – when I'm working and when I'm on set, and I'm just incredibly filled with gratitude to be there.

It was uncomfortable to go back after such a long time and be one of the oldest people around but once I got through just feeling ridiculously uncomfortable and beyond rusty, I ended up in this amazing community and met some really great friends. My life just became completely different.

It also became really frustrating, and continues to be, because it's a really hard industry and tack onto that being transgender and being known as something other than an actor and having the parents that I do – it's been a slog. But there's nothing else I want to do with my life at this point, so I'm in that slog and I enjoy the creativity of it. That's what I'm in it for – I'm the happiest when I'm playing a character as opposite of me as I can, and it is usually characters that are pretty nasty.

RELATIONSHIPS

How do you navigate conflict in relationships?

My girlfriend and I honestly don't have a lot of conflict because neither of us are fighters, which is great – and neither of us is particularly sensitive so there has been very few conflicts and the few times there have been, we have just rationally talked it out. Neither of us are yellers or have hot tempers.

We've known each other since we were 14 - we haven't been together for that long, but that's when we met. We reconnected because we both got sober and we met through that community. I'm 17 years clean and sober and she's 14 years so we have that experience under our belt and have worked on ourselves a lot individually.

The few times that stuff has come up, we've been able to talk about it – but it hasn't been that many instances. We are really different people, and we work because we accept that we are really different, and we enjoy the stuff we enjoy together – we genuinely love and respect each other – and we don't ever try to make the other person into someone else. I think that comes with age, honestly.

You've got to know what works for you and what doesn't, and what you can deal with and what you can't. When you meet someone and you go, "Okay, I really like you and can deal with you, and this is me and I've got some really good characteristics but there are some things about me that could drive somebody crazy." You're willing to accept those things and vice versa, and that's it.

When you're young you have this idea that you are going to be able to shape other people into what you want them to be – and as you get older you realize that that's just a losing proposition.

It's been a lot of trial and error throughout my life, and when I was younger, I was with a lot of women who probably weren't the best for me. Before I was with my girlfriend now, I was single for about 5 years and that ended up being a really good thing.

I think all too often, people are afraid of spending time with themselves, but I think when you're comfortable with yourself – and I am – I am very comfortable with myself. I'm very happy by myself – and when you get into that place, you're choosing somebody because they're really the right person for you versus being terrified of being alone, so I'll be with anybody. And that's how I was a lot when I was younger. My criteria for a girlfriend was "I find you attractive and you seem to think the same thing about me, so let's get together." And that was about it.

Whereas, when I got older, and especially after I transitioned, it changed a lot about how I saw things and what I wanted, and what I would accept and put up with. It put me in a position of being a lot choosier and waiting for the right situation to come along.

BEING A MAN

Has your concept of masculinity changed over time?

It's hard – I had no idea I was transgender at 18. I knew it existed, but not really and not with men. So, it didn't seem at that point in my life a possibility even. It wasn't even something that entered my mind. I had no idea what was happening – but it wasn't until I got to play a man after 4 years of studying acting that I was good at it and felt that I could relate to the character I was playing.

I've always been incredibly masculine for as far back as I remember, but it wasn't okay. So, I went through a life of innately not being okay – which is a difficult thing most men don't have to experience.

I'm a very thoughtful man and I am still fairly masculine and like fairly typical male things – and I've come into it in a time where those things are looked down on a bit, so that's been interesting too.

I wouldn't really call myself being in the transgender community – I don't know what that means.

I get a lot of insight from that and especially with kids – you just see this incredible spectrum of gender expression and then this idea of non-binary gender, which I am completely comfortable with and which I fully validate. It's just not my experience.

I think we are in a time where everyone needs to understand other people's experience and be okay with that, and while I really support someone who is male and whose gender expression is not masculine at all, I think it's also important to be accepting of someone who's male and whose gender expression is more typically masculine.

Actually, when a good friend of mine, Shane Jenek, and I became friends, we would talk about this stuff a lot and at that point, Shane was like, "The problem is the binary". And I was like, "The problem for you is that you don't fit the binary which is okay." I was the first person who said to him, "I think you're probably gender fluid or gender non-binary or something in that realm."

The problem for me isn't that because I do fit in it – so it took a while for him to understand that and say, "You're not pretending to be something you're not – that is who you are."

I remember at one point he said, "If only everyone was okay that you had to transition" and I was like, "I didn't have to – I wanted to."

So, it was a really interesting journey we went on and why we have such a deep friendship – up until then, he didn't have a lot of straight, male friends.

As a male, I experience the world more physically than ever before. Before transitioning, I experienced everything in my head, intellectually, because I was so not in my body. Going through transition, what I discovered is my first experience is with anything new is a much more physical experience first.

I have never been terribly emotional, and that's innately me to a degree. Testosterone allowed me to access anger, which I really couldn't before – in a healthy way. Getting back into acting class and all that has opened up a whole range of emotions that you have to have access to.

My emotional range is a lot bigger, but I would say how I experience something first is still a physical experience.

When I met my girlfriend, for the first few years, we just had that "in love" thing of throwing good eating out the door and both gained about 15 – 20 pounds. We've gotten back on the good eating plan now, which is great, but I was watching something on TV, and I saw this cupcake – I have cut out all sugar and carbs and I don't even like cupcakes – but the reaction I had was purely physical.

My stomach – butterflies went off and I had this physical yearning for this cupcake. I would say that is far more typical of how I experience things now.

Even in acting, I can go into aggressive mode at the snap of a finger. Sarah Paulson – she cries SOOO well – it's phenomenal! I could never in my life do what she does at a moment. And there are certain things you need to do well as an actress – for men, we need to be able to go there, but just not as often.

I did a scene with an actress where she had to aggressively smack me over the head and it was hard for her, and I was like, "C'mon, just do it – just hit me!"

Physicality is just how I experience everything.

What's the most important quality to you as a man?

Character I think – just like integrity and honesty and character. I can't abide people who are in it just for themselves and who lie and cheat and who aren't trying to make things better in some way.

Was there a moment that defined you as a man?

There wasn't an exact moment – there were different moments – and I have heard other trans people talk about this, but for me I was in a state of perpetual adolescence till I transitioned because I wasn't going to grow up as a woman, that wasn't a possibility for me.

I started transitioning at 40 – I didn't grow up until then, until I could reach manhood.

I remember a pivotal, superficial experience that was about 7 months into my transition and my high school friends were having a reunion in Las Vegas, so I went up there for that, and that was the first time in my transition that people were calling me "Sir". That was a superficial standpoint, but in the real sense it was a process of growing and changing and getting to know myself and getting to a place of feeling whole, in and out.

I'm very comfortable in myself and my own masculinity.

Do you have a group of men you can talk to?

Most of my good friends are actors so it's important – because it's talking about our lives, the women in our lives, and our family – but it's also talking about our work and the frustration and everything around that, because everyone is at the point where they have some work, but nobody's career is at the point they want it to be. So, it's the highs and lows that we can share – and we can get so incredibly frustrated. There's a small handful of guys that I know that if any one of us makes it, we are taking the others along.

My girlfriend has her friends, and they have their 'thing' – I don't exactly understand it. It's really different – but there's that bonding that women have with other women and men have with other men. It's great to have the connection with my male friends and just be one of the guys, because for so much of my life I didn't know exactly where I fit in, so it's really nice to experience it.

SCOTT NEESON

FOUNDER, CAMBODIAN CHILDREN'S FUND

 @scottatccf   @scottincambodia   CCFund

When Hollywood marketing executive Scott Neeson embarked on a sabbatical between jobs in 2003, he couldn't have imagined how it would change his life.

On a trip to Phnom Penh, Scott saw hundreds of children and their families living and working on the Steung Meanchey garbage dump, one of the most toxic environments imaginable. It was a moment that changed his life.

Scott had a 26-year career in the film business, including tenure as President of 20th Century Fox International. Scott thought he had it all – a powerful role in the film industry, celebrity friends, a big house, fancy cars and a boat.

But in 2003, Scott's view on life changed completely when he found himself looking out across the Steung Meanchey garbage dump at hundreds of children scavenging through garbage.

Soon after, Scott made the decision to resign from his job, sell all of his possessions and focus his energy and passion into the Cambodian Children's Fund.

What are the issues you are seeing in Cambodia?

Overall, the country has been doing well economically. This growth has lifted most people but there are still areas of poverty and the area we work in has not only poverty but a very broken society. The people around this area have migrated in from the countryside with debt and other deep-rooted problems.

What is your favorite quote or philosophy you live by?

"People say that what we're all seeking is a meaning for life. I don't think that's what we're really seeking. I think that what we're seeking is an experience of being alive, so that our life experiences on the purely physical plane will have resonances with our own innermost being and reality, so that we actually feel the rapture of being alive." - Joseph Campbell

What is the one characteristic about yourself that you are most proud of?

The Cambodian Children's Fund (CCF) has grown quickly in terms of the number of students and the overall number of programs with an education program from kindergarten to university, medical center and very low-cost housing. I am proud of the fact that amidst all this I have never lost track of the individuals in the program - mostly the children but also the grandmothers, the parents and others. I love to be able to talk to them meaningfully, knowing their names, their backgrounds and any recent problems. In short, it is that thing that makes people feel special. Having that connection is wonderful for me too, it keeps me grounded and reminds me of why I moved here.

How is love shown to the kids at CCF?

This is certainly one of the challenges here. The dysfunction in the Steung Meanchey area largely manifests itself as a lack of care, love and what we would generally consider natural parenting skills. This is not a judgmental statement, it's simply that all the parents here are essentially survivors of the killing fields in 1975 - 1979, which were brutal days and broke up families in different parts of the country. Today's parents had no childhood, no exposure to parents, culture, only everyday survival.

Implementing a program to distribute love is no easy task. There is no simple distribution and it certainly cannot be faked. I spend a large portion of my non-office hours down in the community ensuring that the children understand that I very much care about them, that they are special. I've learnt how to express pride, love, care and ensure that each child knows that they have their own identity.

Scaling this has been more challenging. We have a very good foster program now, largely headed by grandmothers in our community. It may not be a precise definition of love but it's an environment where they feel part of a family and cared for.

BEING A MAN

What does "being a man" mean to you?

It's harder these days to define what being a man means when there is greater equality in society and the workforce. However, being a man, in my mind, is to demonstrate the values you believe in, provide a sense of security for family, extended family and the vulnerable, teaching the younger men - not just one's own sons but other boys who are growing up without a father figure - the difference between strength and domination, masculinity and tyranny and that vulnerability is acceptable.

It's concerning that even in the West, boys can grow up without a father figure. With a large number of single mothers and a primary school system that is predominantly staffed with female teachers, boys go without a guiding male figure. That is not to say that mothers and women overall cannot teach the right values, but I think a boy will look to a father figure to learn his own definition of being a man.

What piece of advice would you give young men?

My advice to young men would be to live your life with authenticity and integrity. If you can base your life on what you see as right or wrong and not simply what you can get away with, life will be fuller. You may not be as rich, but you will certainly be far more content with life. Remember, too, that reward is not simply financial or a direct benefit to oneself, the greater rewards lie with giving to those who cannot give back and giving without being recognized.

What needs to happen for these boys to have the insight to stay with the program at CCF?

I find this very challenging. Our retention rate for girls in education is terrific, it's far ahead of measures both within Cambodia and overseas. However, with boys, we don't have that same determination to get an education, to set themselves up for a better future. I think the largest factor is the lack of good role models in this area. Around 10% of the households in the Steung Meanchey district have a functioning male figurehead (in this case, defined as being mostly present, contributing toward the family's well-being and keeping the household free of all abuse such as substance abuse and violence.)

I understand why the girls stay in education: it's not just that they have mothers as role models, they know what the future looks like if they opt out of education early. The girls and young women are more determined to get a better future for themselves, help their mother and siblings out of poverty and make a better life for the next generation. Sadly, the boys don't have the same focus and again, there is no one to teach them this as they grow.

Are there men in popular culture who are shining a light in Cambodia?

I have seen more examples of men starting to lead the way here. The most obvious to me is some of our older students who have either graduated or, in some cases, are completing their studies overseas. They are remarkable role models for the next generation, and I am so proud of how they have overcome their initial difficulties. I can't think of a better role model for the next generation. There are now those in leadership positions in Cambodia who have a broader world view and I feel will be able to serve the country well. There is an increased focus on the welfare of the poor, care for the most vulnerable, understanding the need to equalize women's rights, care of the environment and the need for social security systems, etc.

I have got a great deal of optimism seeing Cambodia moving from simple survival to being a very progressive country.

EMOTIONS

What makes you truly happy?

Essentially, it is being able to help people. After 16 years here, we have developed processes that can effectively and efficiently help those who are sick, those who are subject to abuse, children who have never had an education. I am in the community each evening and simply being able to move a child from a place of vulnerability and no education into a good, consistent education program is a real joy and I get to see it every day. The transformation is fast and usually permanent. I love that.

Similarly, finding a sick person in the community, very often a grandparent, and being able to get them into our medical program - that makes me very happy.

There is also an enormous satisfaction seeing the kids I first brought into CCF in

2004/2005. Of the first 200 children that came off that wretched garbage dump, 135 have gone onto university. That is a wonderful feeling and, as I get older, I can see the legacy of my work. Knowing that the children of these students will never know the same poverty, squalor and neglect is a real wonder to me. Generational poverty has been broken with each graduation.

How do you express your anger? What's your emotional release?

I've lost either my ability or my need to be angry, well, at least most of the time. Being in these dire communities and being within a Buddhist culture, one begins to understand the futility of getting angry.

Most of the time, the anger is a reflection of one's own internal problems, judgment and perspective. These days I like to take a couple of breaths and start to look at the situation more objectively, seeing if there are ways to avoid such a situation in the future, and address the core reason for the anger.

I don't have any specific practices for emotional release. I have returned to doing Yoga and weights. I find that my life overall has enough balance between the suffering and the joys of helping people overcome and achieve better lives, happiness and fulfillment whether it's a child getting an education or a father with a drug problem.

What does vulnerability look like to you?

I have my own issues with vulnerability and being here on the ground and very often being the go-to person for people who have dire situations. I'm not the person that can afford to be vulnerable and there

is an expectation for me to be their rock. Clearly, my upbringing has taught me to live without too much vulnerability. There is a very small group of friends that I can be vulnerable with. Unfortunately, most of them are not actually living in Cambodia.

Do you have a resource to have those discussions?

I don't have a resource. I try not to internalize - I try to work it through in my own place and time. There is another aspect: some of the experiences, the most distressing and traumatic, are best not spoken about. People really don't want to hear it and I feel that by talking about it I am giving additional life to a terrible situation or incident.

LIFE PURPOSE AND SUCCESS

What do you ultimately strive for?

I have never had a grand vision of what I wanted to be either in the film business or what the Cambodian Children's Fund would look like. It has been an organic growth albeit a spectacularly successful organic growth. If I had the vision of an organization that would be medically treating 30,000 people a year, 600 homes built, 2,000 kids in school, I would have laughed and run a mile - I would never have moved here. Mentally, I need to take it one step at a time, more so given the fact I knew nothing about charities or philanthropy when I moved here.

I've achieved more than I ever expected to and the legacy of having helped children from a life of squalor through to university, very good jobs and fuller lives provides me with a great deal of contentment. I am at an age, too, where striving is no longer a priority.

At what point did you define yourself as being successful?

I have issues with looking at myself as being successful, I tend to look forward to what needs to be done next. Admittedly, I understand the need to sit down and reflect on what has been done and how it measures up to my own standards and expectations.

That said, the charity has grown to be an enormous success from the values to the efficiencies and the care provided.

How do you deal with failure?

I would like to be able to say that I take it in my stride and that the number of successes well outstrips the number of failures by a factor of ten. However, the truth is that when you're dealing with such a personal undertaking, bringing in children to school, helping grandmothers get medical care, etc. a failure very often leads to dire consequences and it's hard not to internalize this. The Cambodian Children Fund staff are terrific and I trust them to ensure that no one will unnecessarily fall out of the programs but with such a dysfunctional environment, there are inevitably cases where we can't help.

SPIRITUALITY AND MINDFULNESS

What role does spirituality and mindfulness play for you?

I strongly believe that spirituality and mindfulness are essential. I realize this more so in the work I do now where I see both the best and the worst of humanity. Without a spiritual practice, the work could eat away at me. The grounding that the likes of Yoga, meditation, meaningful time alone bring, allows me to restore and revitalize. I have been the poster child for having a bad balance between work and a healthy social life. I am always being pulled towards overwork.

RELATIONSHIPS

Who has been the most important role model in your life?

I find it very hard to point to role models. Meeting the Dalai Lama was enormously inspiring: his understanding of humanity both in a spiritual and a pragmatic sense was quite an epiphany for me. I find that different individuals have remarkable qualities that I look towards. For example, Tony Robbins has the most remarkable communication skills and the ability to concisely explain difficult concepts.

In terms of philosophy, the work of Joseph Campbell resonates as does the courage and oration of Martin Luther King during his activist years.

What role have women played in your life?

During my time in Cambodia and especially doing the work I do my view of women has changed remarkably. Cambodia was devastated during the Khmer Rouge years of 1975 – 1979, there was a terrible genocide, and the country was left without direction or soul. It was the women who pulled it together, particularly mothers who brought together family, community and eventually a relatively harmonious and sustainable society here. It seems the mothers will always step in when social fabric disintegrates.

STEPHEN "WONDERBOY" THOMPSON

UFC FIGHTER

 @wonderboymma   @wonderboymma   Wonderboymma

Stephen "Wonderboy" Thompson is an American professional mixed martial artist and former professional full-contact kickboxer who currently fights as a welterweight in the Ultimate Fighting Championship. Stephen is undefeated through 37 amateur and 57 professional kickboxing matches, and is a 5-time World Champion.

Do you have a favorite quote or philosophy you live by?

I'm a martial artist, I've been in the martial arts scene since I was 3 years old and my dad fought back in the '70s and '80s. My brothers and sisters fight. So, we lived that warrior life, so to speak.

There was a quote that I used to see as a kid, and my dad used to say it all the time. I guess he wanted to see us handle tough situations and through the training and the martial arts, we were able to be put in those uncomfortable situations and try to fight through those and learn from them.

So, there was a quote he used to say to us whenever training got tough – he would always say, "The more you sweat in peace, the less you bleed in war."

What he meant by that is the harder you train in the gym peacefully; in a street situation or competitive situation the less you are injured.

I think that goes into not just the martial arts but in life itself, and everything you go through in life. So, I've always liked that quote.

That's a great quote. Does your father come from a military background?

It's funny you say that, even though you've never met him before. He does not – there was a time he wanted to go into the military, but it was right after Vietnam, and they were kind of kicking guys out of the military, so he wasn't able to do that. He went to military school though.

His dad was a pretty rough guy – he grew up in Moncks Corner in Charleston, South Carolina. At the age of 18, that was Dad's chance to leave and he got out of there, and moved to Greenville, South Carolina.

Dad has a military mentality, and through the martial arts, he has kept that – he went straight into martial arts after studying.

The man that your father has been to you and your siblings, do you think it's because he lacked that guidance from his own father?

He may not admit it, but I think so. His dad raised him to the best of his ability – his dad was born in West Virginia in a shack and that was his way out of it. He was a pretty rough dude. I saw that sometimes when I was a kid. I think my dad raised us the way he wasn't raised. I think he wants to be the dad that his dad wasn't to him.

I remember getting into trouble – I was afraid of my dad. I know that sounds bad, but I knew that there would be dire consequences if I did something I shouldn't have, and that taught me as a man today not to do certain things because there will be consequences. People today often don't see those consequences and don't fear those consequences.

I got my behind whooped when I was a kid. I would have loved to have been sent to time out or sent to my room – there's a whole lot I could have done in my room! Now, as a man, it's worse than getting a whooping if you do something wrong – you can go to jail and that affects not just you but everyone around you.

My dad would always discuss why I was punished and that kind of helped me through my life. I saw there and then the mistake I made.

I thank him every day for it – even if it's just giving him a hug or telling him I love him.

Do you have a personal trait that you are really proud of?

I would say that I am glad that I am a very patient person – and that has to do with being part of the martial arts as well. People think that martial arts is just about kicking and punching. It's not just about that. It's about showing modesty, courtesy, integrity, self-control, perseverance, and an indomitable spirit. That's what martial arts is about.

Through martial arts, and teaching kids, I've learnt a lot about patience. Nothing really gets to me; nothing really bothers me that much. I think it upsets my mom and my dad that I don't get upset. I take everything with a grain of salt, and you've got to find that fine line between being nice and being taken advantage of. A lot of people I know say, "Don't mistake Stephen being so nice as being a sign of weakness."

I don't know why I am that way – I guess I know that whatever is coming my way, I am able to work around it in the best way possible, and in the nicest way possible. You don't have to be angry at anybody, you don't have to be mean. I hate holding grudges. If I'm upset with somebody or somebody is upset with me, I go out of my way to make sure that things are taken care of and we leave on a good relationship.

Even if I'm done wrong, I like to forgive but I don't forget. I think it's the fact that I'm just nice! I do think martial arts has a lot to do with it. On a daily basis, I am put in an uncomfortable situation.

I think that training, and getting my frustrations out on a bag, or getting a good sweat in has a lot to do with it. So that way, outside of the martial arts, I'm able to live a comfortable and happy life.

Outside of the Octagon, what are some of the things you're passionate about?

I don't have any kids, but I know how I was raised – and I thank Dad every day for it. At the time, of course, it was no fun. Dad wasn't my friend until I was in my late teens... he was a parent first. I see a lot of parents nowadays wanting to be their 5 or 6-year-old kids' friend instead of being their parent.

A lot of parents come to me and say, "I can't make them do anything." And I think, "Wait a second, you're the parent. Why can't you make them? You make them go to school." And the parent responds, "Well they don't want to" but they're not old enough to know what they want.

Here at the school, Dad and I not only teach the kids stuff, we try and teach the parents as well. Sometimes that's a little easier said than done! But there's a lot of training that a lot of our parents need. I think what you're doing with *Men: Real Conversations* could help as well. Kids aren't being raised right nowadays. They're doing what they want to do. Nowadays, when parents are tired of being with their kid, or they're being too loud, they stick a computer or tablet in front of their faces as a babysitter. I was born in the '80s so maybe families were tighter knit then, but now everybody's everywhere, so you don't have that tight-knit family. It's very hard to come by, nowadays.

I think it starts in the home; I see it every day.

Who inspires you?

I would have to say it's my dad. There's a lot of other people who inspire me, but when I really think about it, I find myself looking more and more at my dad and what he does, and how he handles situations.

Even when he's tying his shoe, he tries to do it to the best of his ability. If it's cleaning up, if it's helping others – even the smallest task possible – he does it to the best of his ability. Nowadays, the world is full of lazy people. That rubs off on me, seeing what my dad does. I'm driving down the road, and the person in front of me throws something out of his car, I find myself pulling over and picking up that trash now. It's like, "Wait, what am I doing?" It's him – I think Dad is the reason I do that.

Little things like that are things I think are special.

Outside of my family, it's champions such as Georges St-Pierre, Chris Wiedman, Rashad Evans, and Anderson Silva. I've trained with all these guys and I'm glad I did because I saw what it takes to be a champion and have that champion mindset, and why so few people have made it.

Georges St-Pierre was my inspiration to switch from kickboxing to MMA. I had a kickboxing fight in Montreal, Canada, and lo and behold, in my opponent's corner was George, one of the all-time greatest welterweight fighters. I think I knocked my opponent out in the fifth round, and after the fight they came to me and wanted me to be a part of Georges' training camps. To go and see what he does, and what he puts himself through, I realized I needed to do that in order to get where he's at.

Chris Wiedman – it's funny how these inspirational people end up becoming my family! My baby brother married his sister. I remember helping him get ready to fight for the title against Anderson Silva. What I learnt from him is how to carry yourself, and how to separate your training with your everyday life.

He's a family man, he's got three kids, and I know how stressful training camps can be because you're so exhausted at the end of the day. How does this guy get the energy to spend time with his kids and to love on his wife? It was probably after three training camps that we became really close and good friends, and I saw how he treated his family during those stressful times. As a man, it's your job to bring your family together, even when you're stressed out. Sometimes they see you're in an uncomfortable position, and they learn from that as they get older.

LIFE PURPOSE AND SUCCESS

What do you ultimately strive for? What is your mission in life?

You know, everyone sees me as an MMA fighter, but I do that because I love to compete at my craft, and that's martial arts. I could stop doing that right now and just focus on teaching the martial arts, teaching Karate.

My mission in life is to put as many martial artists out in the world as possible. Not just to be able to kick and punch, but true martial artists. I know what martial arts have done for me, not just as a martial artist, but being a good man. Showing respect to others, showing modesty, showing perseverance when things get tough to be able to push through it. That's what I enjoy, just being a positive influence in a lot of these kid's lives.

I get grown men coming in every day thanking me and my dad for what we do here, and how it helped them in tough situations in their life, and tears come to their eyes when they say that. I think that's something special. Living a life of service is an amazing life. Yeah, we get paid for it, but my dad always told me too, "People don't care how much you know, they only want to know how much you care."

I think that's with everything - your neighbors, your family, your friends. People don't care about how much you know; they only want to know how much you care.

How do you define success? At what point did you identify as being "successful"?

I've never really thought if I'm successful or not. I love to do what I do, and that's all I think about. Do I make money through the UFC? Yes, but I would compete for free, I love it.

I have a lot of people on social media who thank me for being a positive influence on their lives. People say, "Win or lose - the way you carry yourself, the positive attitude you have is inspiring."

If you enjoy doing what you do in life – whether it's art, or it's raising kids, if it's teaching them martial arts, if it's being a nurse – if you enjoy it then you're successful. It's not about how much money you make.

I know the fame and the money is not going to last. My dad tells me that every day. People come to me and ask me for autographs and photos and Dad says, "Hey man, it won't be long before no one wants your autograph and no one wants to take pictures with you, so enjoy it while you can."

OVERCOMING CHALLENGES

How has failure, or apparent failure, set you up for later success? Do you have a "favorite failure" of yours?

We live a very simple life here in South Carolina. We are very simple people – not a whole lot of drama. So, I learnt a lot through competing. I was undefeated for so long. Since I had my first fight at 15 years old until I was about 28, I was undefeated. I was 57 – 0 in kickboxing and I never really knew what it was like to fail on a main stage. Of course, I failed a lot in training. I had sparring partners that beat my behind all the time. I had an older sister who would just crush me on a daily basis, and she probably still could.

But my favorite fight experiences are in my losses, and how I handled those losses. I had my first loss in my second fight in the UFC. I was 28 years old, and that was a long time on a main stage before I failed. I really didn't understand what it was like to lose in front of people, what it was like to lose in front of my family and friends, and all the people who helped me get to where I'm at. You hold a lot of that on your shoulders when you go out to fight.

When I lost, yeah it was upsetting, but for some reason I didn't lose because I didn't give up in that fight. I had to cut a lot of weight to get to 170 pounds. I usually walk around about 190 – 195, and I fight at 170 so I had to cut 25 pounds. When I went through that cutting weight process, it killed me – I passed out a few times; I've never been through anything like that before in my life.

For 30 seconds in that first round, I was done. I had no energy, my muscles were failing, but I told myself I was not giving up – I'm not quitting. I thought, "This guy is going to remember me after this fight, even if he beats me." Just the fact that I didn't quit when most people would have, that's just awesome to me. That indomitable spirit that I didn't even know I had until that point.

There's been a few fights after that when I fought Tyron Woodley when I got knocked down three times in the fourth round, and I was in a deep choke and ready to go out. I told myself in that choke, it's crazy what goes through your head in that moment, "All these people came to watch me fight, I am not going to tap. I am going to go out, I'm not going to quit."

Those are my favorite fights – the ones where most people would have given up, but I didn't.

That rolls into life for me – if I can go through that, I can go through anything. I like to tell myself that.

Things hit you in different ways – losing a family member, having trouble financially, marriages – they all hit you in different ways, but I am somewhat ready for handling things that can get you down because I have that indomitable spirit.

EMOTIONS

What makes you truly happy? What lights up your soul?

Number one is my family. We are tight knit – we are with each other every day in the business. Sometimes your mom and dad aren't your parents, they're your bosses. But every Sunday, Mom cooks dinner for everybody, and we hang out. When we all get together, that puts a smile on my face. Being with family is very, very important for your soul.

You have to find that thing that makes you happy and you got to hold onto it, and my family is it.

Teaching Karate class – I see it every day. I teach the kids that are aged 5 to 10 and they are so excited to do Karate, and they're so excited to see me. When I see them come with a big smile on their face, that's awesome man – it's the best feeling in the world.

You've said you're pretty unflappable and don't often get angry – but when you do get angry how do you deal with it?

For me, I have an outlet – it's martial arts bag work. If you don't know what your outlet is, I encourage you to go and find it. I know people who go and hit golf balls, or ride a bike, or do bag work, or play video games or just read a book. I have an outlet in the bag work, or doing forms, or breaking a sweat. When you break a sweat and work out, you release endorphins and that gives you that positive attitude and makes you feel good.

You've publicly said you don't ever hate your opponents, and there's no anger towards them. When you're standing toe-to-toe and someone's kneeing you in the head, how do you deal with the feeling in that moment?

I know that when the fight is said and done, you learn a lot about somebody's spirit after you've seen them in action and after you fight them. I've hit guys as hard as I could, and they just smile and keep on coming. But I've also hit guys and as soon as I've hit them, they're looking for a way out. They immediately want to give up and quit. The guys that don't give up and have that indomitable spirit are the guys that I want to have my back. I don't care what they say to me, I've been in the game for a long time and I've been around fighters my entire life, and I try to be as observant as possible.

So, I know what they say to me, they don't mean – they're trying to get under my skin. I don't take it to heart.

People like Muhammad Ali and Conor McGregor – they win the fight before they step out there and it's because their opponent is not able to handle their emotions.

That's where it all begins – your emotions – and that's where the self-control comes in. Everybody has self-control to some level – you're taught that when you're younger to control your mouth, to keep your hands and your feet to yourself, but not a whole lot is taught about emotions and I think that's number one. If you can't control your emotions, anybody can get under your skin, and once your emotions control you, that's when the downhill slope starts.

You've got to know how to control yourself before you can do anything else.

When I step on that Octagon, I know what they're trying to do; I know they're trying to upset me, and I have control over my emotions. It's funny how that can have a reverse effect on people – they get upset that I don't get upset! In my last fight, for example, my opponent slipped and fell, and most people would have taken advantage of that and jumped on top of him and try to hit him. I let him back up. I do it for the honor and the glory – I don't want him slipping on the canvas to be the reason I win. In the second round, I slipped and fell and guess what? He let me back up, and he said, "Respect" and we bumped gloves. So, it rubs off on people.

What does vulnerability mean to you? Are you comfortable being vulnerable?

I think so – I think when you step out on the Octagon, you're testing yourself. Am I vulnerable? Or did I do everything to prepare myself? I think that's what gives me confidence to step out there. I train every day – I would never miss a day because I'm a little tired. I see guys at the top of the game make that mistake in training, and not go in because they weren't feeling 100 percent. That's not an excuse. Your opponent is preparing for you now, they're training. You've got to make sure you do the same thing. I keep my training partners accountable, because I'm not missing!

But things happen... the first time I was ever knocked out was three fights ago in front of pretty much my whole hometown. My opponent knocked me out in the second round. I was beating the crap out of the guy and next thing I knew; I woke up in the back and I didn't even know how I got there. I wasn't prepared for that. You've got to be prepared to lose every now and then.

What about emotionally - do you have a network of people you can open up and show the vulnerable side to?

Of course. I wouldn't be the person I am without the one person to talk to, and that's my Pops. Like I said, I keep a very small circle, and I've learned that from a lot of people. Looking at other fighters, they have this entourage of people that aren't in their best interests and are taking advantage of them.

I have one or two friends that I keep very close to me, and the rest are family. A lot of successful people I talk to have that same small network – I don't know if they mean to or if they've been taken advantage of in the past.

But my main man is my Pops. I can always sit down and talk with him. The things he tells me may not always be the things I want to hear, but it's the truth and that's how he is. He is not the sugar-coating type guy, and that's why I go to him every time. Sometimes I go to people who say the things I want to hear, but I find myself not going back to those people. I want people to be honest with me.

What about the fear of pain? Where does fear come into your life?

That's another thing too... I grew up in pain. I grew up getting kicked, getting punched. There's a conditioning process that I went through as a young man in order to take a punch to the face or a kick to the leg. You have to know how to deal with that pain. You may have tears that come to your eyes, but you rub those tears off and you get back out there, and you do it again. You never give up.

But in a fight, you don't feel that. I don't feel the pain, especially when I'm getting punched. A year ago, I broke both my hands in the first round. I felt that! That was painful. But I've felt pain before and I knew how to handle it, I knew how to cope, and I learned that in the gym.

SPIRITUALITY AND MINDFULNESS

Does religion or spirituality play a big part in your life?

Yes, I'm a Christian man. People ask me, "You're Christian – why do you choose this violent sport? You're trying to hurt the other man." I don't see it that way, I see it as a gentleman's sport, a way for two men to test each other's ability in the most primitive way possible.

When it comes down to it, as a man, I want to know I can take care of myself and the people around me, and my property. As a man, we always want to have that feeling.

I don't look at it as though I'm going out to hurt this man, I look at it as a friendly, combative sport. At the end of the day, if you beat me or I beat you, I'm giving you a hug, man.

It's funny – there's a lot of trash talk going into a fight, but at the end of that fight, they are always showing love.

Do you have a practice that enables you to relax and connect with your inner self?

There are certain things I do – things like kata, which is a set form of techniques and it almost looks like you're doing random stuff, but it's Karate techniques that you have in a form. There is a lot of spirituality that's involved with kata. What I love about it is that you don't need anyone else around you. If you do a kata right, you're sweating by the end of it. The goal is to make yourself as 'perfect' as possible, which is impossible. I've been doing kata my whole life and there's still things I do wrong. It makes you more body aware.

Sometimes, if I get frustrated or I just want to find myself, I put on my traditional Karate Gi and I will turn the lights off and I will do kata. It's a way for me to think about the things that are making me frustrated, or things that are on my mind, or things that have to be done. Sometimes it's things that are wearing and tearing on me, on my soul. I really suggest you look up kata, it's really cool stuff.

RELATIONSHIPS AND FAMILY

Talk to me about the women in your life and the respect you have for them.

Man, I think every man can say this. The women in my life... I wish I was as smart as them.

The women in my life – not only are they straight shooters, they're willing to take care of their own.

It's funny, if I have a situation in my life, I don't go to my dad, I go to the women in my life. You can't argue with Mom, she's so smart. They're very loving in the way they talk to you; they're the first one to give you a hug and to cry with you. My dad's not the type of guy to cry.

My dog died recently – he was my buddy. My mom was there to cry with me; she was there with me; she called and texted every day to see how I was going. Not only that, whenever I lose, they're the first ones to say, "Hey you're fine, you're okay – you're strong – you will be back better than ever."

I remember when I first moved into my apartment, my sister came down from Texas, and I had nothing in my apartment; I was sleeping on my cot. I'm a dude, I didn't really care about that stuff. She was so upset! I remember that day, after classes, I went home, and my house was fully furnished. I had a TV, a couch, a dinner table, a queen-sized bed... tears came to my eyes. The women in my life take care of us, they nurture our souls. I haven't even cracked the surface of everything they do for us, it's so cool.

Do you have a dream of being a father yourself some day?

I do, I'm itching to be a father. But I've had a dream ever since I was a kid, and my dad took me to my first UFC event in Charlotte, North Carolina and I told my dad then I was going to do this someday. That was my dream then, I wanted to become the best fighter – and I didn't want anything to distract me. But I have 13 nieces and nephews now, and I kind of envy that. I want that, I love seeing those relationships. I want to be someone's dad and someone's inspiration.

PROFESSOR SEYYED HOSSEIN NASR

UNIVERSITY PROFESSOR OF ISLAMIC STUDIES, THE GEORGE WASHINGTON UNIVERSITY

Professor Seyyed Hossein Nasr is the only Muslim to be included in the Library of Living Philosophers and has written over 50 books and over 500 articles. A University Professor of Islamic Studies at George Washington University, he remains one of the most influential Muslim scholars in the world for his work on Islamic tradition and philosophy.

Born in Iran, he obtained a scholarship to MIT to pursue undergraduate studies in physics and went to obtain a Doctor of Philosophy in the history of science and philosophy from Harvard University.

Upon his return to Iran in 1958, he became a Professor and subsequently the Dean of the Faculty of Letters before becoming Vice-Chancellor of Tehran University, and then President of Aryamehr University. His academic work extends from classical Islamic philosophy, Islamic science, Sufism, and critique of modernity to interfaith relations, Islam–West relations, and the environmental crisis.

Professor Nasr was the first Muslim scholar ever to be invited to give the prestigious Gifford Lectures, which were later published as *Knowledge and the Sacred*.

Do you have a favorite quote or philosophy you live by?

I am a philosopher in the traditional and not modern sense. Plato said that "Philosophy is the practice of death" which means death to everything other than the Truth, which for me is contained in the perennial philosophy. I try to live according to its tenets as embodied in the integral Islamic tradition.

What are the issues - whether social, environmental, political or economic - that you feel are most pressing and for which you feel the greatest personal concern and responsibility?

The most pressing issue concerns traditional wisdom itself with which I have been concerned all my life. On a more outward level there is the issue of the environmental crisis with which I have been involved for decades on the deepest level, being one of the first persons to predict the coming of the environmental crisis in the 1960s before it became recognized by the public at large.

Who inspires you?

Those who are embodiments of traditional wisdom all inspire me whether they be Rumi, Eckhart or Black Elk. But above all it is the Prophet of Islam who is my greatest source of inspiration.

RELIGION AND SPIRITUALITY

You write a lot about the idea of unity. Can you describe the significance of unity in Islam?

Unity (or tawḥīd in Arabic) is the alpha and omega of Islam and everything Islamic is imbued with its reality. Unity implies not only the utter transcendence and at the same time immanence of the one God, but also integration of all aspects of human life and thought. That is why there is in principle no duality between the religious and the secular and there is not even a word for the concept of secularism in Islamic languages.

"It might sound audacious, but I would say that what makes me truly happy is that God be pleased and satisfied with me, with my actions and thoughts. I often repeat to myself the Quranic verse, "O soul that has gained certitude, return to thy Lord, satisfied and satisfying.""

What role have women played in developing the spiritual tradition and heritage in Islam?

Outwardly it might appear that women did not have much of a role, but the reality is something else. It is true that all Islamic philosophers and theologians of note were men, although there were a few notable women who were scholars and especially Sufis such as Rābi'ah al-'Adawiyyah and Sayyidah Nafīsah. But of even greater significance is the role of so many Muslim mothers who were and who remain the first spiritual teachers of their children. Their role in this domain is immense and cannot be confined to a few who were known scholars, mystics or poets. The continuity of the spiritual traditions and heritage of Islam is inconceivable without women.

Sufi Scholar, Shaykh Abdul-Karim al-Jili (ra), has mentioned the term "al-insān al-kāmil" (The perfect man). Can you briefly elaborate on this term and what it means?

The concept of Perfect or Universal Man (al-insān al-kāmil) was developed earlier than the time of Jīlī by other Sufis especially Ibn 'Arabī and is a key concept for the understanding of the Sufi doctrine concerning man. The Universal Man is the mirror which God has created to reflect fully His Divine Names and Qualities. All the positive possibilities of existence are to be found in man, but in the Universal Man are they actualized. The Universal Man is the pole of cosmic existence, the harbinger of Divine revelation, the paragon and example of human perfection, the model of sanctity, and the spiritual guide par excellence. The prophets and the great saints are considered to be universal men, the foremost among them for Muslims being the Prophet of Islam. The Universal Man is not Divine, but he reflects as theophany the Divine Qualities. I must add that insān translated here as Man here does not mean only male but the human being whether male or female.

EMOTIONS

What role do you believe religion and spiritual tradition have on happiness?

Let us remember first of all that religion and spiritual tradition do not concern only the emotions. Rather, they involve the whole being of man especially the spiritual aspect which must not be confused with emotions, but of course they do include the emotional dimension of our reality. Their role in happiness is crucial to the extent that those who reject religion still seek something that they substitute for

religion and cling to "religiously" for as human beings we cannot live happily without meaning in our lives. In Islam it is said that God wants us to live happily and to die happily.

There is a famous Arabic proverb that says, "He who lives happily (which means with faith) dies happily." You have the corresponding Western saying, "He who lives well dies well." Religion and spirituality play the central role in human happiness in the Islamic perspective.

What makes you truly happy?

It might sound audacious, but I would say that what makes me truly happy is that God be pleased and satisfied with me, with my actions and thoughts. I often repeat to myself the Quranic verse, "O soul that has gained certitude, return to thy Lord, satisfied and satisfying."

There is no greater happiness for me than this satisfaction. If I perform an act, intellectual, spiritual, psychological or even physical that I believe is pleasing to God, that makes me truly happy, whether it be writing, helping a student or performing an act of charity.

How do you express anger? What do you do to release frustration?

There are two types of anger: ordinary psychological anger and what Christians have called "holy anger". In the face of falsehood or injustice one can and even should display "holy anger" which is objective and does not destroy the peace of the soul. I am confronted by that reality often. But when something comes up that arouses personal and psychological anger, I try my best to control it inwardly, but that is not always easy. When occasionally I do get angry in this manner, I try my best to quiet myself down and I ask for God's pardon, what we call *istighfār* in Islam. It is not easy to control anger which can have a very negative effect on the soul. It is not accidental that in traditional Christianity, anger is considered one of the seven deadly sins.

To release frustration, I re-examine my actions and thoughts concerning a particular situation and see if I did the best that I could. If I had done so, I try to resign myself to what was ordained by God and was my lot or *qismah* (which has entered the English language as *kismah* or *kismet*). If I had not done so, I try to learn from my mistakes so that I can draw a positive lesson from even a frustrating situation.

What does strength look like to you?

The strength of a real man should not be confused with simply being macho in the present understanding of this term.

Yes, strength means being able to endure hardship, bear difficulties with patience, and on the mental and spiritual level to be truthful and trustworthy so that one's words are "a man's word". But it also means to be kind and generous, charitable and humble, helpful and understanding.

In Islamic terms it means not only to reflect the Divine Qualities of majesty, justice and power, called Names of Majesty (*Jalāl*), but also to display love, beauty, charity, generosity and nobility, or the Divine Names of Beauty (*Jamāl*).

In the West you have the example of the medieval knight who was the exemplar of strength and also chivalry, who was a selfless warrior but also kind and gentle especially towards women, the knight who fought for truth and justice but was always caring and considerate towards the weak and even his enemies. An outstanding example of the strength of a real man in Islam is to be found in Saladin, who became famous in the West because of his combining strength with wisdom and generosity.

What does vulnerability mean to you?

Vulnerability has both a negative and positive aspect. Negatively it means to be weak, to lack the strength to withstand external and internal pressure and therefore not to be firm in clinging to one's principles when they are challenged. Positively it means to be sensitive to the suffering of others and to be open to accepting the truth even if it is against the errors one has harbored within oneself in a dogmatic fashion, absolutizing one's errors as truth. A real man avoids vulnerability in its negative sense but cultivates it within himself in the positive sense.

"Yes, strength means being able to endure hardship, bear difficulties with patience, and on the mental and spiritual level to be truthful and trustworthy so that one's words are "a man's word." But it also means to be kind and generous, charitable and humble, helpful and understanding."

What pastime or practice enables you to relax and connect with your inner self?

The practices that enable me to connect with my inner self are first and foremost prayer and then meditation, reflection and contemplation complemented from time to time by listening to traditional and sacred music or experiencing other forms of traditional art including the reading of mystical poetry. As for pastimes to relax, besides sports especially tennis and squash which I played for decades until a short while ago, I do not really have a pastime outside those practices that enable me to connect to the inner self.

RELATIONSHIPS AND FAMILY

Who has been the most important role model in your life? Has there been someone who has led by example?

The most important role models for me on the highest plane have been the Prophet of Islam and the great Muslim saints. On the ordinary human plane, my father has played that role for me along with my direct Sufi teachers.

In what ways have the women in your life influenced the man you have become?

There is first of all my mother to whom I owe much and who had a major role to play along with my father in the training of my character during my childhood and early youth. Then there are the women whom I have loved and through whom I have experienced what it means to love not only romantically but even in general. I have been married for over sixty years and in that relationship that is both the domain of love and a battlefield of contending personalities I have learned much about myself through these experiences. I have also known a few women Sufis, some saints, who have influenced me.

What key piece of advice would you pass onto your children?

I have a son and a daughter, both of whom are now middle-aged. From their childhood I sought to teach them about their religion and culture, to give them the best education possible and also to inculcate in them virtue and strength of character.

My main advice to them was and remains to remain true to their real selves and to try to live a life that has meaning in the deepest sense of the word.

KHALIL A. CUMBERBATCH

DIRECTOR OF STRATEGIC PARTNERSHIPS, COUNCIL ON CRIMINAL JUSTICE

 @khacumberbatch   @khacumberbatch

Khalil A. Cumberbatch is a nationally recognized formerly incarcerated advocate for criminal justice and deportation policy change.

His advocacy work began in 2010 shortly after his release from serving almost seven years in the NYS prison system.

Khalil currently serves as Director of Strategic Partnerships at the Council on Criminal Justice. Most recently, he served as Chief Strategist at New Yorkers United for Justice, where he maintains the role of Senior Advisor. Prior to NYUJ, he served as Associate Vice President of Policy at the Fortune Society, a re-entry organization whose goal is to build people and not prisons.

Do you have a favorite quote or philosophy you live by?

Yes, I do. It's a quote by Nelson Mandela, "To be free is not merely to cast off one's chains, but to live in a way that respects and enhances the freedom of others."

One, they're powerful words, and two, it's by Nelson Mandela and as someone who was formerly incarcerated, as someone who has spent time in prison, I think that there are very few examples of other formerly incarcerated people who rise to the level of Nelson Mandela.

He was a political prisoner, and he believed deeply in his country's ability to transcend its current status. The moment he was given access to power and opportunity, he didn't do what I think the majority of people would do in his circumstance, which is to use that power to seek revenge towards the people that imprisoned him. Instead, of course, he becomes the President of South Africa.

Here, in the States, we are many, many years away from having someone who has been in jail, let alone prison, become the President.

That's why it inspires me.

If you look at the wording of it, and if you think of "freedom" as literally gaining your physical freedom, and you also look at it in a figurative sense and say, freedom can really mean a release from mental oppression, a release from anxiety and worry that you constantly have as a person of color in the United States. Unfortunately, there are deeply rooted and entrenched systemic issues people of color face here.

It literally inspired me from the day that I read it, and it's one of the guiding philosophies that inspires me to change our criminal justice system.

What is one personal quality that you are most proud of?

One of the traits that I'm most proud of is the ability to see the humanity in other people, even when they're often the most difficult people to see it in.

I learned this in prison. Prison is a place where, from the time you walk in the door, to the time you leave, the ultimate goal of the correctional is to not treat you as a human being. It's also a place where inhumane things can happen, and at the same time there is also a tremendous amount of humanity that exists among people who are incarcerated.

That doesn't mean everything in prison is rosy and nice – of course not – there are some very violent and dangerous places. But I would argue those places are that way because people there have adopted the narrative that the system gives you, which is that you are less than human. And we know from history that one of the first things needed to do the most dehumanizing acts, is first view them as less than human.

During your time being incarcerated, and locked in a cell, how did you deal with emotions that came up in that space? How did you deal with anger and not let it override you?

My incarceration came at a point when I was very young and naive. I didn't have an understanding of how much my anger drove the decisions I made – until my incarceration. Being incarcerated forced me to understand that I had anger that drove me to make unhealthy decisions for myself and others.

Time in prison was the reinvention of my entire being - emotionally, psychologically, physically and spiritually. This reinvention taught me to contain and control my anger and frustration.

My overall transformation helped me to control my anger as well. I started to develop myself spiritually while simultaneously developing myself physically. I started to exercise more, paid attention to my diet and began fasting. My transformation was intellectually as well. I enrolled in a college program which helped me to develop academic skills in a collegiate setting.

I realized in order for me to be a well-rounded individual, I needed to critique and change all these aspects of my life.

I was more frustrated than any other emotion during my incarceration and I really used that frustration as motivation to complete college and have a positive leadership role in prison.

Who were the positive male role models prior to your time in prison?

Interestingly, I grew up with a ton of positive role models, including my father. He may not have been in my life on a daily basis, but he was there enough for me to know he was a working-class guy.

I had other men that were friends of the family, but in West Indian culture you have a bunch of uncles and aunts who don't relate to you in the blood-sense, but they are family through other ties. I had "uncles" who were working class – I had one I shared a house with for 8 or 9 years, and he would work every day. He would shine his boots the night before, get up at the crack of dawn, put them on and went to work as a delivery driver. He provided for his family in that way.

So, I had great role models, but when I was 17 or 18, they weren't fitting the persona that I wanted to portray. I didn't want to "be that" to be honest with you. I started to gravitate towards people who had the same ideology as me at the time. The irony is that I chose to move away from the great role models, and I chose to hang out with people who I knew weren't the best, but in the end, they fitted the persona I wanted to emulate.

How has your concept of masculinity evolved since that time?

My concept of masculinity has changed so much since I was 13 or 14. Again, I grew up in a household and family where men weren't expected to cry or talk. I had an uncle whose son was my best friend, and I spent many nights at his house. I can tell you that there were only a handful of occasions when I heard him speak, quite literally, because he was just that figure in the house.

He was working, came home, and he was usually doing something in the garage – so he might have been home, but he was never really "there".

For all of the traditional negative characterizations of what a man is supposed to be and what masculinity is supposed to look like – the thought of crying was not even in my psyche at the time. Now, I understand that masculinity is relative. It's something that the moment you accept it, you have to understand that the contrast to that is femininity and that those terms are not necessarily distinct to gender.

That what it really means is to know what masculinity looks like, you have to have some proximity and understanding of what femininity looks like.

I'm a huge Star Wars fan, and in one of the movies, Obi-Wan said, "You can't truly understand the light until you understand the dark." It's two ends of the spectrum. I understand that now.

We have three girls and one boy, and I always try to talk to them about how I feel, I try to listen to them about how they feel, they see me cry which is something that I'm proud of, actually.

From my perspective, it completely goes against the stereotypes that I was ingrained with, that when I got into adolescence, it really dwarfed my understanding of what true masculinity is.

With my son, I intend a complete strengthening, emotional experience with him and I vow to be the one to break the negative stereotype, negative cycle that has happened in my generation and my father's generation which is this false concept that men don't cry, that boys don't cry.

I really want him to understand that, as he gets older, he can say, "Yes, I've seen my father cry, yes I've seen him express emotion, yes I've seen him talk in the house."

Looking at the women in your life, your wife has been such a critical person for you. What role have women and femininity played in your life?

I was raised in a single-parent household, my mother was the breadwinner, she was the decision-maker, the buck stopped with her. My aunts in my family were similarly so – growing up, they were the ones we engaged with the most.

When I went to prison, it was women who were there for me, especially during the hardest times, my wife included.

When I went through a 5-month immigration detention in 2014, it was also my wife who bore the brunt of that part of our lives. She woke up one morning and she was a partner in a two-parent household, and by the end of the day, she was a single parent. It was her strength that, quite honestly, got me through it.

As I've become more attuned with my masculinity and my understanding of how important women are, you start to see pieces of history where women were critical, and you realize, "Of course, you can't wait for a man to do that."

Here in the States, many of the social justice movements of the past 50 - 60 years, you can't really talk about them without highlighting a woman, and often a woman of color. If you have a look at the more recent social justice movements, including the #Metoo and the Black Lives Matter – those were led by African American women.

This mixture of historical and personal perspective has made me understand how important women are. In my personal life, my wife is the glue that holds us all together. She's been someone who, in my darkest moments where I have quite

literally given up on myself, she was my light.

Women, throughout my entire life, have always been pivotal. So, when I think of masculinity, I can't help but to immerse that within my experience with women.

You're very comfortable opening up your life – what strength do you take from being so vulnerable?

Vulnerability was really foreign to me, growing up. I really only started experiencing the practice of being vulnerable when I was in prison – I learnt that from other men.

The first time I ever said, "I love you" to another man, outside the family (which almost never happened), was in prison. If you think about that, even my uncles – I don't remember telling them that I loved them.

Vulnerability was clunky to me, it wasn't natural. I also remember in prison, how liberating that could be if you were vulnerable. There was a moment that we were committing the crime that I was ultimately incarcerated for, where I was scared, and I didn't want to come out of the car to commit the robbery.

But there was something in me that would not allow myself to physically say I was scared. Part of that was I didn't want to be vulnerable; I didn't want to be viewed as someone who was weak.

That moment, that I always think about, that had I been strong enough, vulnerable enough, to say, "I'm scared, and I don't want to do this" how differently everything would have turned out in my life.

I went to prison because I was scared, and I wasn't the leader I should have been at that moment, which was to say, "I don't want to do this, and we shouldn't be doing this." Instead, I just followed.

Now, I try to be vulnerable with my wife – she's my partner in all of this madness.

Growing up in a single-parent household, I've never seen first-hand the parental and marital experience of one parent being vulnerable to another. My mother and father all too often weren't on speaking terms – it was volatile.

I try to be vulnerable with my wife and share my thoughts, my dreams, my concerns, my fears, and I try to do it not only for us but to show my children that their partner needs to be vulnerable with them, and that that is a true level of trust.

The relationships you developed in prison with other prisoners – were there some mentorship in there that you had shared experiences with. What were some of the strengths of those men?

When I went into prison, I was 21, turning 22. Because of the prison sentence I had received, I went to a maximum-security prison. Here I was a 21-year-old, baby faced, kid in a maximum-security prison. You talk about a worst-case scenario? That was it. The prison that I went to had a 40-foot wall. It was notorious throughout the state, it was myth or law or legend that it was also 40-foot underneath so you couldn't dig out. It was terrifying to see that wall.

Something I was told, entering the system as a young man, was to be mindful of older men who had served lengthy periods of time in prison because they could have intentions that were of a sexual nature, where you could be ambushed or have to physically defend yourself.

So, I went into prison with a very guarded attitude – add to that I was very young, with a chip on my shoulder. I thought I knew it all. You could see how I walked into that experience with my eyes completely shut.

I was maybe about 5 or 6 months into my prison sentence, and on Saturdays in New York everyone is let out of their cells for about 15 – 20 minutes to clean up their cell. At that point, I was fresh in the system and I stepped out of my cell. My cellmate was cleaning the cell, and I was standing on the tier and I was approached by this older individual, his name was Chico. Chico said to me, "Hey man, I work in this program – it's a youth assistance program and we are trying to get more young guys involved. I want to invite you to come down there and just see what it's about."

Automatically, my red flag went up and I said, "Nope, I'm not doing it. I don't need anyone to be my father, I don't need anyone to feel sorry for me."

He could tell from my body language that I just wasn't going for it, so he said, "I know you need some time to think about it. But what you really need to think about is do you want to continue to be part of the problem, or do you want to be part of the solution?" And he just ended the conversation and walked away.

Of course, in that moment I'm thinking, "What kind of Machiavellian stunt is this guy trying to pull? Is he trying to psychologically trick me into feeling guilty? Whatever."

But the more I thought about that question, the more I understood I was not a part of the solution. I had made decisions that hurt other people, that hurt my community to a large extent, my family, my mother, my wife, people that loved me. So, it really made me think about how to get involved in these programs, and I did go down to that program and into many others after that.

Ultimately, I got mentored by Chico and other older men who guided me throughout the entire duration of my incarceration and made me succeed. If it wasn't for those men in that part of my life, I don't know how my incarceration would have turned out.

LIFE PURPOSE AND SUCCESS

What do you ultimately strive for? What is your mission in life?

In terms of the work that I do, I ultimately strive for society to create a criminal justice system that is indeed fair, just and balanced. In terms of my personal life, I want my children to look back on their experiences with me and have enjoyable, good moments.

My father never took me to school, I've never had that experience. My father never picked me up from school, I've never had that experience. I've never lived with my father. I've never woken up to him and had those experiences that you should have. I want them to have the image of me being human but also being there when it counts the most.

On a larger scale, I want to inspire people the same way that other people have inspired me. I want to tell people something we imagine as possible, is indeed very much possible. The people we hold in high regard for doing amazing things wholeheartedly believed those things were possible. They talked about it, they thought about it, and they advocated for it, even when other people around them didn't believe in it.

One of the people I constantly reflect on is Martin Luther King Jr. One of his last speeches, he talked about reaching for the mountaintop. He said, "It really doesn't matter with me now, because I've been to the mountaintop. I've seen the Promised Land. I may not get there with you. But I want you to know tonight, that we, as a people, will get to the promised land."

That's what I think about – he was one of many who were saying, "The system isn't working – but we can have a better one and we will have a better one."

What has to change to reach the mountaintop?

You have to talk about the foundation and the beginning of this country, including the treatment of Indigenous people and slaves. We haven't yet really acknowledged that openly.

Greed is also deeply ingrained into every single aspect of our society – particularly in aspects where people shouldn't be. It's that greed that hinders the country from being the best it can be.

In order for the States to grow, we have to acknowledge all of that, and particularly its bloody history, and the reality that it's a fractured nation. That's long before Donald Trump came. Many people would love to blame him for much of the division that exists in this country, but the reality is he has been the great exacerbator of it, but he hasn't been the one to cause it.

We need to acknowledge how systemic racism has completely stopped the growth of entire communities in this country. We need to talk about how there's always been this need to "other-ize" some group, whether it was indigenous people, slaves from Africa, Mexicans, immigrants, Muslims, etc. We've always had this need to pick a fight with some group, and to villainize and de-humanize them to a point where you can implement policies that have severe impacts on them for generations.

I don't know what kind of event it would take to have those deep-seated conversations, but those conversations are vital.

What makes you truly happy and lights up your soul?

What fuels my soul is the idea that, as a country, we have the opportunity to make better decisions. That lights me up in terms of the work that I do.

What lights me up on a personal level is my interaction with my children. Growing up I was an only child, I didn't have that ability to have those interactions. When I think of family moments, it was my mother and myself.

Coming from that background, I never expected to have four children – my wife and I laugh about that all the time. It is really something to see that these little human beings are developing because of their interactions with me. That puts so much more emphasis on making sure those interactions are healthy.

On a larger perspective, I want people to remember my work and my legacy as helping to pave the road, leading to the mountaintop.

Some people pave much more than I did, but I want to be able to say I helped pave that road as well

What advice would you give your younger self?

I would tell myself to think about how connected other people are to my

decisions. It was something that I didn't understand as my younger self and became clear to me after I was arrested for armed robbery.

My wife and I were just dating at the time, we were young kids. It was in my mother's house at night, it was just her and I, and she asked me if I had ever stopped to think what my decisions would mean for her, and what they would mean for my mother? In particular, what would it mean if I wasn't there? If that night had turned out differently, and I had died, how would that have impacted them?

It's sad to say, as a 19 or 20-year-old man – legally but definitely not emotionally and maturity-wise – that was the first time I was forced to think from other people's experience about my decisions. That's completely sad that I was that person.

So, I would tell my younger self that, whether I liked it or night, other people are intimately connected to my decisions and they're intimately connected to the outcomes of those decisions.

By the time I understood that, and embraced that, I was already serving a prison sentence.

Do you carry any guilt about it?

Oh yeah – a tremendous amount of guilt. I would say my spiritual journey helped me to forgive myself. I was incarcerated for almost three years before I truly forgave myself and forgave myself for committing a crime where I physically, at gunpoint, robbed two people but also for the accident that happened afterwards, where we got into a police chase and hit another car and that person almost died.

I had to forgive myself for decisions I made up until that point, including ones that hurt my family at a very deep level.

JOHN BEEDE

EVEREST CLIMBER, GLOBAL ADVENTURER, ENTREPRENEUR AND SPEAKER

 @johnbeede   @johnbeede   Jbeede

John Beede is an Everest climber, global adventurer, entrepreneur, author, humanitarian, and keynote speaker. He has climbed the tallest mountain on every continent and survived hurricanes, earthquakes, avalanches, tribal warfare, and was once even struck by lightning.

A life-enthusiast who lives his message of goal setting, productivity, and high performance, John is in the constant process of architecting his life into a great adventure.

John is the author of *The Warrior Challenge: 8 Quests for Boys to Grow Up with Kindness, Courage, and Grit.*

Do you have a favorite quote or philosophy you live by?

I do – it is a synthesis of words from Sir Edmund Hillary, Ed Viesturs, Ryan Holden-Messner, all of these classic mountaineers that I modelled my 20s and early 30s of life after. I brought all of their quotes together, and here is my synthesis of all of those quotes:

"The mountains will never lower themselves to your level. You must rise up to the demands presented to you by the climb."

What is one personal quality that you are most proud of?

I think that self-awareness is my most valued quality. The reason is that if you're not self-aware – if you can't look at yourself in the mirror and see what's actually going on and who you really are, you don't stand a chance for any sort of self-improvement. All you're going to be doing is acting like an animal – going off on reactions to every single thing that happens.

But if you can see yourself in a moment, both what your mind is saying to you,

your emotions are trying to direct you to do, and how people are reacting to you – if you can take yourself out of your own head and see what's really going on and be aware of that, you're going to have a much much better chance of being a man who can make a difference in the world.

What are the issues - whether social, environmental, political or economic - that you feel are most pressing and for which you feel the greatest personal concern and responsibility?

I have two issues that concern me. The biggest and most concerning to me is the environment. I'm shifting almost everything I'm doing to become an activist and start creating sustainable solutions for every aspect of how we are destroying the planet. From plastic over-production and over-usage to carbon emissions. That's the new direction I'm going in – that's my new Everest.

As far as social issues – narcissism is the biggest one that concerns me. Every single time I look at a news story or hear from a politician or celebrity, there are traces of self-involvement and narcissism that are on the rise at an uncontrollable rate.

To me, when we are talking about this subject of being a man, if you look back historically, to become a man in past cultures, you had to go through a rite of passage which typically involved being part of a community, adopting their set of values, and then going through the most intense pain possible in order to defend your community. It wasn't just for the sake of being in pain, it was learning how to defend your tribe.

Now, there is no sense of defending a tribe – it's only a sense of "How do I make myself be more important?" We have it backwards. To become a man, you have

to look after your people. If you're only looking after yourself, you're missing the point, you're missing the whole concept of what it is to be a real man.

BEING A MAN

What does "being a man" mean to you?

That's an awesome question and it's a huge question. I've split it into 2 categories.

I think being a man means you're able to take care of yourself and you're able to protect your tribe. If either of those is missing, then there's room to improve as a man.

It also means being humble – none of us are perfect, and so there's always room for improvement, and acknowledging there's room for improvement is a huge part of it.

But if I can break those two categories down – that you are self-sufficient and that you can look after your tribe. Self-sufficient basically means you have the mindset that whatever comes your way, you have the ability, or the skills to learn or learn from other people about how to make the most of that moment or situation, or how you are going to perform well in that scenario.

It's about the values and the person that you are, and what you bring to the things that you do.

Have your concepts of masculinity/ being a man changed over time?

When I was young, I would watch Terminator 2 or the Die Hard movies, and I would think, "That's what it is to be a man!' It's a guy who can walk across glass and grit and then beat up the bad guy, or the Terminator - he could take an endless number of bullets and it doesn't faze him at all."

This concept of being a man was only about gritting through pain. That's just flat out false and wrong.

I became a scout when I was about 8 years old and I continued with the scouting program through to when I was about 22. What I love about the scouting program is they taught the scout oath and the scout law.

So, the values that I live by are all about how I deal with people. It's all about the tribe. Trustworthy, loyal, helpful, friendly, courteous, kind, obedient, cheerful, thrifty, brave, clean, reverent. These are the things that were drilled into my mind and they got into my heart.

It's shifted from this idea that you've just got to be tough, you can never shed a tear, you can never cry, which is only a formula for a mental health problem – that is all that will ever result in.

It's shifted from that perspective through to one of embracing values and then eventually where it is now, after having climbed the world's tallest mountain, having had some wonderful relationships with incredible people – it shifted into a sense of "What's the legacy I am going to leave? How am I going to improve the world for people who come behind me? How do I live in a way that I am proud of who I am as a human – I'm present with the people I'm interacting with and living by my values."

That to me is how you handle yourself as a tribe, and how you live as a man.

If there's one piece of advice you could give every young man, what would it be?

I think it would be that the only person that has a plan that's right for your life is yourself. You can learn from others, you can see what others have done, you can take advice from others, but at the end of the day you are the captain of your own ship and you don't have to live your life by anyone's standards or path except the one you want to live.

EMOTIONS

What makes you truly happy?

Oh man – what lights up my soul is connecting with other human beings in an intense scenario.

I don't know why but for some reason I've always been drawn to "Let's go climb a 1000-foot cliff face and while we are hanging 700 feet above the ground, let's have a real conversation or real moment."

I've been a kitesurfing instructor – I've got students who are facing 60-foot waves and 35 mile an hour winds on a kite that can rip people 50 feet in the air, and I'm teaching people how to control this thing. In that moment, the students are scared – they're terrified – and they're raw and that's when I'm like, "Hey, what's going on in your life?"

It's in those moments that I really become happy – because when we drop our guard and we're faced with just the raw elements of our emotions and what our brain is reacting to in fearful moments, that's when our real self comes out.

People say, "Dude, you're an adrenaline junkie – that's unhealthy!"

To me, it's not that at all – to me, I do these things not to feel adrenaline, but I do it so I can express calm in that moment. How do you breathe through that moment, how do you collect yourself, and how do you let it not rattle you? It's calming yourself.

Everything is just clean when it's right – it doesn't feel messy.

How do you express anger? What do you do to release frustration?

Anger, I've learnt, is a good thing. I don't believe there is any negative emotion. There is a negative *expression* of anger. Early in my life, I would feel anger without even recognizing it was anger, and I became very good at turning that inward and then getting depressed because I was angry with myself and what is a person who is angry with themselves going to do except having negative self-talk and then get depressed?

Now I've learnt that anger is simply your body's way of telling you something needs to change or that a value has been violated. If you act out violently with that knowledge, then you're poorly expressing that anger. But the anger is just an emotion expressing that feeling that you're not being treated right, or that your code of ethics is not being honored.

To me, at this point in life, my healthy way of understanding anger, when I feel that emotion, is to pause and to breathe through it. I will take 3 or 4 deep breaths just observing what's going on in my body and once I've done that, I will also have the space to see which value has been violated. Then I will just speak assertively and clearly to the person who has upset me.

Sometimes if I am just upset with myself, I kind of get real and self-aware and get real honest with myself in the mirror, "John, you've got to treat yourself better. You're angry because you're not treating yourself right."

Or if it's somebody else who has upset me, I'll just bluntly say, "I observed this thing.

This is how I would like to be treated. Would you please treat me this way."

It's not yelling or reacting – it's just stating facts. And if they say, "No, I am not going to treat you that way," I'll just say, "Thanks for your input and time, but unfortunately we won't be interacting any longer."

What does strength look like to you?

It's a good question.

Let me give you an analogy with a bodybuilder – if you look at the bodybuilder and you said, "That guy is huge – he can bench-press 300 pounds!" You would be impressed and say that guy has strength.

But if you look at a rock-climber – they're very sinewy and they have different kinds of strength. Per pound, they're much stronger than a bodybuilder.

Using this analogy, if we look at emotions or inner strength. Inner strength is that quiet, humble, unassuming inner rock-climber than can always dig within to find more strength. I'm not the tallest guy, I'm not the longest-legged guy. I have no business being on mountains like Everest. But in those moments, when I'm at 28,000 feet, there are people turning around, there are people who've died in the days before me... I can look within, even though I physically don't feel like I can take another step. Where am I going to find that strength from? And I can find it within.

Same thing with giving a speech – sometimes there's 1000 people in front of you and you've got an hour to give a speech, and you're 40 minutes in, and you start to drain because you've given everything you have. In that moment, you've got to look within, dig deeper than you ever thought you could, find what else is within there. If you get in that habit of continually looking, then just like a bodybuilder who lifts 20 pounds one day, 22 the next day and then 25 a week later, by continually trying to look deeper you will gain more skill at finding that inner strength in all areas of your life.

What does vulnerability mean to you?

I never thought of vulnerability as enjoyable. I guess the reason is when I was growing up, when I heard the word 'vulnerable' and when I first heard Brené Brown's work around embracing your vulnerability, I kind of scoffed at it. Embrace what's weak about you and show off your weaknesses?? If you were Achilles would you just flaunt your heel in front of everybody? That's how I saw it.

As I've studied more and more and read all of Brené's work and learned to be required to be vulnerable in some of the more intense situations I've described to you. I define vulnerability as being radically honest – just flat out say what's going on in the moment without worrying what other people may judge you for. As an example, I go up on stage and get in front of a crowd. I get a few minutes into it, and say, "Hey guys, I'm feeling a little bit nervous and scared right now." That would be an expression of vulnerability. It's saying, "Here's my Achilles Heel."

Or if I'm climbing and I said, "Gosh, I'm really scared. I don't know if I can do this."

"Vulnerability – what does it mean to me? It means how you honestly connect with people. It shows people that you're human."

Kevin Jorgenson and Tommy Caldwell, when they climbed the Dawn Wall in Yosemite, said, "I don't even know if this is possible." They were radically honest and vulnerable about their situation.

What this does is allows people – in the first case, the audience members, or in the example of Kevin and Tony – the entire country got behind them and cheered for them and celebrated.

With an audience, if you say, "I'm feeling nervous right now" the whole audience is going to feel "Dude, we're here for you – we want you to succeed! We've got your back!" People know what it's like to feel scared.

So, vulnerability – what does it mean to me? It means how you honestly connect with people. It shows people that you're human.

LIFE PURPOSE AND SUCCESS

You've climbed all seven summits – most people would look at you and say you've been hugely successful. How do you define success? At what point did you identify as being "successful"?

All those things – climbing the summits, all the achievements – are bullshit.

Here's what I mean by that; I climbed some big mountains in the past, I've given speeches, I wrote books – those are just factual statements.

Here's the thing – if you and I get on the phone right now and I'm a jerk to you, I'm not a success.

The only way I determine success is who you are, right now, in this moment. I think the only way to earn the figurative summits that you've climbed, is to bring a better self to your current moment.

Had I done all those things you've listed in the John Beede resume and then I'd spoken to you and I'm not paying attention, or I'm not caring about the answers or I'm talking smack to you or trying to talk myself up – how successful am I? I'm just some blowhard. That sucks – no one wants to hear about that right?

None of those things matter now. The only way they matter is how they shaped me then to become who I am right now.

That's how I define success – it's who you bring to this moment.

How important is collaboration and teamwork to achieving success?

Have you ever heard the phrase "Self-made man" or "Self-made millionaire?" I think that anyone who calls themselves that is a liar and a probably a narcissist.

No human being is self-made – that is completely ignorant of reality and blind. Here's why – that person had parents, an education, employees working for them, an infrastructure from a government and a country that had to defend itself in a multitude of wars, technology from thousands of years that have gone to support them.

A lot of mountaineers will just post a photo of themselves on top of a mountain, "Here am I, doing the thing I did on my own". That was my own mindset too for a long time.

But if I zoom out a little bit, I look at the team immediately with me. If I zoom out a little bit more, I look at who are the rangers, who are the porters, who are the Sherpas on the mountain who helped find the route that year.

If I zoom out even further, I look at the historical figures who found the routes way back when and made mountaineering

possible. Who are the companies that created the technologies to create the clothes that I'm wearing at the moment, from the crampons on the bottom of my feet to the headlamps on my head. There are heaps of teams that put that stuff together for me.

So, collaboration and teamwork – it's almost like saying "How important is an engine in a car if you want to drive the thing?"

OVERCOMING CHALLENGES

Have there been any key challenges that you have had to face in your life? How have you faced them?

I will live by what we've talked about and get a little bit vulnerable and the thing that makes me kind of nervous to talk about and to share, but I'm going to learn from you and try to enjoy this.

When I was 15, a very close friend of mine was killed in a car accident. I went to my school counsellor in tears, and he said, "I don't know what to tell you." And I didn't know the difference between a counsellor and a psychologist – I thought they were the same thing. He was just a guidance counsellor, putting me through classes. He wasn't trained or skilled.

I went back to my classroom, still crying, and a kid stabbed me in the back with a pencil and there was blood coming down my shirt and said, "Quit being a little bitch." I get up, and go talk to my math teacher and say, "I just got stabbed in the back" and he doesn't care, he said, "Go sit down and stop disrupting class."

So, I got this thought that when things hurt emotionally, when things hurt physically, the right thing to do and the only way to avoid embarrassment is to bottle them up and to lock it in. That set a direction of my mindset.

When I was 22 and I saw a DUI and a guy who passed away, when I was then 23 and saw 3 people die on Aconcagua in South America, one of the tallest mountains there. Fast forward to the last death I saw on Mount Everest, there was a collective of 16 deaths – all of them I said to myself, "Well, there's nothing I can do about this. I've just got to bottle all this up. If I reveal the pain that all of these brought to me, it's just going to be embarrassing. So, keep your mouth shut, be tough, and go climb another mountain."

What that mindset resulted in was Post-Traumatic Stress Disorder.

When I was about to give my first TED talk, that morning I saw dead bodies in the shower with me. Imagine preparing for your speech and opening your eyes in the shower and reviewing what you're going to say, and you look down and at your feet, you see dead bodies. I was like "What is going on here? I've got to talk to somebody – this is not right."

The psychologist suggested it was Post-Traumatic Stress Disorder, and my first thought was, "That's impossible – I wasn't in the military," and I didn't understand that the brain physically looks exactly the same whether you're in the military, you're a fire-fighter, you're a police officer, a paramedic or a mountain climber. If you've gone through a trauma, even if you've just experienced a loved one pass away, the brain has the same physical appearance in that trauma.

So, the key challenges that I really faced, even bigger than Mount Everest, was overcoming this condition, which is curable. It's completely reversible. I've been through about 4 years of pretty close and intensive therapy with skilled practitioners and the technology that exists to guide someone who's hurting out of their hurt is really incredible.

That was a key challenge that I would like to vulnerably share.

How has failure, or apparent failure, set you up for later success? Do you have a "favorite failure" of yours?

I have about a 50 per cent failure rate on mountains I attempt. It took me 3 attempts to get to the top of Aconcagua. The first time, there was a storm and 5 people passed away during the time I was there, on the second attempt I had to be helicoptered off because I had pulmonary edema. You could easily call those things failures.

My favorite failure is what I learned from those. I recently went to climb Kilimanjaro and, on the way, up I started recognizing some of these symptoms of pulmonary edema – this is when the lungs fill with fluid – and you can die.

I recognized these symptoms, and I was there in a leadership capacity, helping these teams get to the top. Rather than think, "I'm a failure for not getting to the top with these guys" or thinking, "I'm just going to push through it and endanger myself for the sake of my pride."

Instead, it was a very calm and decided thought, "Hey I'm here for you guys, I'm here for the team. You guys get to the top – I don't want to endanger you and for me, it's not worth it to endanger myself. So, I am going to go down." They had another experienced guide with them, so they were able to get to the top.

My favorite failure is that moment, without any sense of ego or loss or failure, it was just saying "Thank you" to this mountain.

TONY GASKINS

AUTHOR, SPEAKER AND LIFE COACH

 @tonygaskins   @tonygaskins   TonyGaskins

Tony A. Gaskins Jr. is a husband, father of two boys, author, celebrity life coach, and intercontinental speaker. It's been an interesting journey.

Tony built his brand from scratch. At 22, he became an author. At 23, he became a husband and father. At 25, he started his first company, Soul Writers LLC.

Tony made his fair share of mistakes like most young men from areas like where he grew up. Many of his childhood friends are serving life sentences in prison. Although Tony was introduced to the street life between the ages of 18–23, he finally found his way. At 23, he allowed love to change his life. His wife was unwilling to be with a man who wouldn't live up to his full potential. That tough love pushed Tony to be more and to do more.

He first became known for his love and relationship advice. This wasn't a popular topic for a man to be so passionate about, but it was organic for Tony because love transformed him. He spoke from the heart on love and relationships and it helped him amass millions of followers online.

By combining all of his passions Tony became an author, life coach, and speaker.

RELATIONSHIPS

A lot of the work you do is around relationships, sex in relationships, sex before marriage – does this draw on your own experiences?

It is from my own experience – I was a huge womanizer. I was a player from 15 to 21 and I was with over 100 women in that short time span. After that, one of my female friends said, "Tony, you should write a book. You are the biggest player that I know, and you need to give us the secrets."

I was retiring from the game – I had met my wife, and I knew she was my wife, and I kind of had this moment of "Let me right my wrongs. I've lied to a lot of women, broken a lot of hearts, done a lot damage, so let me right my wrongs." It became like a sense of purpose, more so than a profession.

It was 2007, and I was 22 years old when I wrote a book, so I knew nothing about it becoming a business. It was just a passion for writing, and passion for sharing knowledge.

What really hit me was when women who were twice my age started asking me questions based on what they had read from me. So that really piqued my interest because I wrote this book at 22 years old, and women older than my mother did not already know this, they didn't have this information.

So that's when I realized this was something I really needed to do, because this is a space where men aren't really in.

"If I'm rude, disrespectful, controlling, cheating, manipulative, deceptive – my sons will see that – and they will despise me. And if they despise me, I create a cycle that, when I'm dead and gone, I won't be able to correct."

It's true – there are 'man laws.' Just like laws in every area of life, everyone has these secrets that they keep. So, with men, it was like "Don't break the code! Don't tell a woman that you cheated on her, don't tell a woman that we all cheat, don't tell a woman how and why we lie, don't tell a woman how we think."

The women either became a reflection of that man, or a deer in the headlights, so a relationship became two opponents instead of two teammates.

Then that trickles down to the children, seeing this toxic relationship, and then this relationship may fail – then you have a divorce, a child raised in a single-parent home.

What I realized, especially for my race in America, I saw it very rampant and it became an epidemic. I thought, "This must be my purpose to help put a dent in the divorce rates and the toxic relationships."

How did you know your wife, Sheri, was "the one"?

The first time we talked, we talked for about six hours, and when we sat and we talked, she kind of covered every base – she had faith, which was big to me that a person shares the same faith; she had ambition, she was in college as a biomedical science major, with a goal of becoming a doctor; she had patience, she listened to me talk; and she was a conversationalist, she knew something about everything.

We talked about faith, we talked about finances, we talked about family, we talked about sports, and she could just flow with me.

Sheri apparently said she "refused to marry a man who didn't live up to his potential." Is that right?

Yes, and she held me to it. I let her meet my "representative" which is always a better version of myself. But when I spoke that, she held me to that. So, when I wanted to go back on that, and I wanted to go hang out on the streets and be with my friends and do what young men were doing, she said, "No, that's not who I met. That's not what you told me."

When she held me to that, I realized at that point, I had to go ahead and grow.

She holds me to that standard 100 percent.

What impacts do the lack of conversations around relationships, women and masculinity have on the wider community?

It affects us greatly. As the great book says, "My people perish due to a lack of knowledge."

When you don't have the knowledge to create a happy and healthy life, then you self-destruct. The conversation is being avoided because it requires sacrifice, and as humans, most of us don't want to sacrifice in the areas that cause the most pain or require the most discipline.

I notice a lot of men will sacrifice for financial gain – to be a beast in the boardroom and in business. Men will sacrifice, they will dedicate – a lot of people will sacrifice for their body, to get ripped, to get chiselled.

But a lot of men don't want to sacrifice to be with one woman, and to be an example to our children of what love and a healthy relationship should look like.

Without it, fragile men are being raised and those men are becoming leaders and in a position of power but yet are broken, weak and insecure because they don't understand real love.

Who has been the most important role model in your life? Has there been someone who has led by example?

I would say look within, because the solution and your purpose is first found within yourself, and then it will be confirmed outside yourself.

What you need to do, deep down you know it, but you don't trust your own voice. When you trust your own voice, what you will realize is that as you start seeking mentors and hearing and learning from others, you will hear a lot of confirmation and you will think, "This person thinks the way I think," or "This person knows what I know."

We all have the tools to fulfil our own unique purpose, and then others confirm that. Some people will bring revelation, but most people will bring confirmation. Even when you receive revelation, it still needs confirmation within your own spirit.

I believe there is wisdom in a multitude of counsel. I've never had a mentor, and I've reached hundreds of millions of people online, and written 17 books, and got a book deal with a big 5 publisher by the age of 33. I've been on Oprah and Tyra and, been the life coach of some of the top athletes in the entire world.

To do everything I've been fortunate enough to do, one would assume that either my father did it, and I walked into it and was introduced to it, or that I had an amazing personal mentor, or that I had a huge team.

But to be honest, it's just been me and purpose. It's just been me being obedient to the call of my purpose, and hearing and having that feeling and pushing past the weariness and the isolation and the alienation. I've continued to go, regardless of how lonely it is, or how painful it is, and utilizing the voices of the people who show appreciation as my fuel.

If people don't understand your mission, they may be older than you, have more money than you, "wiser than you" but they can derail your mission if you are trapped in the mindset that you must have a mentor.

That's why I say you have to come back to self, and sit with self, and hear everything and weigh it with your own heart and ask if it's confirmed in your spirit.

How did you learn or decide what the values of being a good husband were?

When I tried being a husband, and when I tried it, everything changed for the better in my life. It became so sweet on this side of life; I'm convinced I will never go back to the other side. My thing for every man is to try love, and to try being selfless. I treat my wife like a queen.

Sheri's focus is the family – so with her focus being the family, my focus has to be her. My focus is making sure she's energized, uplifted, motivated and loved – that her love account is always running over – so she has the fuel necessary to love our two sons with an otherworldly love that only a mother can give.

If she's drained, and she feels empty, then my sons will be empty. If she's empty and they're empty, then the home is empty.

When the home is empty, nothing good comes from that home.

My inspiration and motivation to be an amazing husband is because life is no longer about me because I've brought two children into the world. So, I have to think about legacy, which by definition is the gift you leave to the world.

What I share with my sons and the example I show them about what it is to be a real man – the aspect that they will care about most is how I treat their mother, because that is what they love more than my money, more than my success, more than my business. They want to know that their mother is treated like an absolute goddess. She is the queen because that's how they view her.

If I'm rude, disrespectful, controlling, cheating, manipulative, deceptive – my sons will see that – and they will despise me. And if they despise me, I create a cycle that, when I'm dead and gone, I won't be able to correct.

What are some of the other principles behind your relationship with Sheri?

When I speak of my love for my wife, a lot of men go into a little shell. It's not common and so it becomes uncomfortable. No man wants to be less of a man than another man. When a man hears that I treat my wife 10 times better than he treats his wife, it kind of confuses him and it makes him become defensive or he pulls back.

I have friends who laugh at me – any time we are on the road at a speaking engagement, and we are coming home, I will stop at one of the shops in the airport and spend up to a few thousand dollars, but typically around $500 for a "for nothing gift."

They could spring and get something, even if it's $25, but they don't.

It's like, "No – I'm not going to give her the pleasure and the upper hand of believing I was thinking about her!" And I think, "Why not?! It's going to make your life better." And it's because they think it's going to give her more power and more leverage, and it does - my wife has me wrapped around her little finger. She has a lot of power; she has a lot of influence.

But I know when I need to stand my ground on something, and when I do that, that's when I get to see her true love for me because if I'm passionate about something, she'll fall right in line, and she'll say, "Okay, that's what we're going to do."

That's when I get to see that she truly loves me the way I love her.

What challenges have you faced as a couple and how have you overcome them?

My wife is not crazy about a savings account – she's the type of person who thinks, "You live today – you can be gone tomorrow. Why would it benefit you to have all this money sitting in the bank?" We did a 6-week vacation in Europe, 20 cities and 8 countries. After about $50,000 spent, I stopped counting because I was going to lose it.

I had to weigh the consequences and calculate the risks. I risked spending all of my money, but then I can earn all of it back tomorrow. The result of this is going to be peace, joy, love and happiness. But if I don't do it – then what am I giving up? Giving my kids the opportunity to see the world and experience different cultures. And what would it mean for me to have the opportunity to do that and not offer them that?

Our personalities are the total opposite too – I go to a soccer game and I don't say a single word. But my wife – she coaches every second of the game! Mind you, the coach has played for Team USA and my wife will out-coach the coach and has never played a game of soccer in her life.

But that is her personality, so what would it benefit me to change her? She has a passion and a zest for life. I play in a men's pick-up league so it's just a bunch of old men who are out of shape playing basketball and she comes to the game with the same energy, for a league that does not matter.

So, although it's the complete opposite from my introverted, quiet, reserved nature – just let her be her.

Our rule is, if it's not worth breaking up over, it's not worth arguing over.

We discuss it all, but we argue over nothing.

How do you deal with conflict and diffusing difficult situations?

Our first two years were the hardest – Sheri and I were in a power struggle. I was 23 – I turned 23 three weeks before we got married, and she was 20. So being that young, and married, and her being used to being catered to by past guys and me being used to being catered to by women I dated. We were both strong personalities, in the sense of being head-strong and confident, and who was going to lead the household. We learned that we were going to have to submit to one another, we were going to have to identify our strengths and let me operate in my strengths and let her operate in her strengths. She submits to me in my strong areas, and I submit to her in her strong areas. We had to build that strength, and it took us about two years.

It's helped me grow as a person because it has helped build real confidence in me as a man. Because when you operate from love, you build real strength, but when you operate from control and you're cheating, you are operating from insecurity.

So whatever side of you that you are feeding is going to get stronger.

And within every man is a lion and a lamb and unless he learns how to balance and when to be vulnerable in love then he becomes unfit in the world and in his life.

It's made me better in business – I can go to the negotiating table and state exactly what I need from this deal without being irate or disrespectful. I can be intelligent and completely calm and confident, because of what I've gained through learning how to love properly and selflessly.

You coach a lot of high-profile athletes and celebrities. Are there any challenges that you see regularly, regardless of the person's stage in life?

For most people, including celebrities, the root cause of challenges is the same.

When I deal with individuals of high, high, high net worth, their challenges become different – that becomes a challenge of having too much money and not feeling a sense of purpose and not having anything to aspire to, because most people aspire to a higher net worth.

When you're worth everything that you can be worth, what do you have to live for? What good can be done that can make them truly feel good, versus just throwing money at a problem. They can say, "I can donate $100 million to charity but what will that do for me? How is that $100 million really going to be used in those charities?"

After that unique challenge – all other challenges are the same. Relationships are a challenge that rich and poor all have; the other challenge is confidence – knowing that you're good enough, feeling worthy. That's another one of the big challenges that we all face.

If I could pinpoint it, the thing I see the most with everybody is insecurity and love. Not knowing how to love oneself, not knowing how to love someone else, how to require someone to love them in return, and then how to believe in yourself and get beyond your insecurities.

My clients are from the ages of 16 to 68 on six different continents, and all religions, and the challenges are the same for all of them.

BEING A MAN

What does "being a man" mean to you?

To me, manhood means accepting full responsibility for your life. It means you are not pointing the blame at anyone outside of yourself. Manhood means you accept whatever responsibility is before you in love, in raising your children, in providing for yourself, in providing for your family. You do whatever you have to do inside of your legal abilities to take care of yourself. That's manhood.

I feel like, today, men are blaming someone else for their problems.

I would rather not see it like that – I have no problems, I only have solutions to whatever problems I have created, or someone else has created for me. I focus on the solution and how I can overcome that.

I feel like that is what has produced peace

and prosperity in my life, by focusing on solutions, instead of just focusing, and dwelling and complaining about the problems.

What are some moments where you have truly felt connected to your "inner man"?

The moments I feel most like a man is when I put my responsibilities before myself, meaning when I put my wife and my sons before myself, because my desires are different to their desires. My interests are different to their interests, but the one thing I feel responsible for is the woman that I married and the children I brought into the world.

Outside of that, I have no responsibility. Not my mother, my father, my sister, and not the world at large; not my interests or my hobbies. I have no other responsibilities other than my wife and my sons.

When I turn down a speaking engagement for my son's birthday, when I turn down an engagement for my wife's birthday or our anniversary, when I cut off work for a period of time or family time, when I leave for 6 weeks to take my family through Europe, that's when I feel most like a man.

In order to do that, I have to identify what truly are my responsibilities, and what truly is my priority.

That's a struggle and I hear so many men praise their grind, and they spend much more time on work than they do with their family. You see them online everywhere. I heard one guy say, "How many of your kid's birthdays have you missed? How many anniversaries will you skip to work? If you aren't willing to skip those birthdays and anniversaries, you don't want it bad enough!"

I thought, "Wow, you take pride in putting your wife and your children behind your business?"

Men will show you their business, but they won't show you their wife.

They'll show you their accolades in business, but they won't show you their child's report card, and that's where I lose respect for those "leaders".

If a man doesn't understand that his greatest responsibility is to the woman he made a lifetime vow to, and the children he brought into the world against their will, then he doesn't understand life.

What is money? What is business? Businesses that have been around for 50 – 100 years are going out of business today, so the business that the great leaders today pride themselves on will one day extinct. Everything that goes up comes down.

The one thing that will be most important on your deathbed will be the memories that you created with your responsibilities – your partner and your children, if you have them.

That, to me, is what being a man is about.

EMOTIONS AND MINDFULNESS

Do you talk with anyone about how you feel when things are happening in your life, or do you keep these thoughts internalized?

I have a men's golfing group where we can get together and go learn golf and have real conversations before and after it, and I'm actively trying to create opportunities where men can connect. I have an online men's group and there's probably 20 of us in the group every day just talking – and of course it's men only.

I feel every man needs to be part of a tribe – where he can go and be open and be real, be honest and have some laughter. Sometimes in those conversations, you're going to have some tears too.

Having that and creating that time where you can be a man around men who understand and support one another and uplift one another and allow each other to just be. A no-judgment zone, and a loving and caring space, where everyone wants to see you be your best and reach your full potential.

I'm trying to create that more and more, and I know I need it more and more and one thing I've found when I'm in those spaces is that men don't judge me as bad as I think they do. They actually respect and admire me, and they don't refute what I'm saying or say, "You're telling lies, Tony." They say, "You're telling the truth, even if it's a truth I'm not ready to hear."

What pastime or practice enables you to connect with your inner self?

For me, unfortunately, my time typically has to be 11pm and midnight when everyone else is asleep. My wife wakes up at 5am so it wouldn't be healthy for me to be up with her that early. The only time I can think is when everyone is asleep, so I would rather stay awake late than get up at 4am.

What is the method you use for understanding your purpose, and listening to your "higher self"?

It really comes to a routine stillness, where you can sit with yourself. I create time every day to be alone with my thoughts. That's the scariest place for most people to visit.

But when you can get comfortable being in that uncomfortable space, that's when you discover your uniqueness, and your purpose and how you are.

If you can spend time there, you will also be introduced to your insecurities and your secular desires, but the more time you spend there, you will be able to get to the root of those insecurities and to the root of those desires.

You can also ask yourself the "whys". Why do I want more money? Why do I want more fame? Why do I want more notoriety? Why do I want to look different? To walk differently, to talk differently, to be shaped differently?

Then you would hear those answers, which may still bring you back to insecurity. Because I want to appear this way, I want

"My focus is making sure she's energized, uplifted, motivated and loved – that her love account is always running over – so she has the fuel necessary to love our two sons with an otherworldly love that only a mother can give."

to be seen this way, or to be liked, or to be accepted, or to be respected.

The more time you spend with yourself, the more "whys" you can ask yourself, and then you will find the resolve within, and the confidence to do what you were put here to do, but that's a daily battle.

I would much rather do something else than talk about relationships with women, I would much rather do what Tony Robbins does, and talk about business, real estate and investing and building a personal brand. Those things would be so much more fun, and so much lighter, and probably way more financially rewarding – but it's not my call.

The way you can identify your call is by asking yourself what can you do, or what do you do, that not everyone can do equally as well?

If I talk about real estate, I can find 1 million people who impress me more than I impress myself on that topic. But when I talk about love and relationships, I can count on one hand how many people who have as deep or deeper an understanding of intimate relationships. That lets me know that I have to stay in this space because my voice is valuable here. I can speak on other things, but I need to come back and remember what my core message is.

It's tough – I can't have male friends until they get on what I'm on, and it's so rare. Even then, a man may not be cheating on his wife, but it's still hard for him to serve his wife, meaning to be selfless, and not give her what he thinks she deserves but to love her for the sake of love. To love her beyond what she deserves, to love her because of the love in you, not loving her contingent on how she makes you feel.

Is there anything further you would like to add to anyone reading this?

I would say that this is the probably the most important interview that I've ever done, out of the hundreds or thousands I've been involved in.

I want for everyone who reads this to understand the gravity and the importance of this topic and how serious we have to take the role and responsibility of manhood. If we, as men, can accept that responsibility it can change our world across the globe because the men who become real men will become true leaders, rather than men and leaders operating from fragile masculinity, insecurity and pain.

NICK SANTONASTASSO

SPEAKER AND ENTREPRENEUR

 @nicksantonastasso   @nicksanto534   NickSanto534

Nick Santonastasso is constantly defying the odds. Despite being born with no legs and one arm, Nick is a bodybuilder, internationally known public speaker and internet sensation.

Nick only had a 30 percent chance of surviving birth. Nick was 1 of 12 people in the world at the time who was born with Hanhart Syndrome, a rare genetic disorder. Nick was self-loathing and thought about ending his life. Fortunately, he was able to find his "why" through wrestling in high school.

At the same time, he rose to "Vine" stardom, with a series of zombie prank videos. His social media stardom has since outlived Vine, and he has gone on to become a successful bodybuilder, speaker and entrepreneur.

Do you have a favorite quote or philosophy you live by?

I do – it's by Nelson Mandela and it's "I don't lose. I only win or learn."

The reason behind that is that so many people are afraid of failure or afraid of challenges, or have the wrong meaning attached to failure and challenges. When you view life as you "only win or learn" regardless of whether you think the situation was a loss, you can extract pieces of good from it.

You may not realize it when you're in the middle of it – but eventually you realize it happened for you and not to you.

There are so many things in my past that in the moment I thought were negative – for the majority of my life I thought my body was negative, or not "the biggest plus" but now I see it differently.

What is one personal quality that you are most proud of?

I think I have a superpower of making a room feel comfortable. Whether it's a room of five or a room of 10,000 – I have the power to make them feel comfortable and that's super key when teaching or leading, because when people are comfortable, they don't have a barrier.

Now they're taking information with an open mind, which allows transformation and evolution.

A lot of times you can sit in a seminar and see a full-bodied guy, you can see Tony Robbins and still think "I'm a little bit skeptical."

But for me, when I come out, I hop-the-hop and talk-the-talk and I use humor to warm up the audience, and they can see me make fun of myself, and they laugh and get comfortable.

What are the issues - whether social, environmental, political or economic - that you feel are most pressing and for which you feel the greatest personal concern and responsibility?

Suicide prevention and awareness, the comparison epidemic and bringing back human interaction.

The comparison epidemic – the majority of not only adults, but kids, are basically comparing the lowest of their lows with the highest of the highs on social media reels and they're getting a version of success that isn't real, and they're getting depressed and suicidal and kids are taking their lives because they think their lives are so low and success is so far away.

So that's something I'm really passionate about – I released a song called 'Do you hear me?' and basically it talks about suicide awareness and the comparison epidemic and how the biggest superpower is your mind, and that your mind is your guardian.

Music has always been my number one passion – and I realized I could only reach a certain number of people on personal development stages – and so how can I get to the masses? Everyone loves music so if I can release hot, super cool music

that has a really good meaning, then I can plant seeds for the good, because there is so much programming for the bad.

Especially with phones and technology, human interaction is dwindling – so my generation and the generations coming through now don't know how to have conversations. And really, where all the zest and juice and transformation of life comes from is through human interaction. We need to get back to having present conversations. Human interaction is dwindling and it's shitty!

I meet a lot of people in meet and greets and that could be the first time someone's ever met me, and I don't want to not be engaged – I want to be locked in and laser focused on that person, because they may never have that time with me again.

Who inspires you?

I'm a big believer in modelling people who have the results that you want. There's three people in the world that I model – Tony Robbins, Ed Mylett and Andy Frisella.

These are my top three that I look to for guidance and to see their core values and to see what they've built.

As a kid, I looked to Nick Vujicic – basically when I was younger, there weren't many people I could relate to and without sounding arrogant, not too many people inspired me because I couldn't really relate to someone who wasn't in my situation.

My parents saw Nick online and I went to a church in New York – I'm not religious – but I saw him when I was 12 and I met him backstage and I cried. It was just a moment of proof-of-concept to see this guy living a happy, fulfilled life.

One of my biggest fears was 'How am I going to be independent?', 'How am I going to be financially free?', all these things. I can't work a regular job, so what am I going to do? So, to see someone who was successful in my situation was extremely inspiring.

He knows of me; I know of him and we can co-exist in the space. He's very religious, and I bring a different dynamic, but he was very powerful for me when I was younger. Seeing someone do something, it gives you the belief that "Oh! I can do that."

BEING A MAN

What does "being a man" mean to you?

That's a great question. I think being a man means being a provider to both yourself and those around you but also being tapped into your emotions.

I think a lot of men aren't really in tune with their spiritual side or their emotional side because they think it's feminine, or at least not masculine.

I think a well-rounded man serves himself, serves his people, is a leader, and is a protector – protecting not only physically but emotionally and being there when people need emotional support. He's also someone who can tap into his own emotions.

Feel people, be empathetic, see both sides of things – and just be well rounded.

There have been times when I thought crying was not cool, or not manly, but now I know being able to tap into all of your emotions and all of yours senses is important.

Dad is this kind of man – if we didn't have enough food, he would eat last, or he would give the shirt off his back for someone. He just gives, gives, gives and gives. That's been my personal core value – even if you get f*cked over, you still did your part and you still put good in the world, so you can't lose.

Have your concepts of masculinity/being a man changed over time?

That's a great question – we always look to our dads. I always thought Dad was superman. I think you can look up to people, and a lot of times we look up to being our parents, but also being self-aware and realizing what you don't want to be. There are certain ways you don't want to act like your parents.

Being a man, as I said, is being a leader, being a provider but also having that soft side. I think you're closed off if you're always trying to be hard and 'masculine'.

But being in tap with your emotions and talking about things that other guys won't talk about. I think being a man is being so comfortable with yourself that you can talk about anything with anyone and not have a fear of what people think of you. I think that's what being masculine is. It's liberating.

If there was a single piece of advice that you could give every young man in this world, what would it be?

I think so many young guys are seeking validation and acceptance from someone else. When you are a man and you are laser-focused on your purpose and you have goals, and you're driven and you know where you're going – that's when you will meet the right girl, the right partner, or the right teammate, whatever that may be.

There's a whole thing around men being beta or alpha males – if I could give one piece of advice it's to find out what you love to do, find your purpose, chase what you want. That's going to be extremely hot and extremely attractive to women.

I think when you focus on yourself first and build yourself up and crush your goals and your ambitions, the right stuff and the right women will come because they will see your work ethic, and they'll see your passion.

Another rule is open communication – I don't care if it's in your personal life, or in your business or your parents and family – but open communication is key because otherwise things build up and it's no good for you and it's no good for your nervous system.

I think some guys don't want to talk about how they feel because they think it's stupid or feminine, but open communication is the massive key to life.

EMOTIONS

What makes you truly happy?

Giving people experiences that they didn't think they could ever have or taking someone somewhere they didn't think they could ever go.

Like Dad, I'm just a giver – it just came to me now that I ask Dad what he wants for Christmas and he says, "Nothing – I like seeing you guys open the presents." Now it makes sense – I don't want anything, I just want to have money to be able to take people on a snowboard trip, or say, "Hey, surprise! We're going to Italy." That fulfils me.

Being able to do cool stuff with the people I love really fires me up.

"There have been times when I thought crying was not cool, or not manly, but now I know being able to tap into all of your emotions and all of yours senses is important."

Also – contributing. This is not something I usually share, but I work alongside a non-profit in Uganda and we educate people on a range of things. For example, they don't know the symptoms of malaria, and they die without knowing why. There was a kid who broke his knee and couldn't afford his surgery, and they were going to amputate his leg, and so I paid for his surgery which was only $500, which in that situation isn't much.

If I'm having a low day, I can just self-reflect, and say, "Bro, you saved that kid's life."

Tony Robbins always talks about the two needs that you need to meet in order to lead a fulfilled life, and that's contribution and growth, and what fires me up is evolving and growing and progress, whether it's in my personal life or in business, and being able to spoil people – being able to pay for their meal, or say, "Don't worry about that plane ticket, I've got it."

That's dope to me.

What does strength look like to you?

Inner strength is like entrepreneurship – how long can you eat shit for? How many times can you get punched in the face, and get up and smile?

I think we build inner strength by continuously putting ourselves in uncomfortable situations and stepping into the moments, rather than veering away from them. I think a lot of kids are coddled nowadays – especially in a generation where everything's quick. I can Facetime you right away, I can watch my favorite movie on Netflix, I can get Uber Eats, I can get everything quick, but when I build a business and I'm not successful in 2 years, I cry.

I think inner strength is necessary, but I think it's built. It's grit, it's resilience and not giving up.

We all have power and a strength inside – it just needs to be unlocked.

What does vulnerability mean to you?

This is something else I'm passionate about – it's a shitty time for relationships with so much cheating going on. It's normal for guys and girls to cheat on each other. The only way you can find love and receive love is being vulnerable. A lot of times, speaking for myself, you get hurt in the past, so you're like, "I don't want to do that again, because I'll get hurt." But at least you do your part, and you open up for the opportunity.

I personally think I'm getting better – being vulnerable also ties into ego. If your ego is massive, then you don't want to be vulnerable. I think it comes with an ego check and putting your ego to the side and opening up to things that trigger you. Being super self-aware and communication all ties into vulnerability. Communicating what upsets you, what angers you, working through your shit, and opening up to people who can help you.

A lot of men want to be hard – they don't want to crack themselves open, but it's

important to let people know what's truly inside.

How do you express anger? What do you do to release frustration?

That was one of the things I learned from watching Dad. When I was younger, he had a very bad temper. Dad grew up in the ghetto, dropped out of high school, and was carrying pistols to lunch.

He has always talked about his anger getting the best of him and saying, "Thank god I got my anger in check, or I would be in jail."

That was something I was always conscious and self-aware of – I don't want to have anger issues. When I was a kid, I would get pissed off – I would mainly get pissed off if I couldn't figure out how to do something on my own – because I was always trying to be independent.

Anger is okay – it depends on how you channel it.

You can have anger, and go into a deep, dark depression and hurt yourself, or hurt others; or you can channel it and focus it on your purpose and say, "Just watch." That's what I've chosen to do.

It's funny – my guys told me they used to have a company in the past, and they used to write down the names of people that doubted them and they put them on a wall, and when they were grinding and building their company they would look up at the wall and think "F*ck that guy!"

Do you talk with anyone about how you feel when things are happening in your life, or do you keep these thoughts internalized?

There's a guy that comes to mind - his name is Nino - and at the events that I speak at, he is my escort and helps me to be where I need to be.

One of the things I took notice of is he's always asking me about how my energy is, or how am I feeling?

Not many people ask me that – they just see me on stage and just expect that I'm a master of life and my energy is never off. I love and commend people who ping other people and ask them how their energy is – which is another tie into communication.

If you don't communicate about your emotional state, and you need help, you're not going to get help.

It's one of the core values of my company – communicate whether you're pissed off, angry, or triggered. Let it all out, otherwise it's just going to build up and lead to remorse.

You need to be self-aware of what you're feeling and what the thoughts are that are inside your head – a lot of the times as hustlers and winners, we are the ones that beat ourselves up internally.

It's important to build praise and positive self-talk into your nervous system because that helps your emotional state.

If your emotional state is rocky and rough, it's probably because your internal dialogue is so harsh and negative.

SPIRITUALITY AND MINDFULNESS

What role does religion or spirituality play for you?

I'm not religious – I'm spiritual – I believe in a higher energy. It's a fact that we are electrical beings, we vibrate from a certain frequency.

Spirituality is something I want to engage with more – I want to read more about Buddha and Buddhism, because it's about love and floating through the river of life.

I think the power of meditation and visualization is something I need to practice more and incorporate more into my daily routine. It's called neuron-mirroring and basically the mind can't tell whether something is real or not, so when you really crack visualization, your mind can't decipher whether it's real or not and that's when we attract things into our lives.

I visualized being on Tony's stage at *Unleash the Power Within* over and over again, so that way when I get out there, it's like "Oh, I'm here. I've been here already."

Spirituality is not only manifesting, but vibrating off a certain frequency and giving, serving and contributing and the universe will repay you.

It's all a game, and once you realize you can alter your own reality through thoughts and visualizations, that's what I'm on right now.

What do you do to relax?

Video games. I love video games – being a kid, I was the biggest nerd. I figured out how to play an XBox controller in my situation – I use my chin; I use all of it. When I was younger, there was a game where I was one of the best in the world and no-one even knew I was playing with my chin. They would have been freaked out if they knew!

For the longest time, I thought "I can't be successful if I play video games," because I had a different version of success that was implanted by an ex-mentor.

I tell people to go back to the things that their "inner-kid" enjoys. Those things you do where time goes by, and you don't even realize it and you're having a blast. We need to do more of that in our lives.

In most of the situations, I have to be extroverted, and have to be the guy who's talking to everyone, but my idea of a vacation is sitting and not moving.

LIFE PURPOSE AND SUCCESS

What do you ultimately strive for? What is your mission in life?

I want to do everything. When I met The Rock, I said, "I want to do what you did," and by that I meant that he is everywhere, he does everything. My whole mantra is "Why not?"

There's two ways I can view my life – one is that I was a freak accident, or two is that I was strategically put here in this body because the world is hurting, and it needs some light. For me, take over speaking, take over modelling, take over entertainment, take over acting – I want to do it all.

"You can have anger, and go into a deep, dark depression and hurt yourself, or hurt others; or you can channel it and focus it on your purpose and say, "Just watch." That's what I've chosen to do."

If I can get in front of as many people as I can – I don't want to motivate, I want to shift perspectives. Two things that will always ground us is gratitude and perspective.

If you want to describe life in one word, it's "perspective."

I want to change people's lives for the better and impact as many people as I can before I leave. I just feel like I've been put in this strategic body, my soul knew I could hang and handle it and do the amazing things that I'm able to do for a reason.

I just want to max out and squeeze as much juice and life out of this as I can and give as much as I can. When I die, people will say, "Dude, that guy gave everything!"

Do you define yourself as "successful"?

Yeah and no. There was a documentary series on Bill Gates, and they asked him that, and he said "No." One of the things that moved me is that his mom passed away and they asked him "Would your mom be proud of you?" and he hesitated.

I'm successful, but I'm not where I want to be. I know I've got cool shit going on, and I know I'm doing amazing things and helping a lot of people but I'm not to where I want to be.

I think just being fulfilled is success, because I've met millionaires and billionaires who have all the money and "success" in the world and who are still empty inside, because they're not doing something that fulfils them.

I know my purpose and I know where I'm headed, and we're doing all the right things and we are laying the bricks right now.

I don't like saying I'm successful, but I feel pretty good.

Image supplied.

OVERCOMING CHALLENGES

How has failure, or apparent failure, set you up for later success? Do you have a "favorite failure" of yours?

I got accepted to the only college I applied to with my best friend. I was going to go to college, and I went to orientation and I was like, "I don't wanna do this." I was a famous prankster at the time, and I had the opportunity to do a practical joker show where the whole cast was disabled so you could do some pretty messed-up pranks.

They said, "Dude, we need you out in LA, we want you to be a core cast member, we're going to film a pilot." I was 19, and I thought "Great, I'm going to be on a big TV show," and so I convinced my parents to let me move out to LA with a roommate.

I moved out to LA and signed a lease for this shit apartment, a one-bedroom loft, outside Hollywood for $1800 per month. I moved in, and then my roommate stopped paying rent, and I was sleeping on a pile of towels in my laundry, I didn't have much food – I was eating peanut butter and tortillas and ramen noodles

– and I refused to tell my parents I was broke. I lived like that for 6 months before moving home.

It's one of the greatest failures I've ever had, because I know how to live with absolutely nothing. No food, no bed, sleeping on floors.... I know how to do it, and I know I can do it.

I'm not really afraid of losing it all because I've been there. It was guided, that's for sure, I needed to do it. I needed to move out of the state on my own and fall on my face real hard.

It also taught me a whole lot about budgeting and realizing you've got to take account of gas and food and electrical bills. I knew nothing, so it was a fast-learning experience!

RELATIONSHIPS AND FAMILY

Who has been the most important role model in your life? Has there been someone who has led by example?

It goes back to the three guys – Tony Robbins, Andy Frisella and Ed Mylett. Being in this industry and going into this life of speaking and stuff, we vetted out the fake people, the people our core values didn't align with.

Ed Mylett, for example, the guy is worth over $400 million, and is probably the best communicator in the world, has a wife, has a family and is just awesome! It's still grind, and it's still hustle but he's an amazing dude. I see that and I think

"That guy can take his family anywhere he wants on a private jet." That's sick. That's a role model to me.

In what ways have the women in your life influenced the man you have become?

Mom's rule was "So long as you're happy, I'm happy" and that's what we're all chasing, right?

The emotion of happiness – we think it's cars and watches – but it's really the emotion we feel.

The strength that my mom has – the pregnancy that she went through and not knowing if I was going to survive, the way they parented me, all that stuff is super motivating.

I'm inspired by women who know what they want, they're driven, they're focused – they're go-getters. My girlfriend is like that – and she's super loving and our communication is on point. I'm always throwing her into uncomfortable situations and she always embraces it.

In a world where there's so much cheating going on and so much negativity – I don't have to worry about anything with her. She's the first girl I've ever committed to because I wouldn't commit, I wasn't vulnerable, I had trust issues.

She was guided into my life – it came out of nowhere for both of us.

You've got to have a badass teammate in life.

JOHN WAYNE PARR

10-TIME WORLD CHAMPION MUAY THAI AND BOXING CHAMPION

 @johnwayneparr   @johnwayneparr

John Wayne Parr is an Australian Muay Thai superstar and 10-time World Champion.

Growing up as a single child and moving across Australia with his family, John Wayne took to the gym where he found a structure of life that he was looking for: the rules of the ring.

In 1996 John Wayne moved to Thailand, living in Pattaya and training for three months out of Sidyodtong gym, eventually moving to Nonthaburi, Bangkok to train with legendary Thai fighter, Sangtien Noi.

John Wayne has had a long career, over 3 decades. His biggest achievements are S1 Champion, King Cup, K1 Max, The Contender Asia Finalist, and CMT promoter & Champion & Australian Boxing Champion.

In 2021, John Wayne returned to fighting after retiring in 2019.

Do you have a favorite quote or philosophy you live by?

"Never give up" – very easy and straight to the point!

So many times, I've been knocked down in the ring, and thought, "I've got to keep going, I can't stop, I can't stop." If I lose, I'm going to hate myself, so I can't give up.

The only time I've stopped it was when I got my orbital bone in my eye broken in 2 places. As the referee was counting,

that was the first time I've ever said to the referee, "Oh don't bother – my face is gone!"

But any other time, whether it be a tap or a knockdown – just get up and you know you are only one punch away from winning. I might get knocked down, but that doesn't mean you're going to beat me.

It's hard to know what you're going to do until you're in the situation – it's nice to say, "I'll do this, or I'll do that" but when

you're in that predicament all of a sudden, it's like, "Ohhh, this really hurts."

Especially being a gym owner, I've been lucky to be in the corner for so many people – and people handle adversity in so many different ways. But I'm lucky in that if I'm focused on something, it doesn't matter how much pain I'm in. Nine times out of ten, I'll still try to win, no matter what.

You have had a big career in Thailand and fighting in some of the biggest stadiums in Asia. How did you keep yourself centered?

I was fighting on TV, and was in the newspapers, and it's really, really cool but at the same time being a Westerner in their country and doing their sport – sure I might win today but I know there are 50 guys in a line ready to smash me.

You learn to be very humble – you might win today but someone is going to be stronger and smarter and harder next time.

You train hard and you get the win and then you get told, "Your next opponent is going to be this guy," and you think, "Holy shit, how am I going to fight that guy?" and then you get in there, and nine times out of ten you might win, and you think, "That's awesome." But then you get the next guy, and he's even stronger again, and it's like, "Oh man!"

You have recently announced you are coming out of retirement. Being in your 40s and having the opportunity to get back in the ring, what does that mean to you?

I retired in 2012, I was at the stage where my body was burnt out. After around 6 months, there was this void, I had been

training and fighting my whole life since I was 11 years old and, all of a sudden, I faced waking up each day without having a date to plan for. Training people was fun and exciting but it's not the same as stepping into the ring and knowing that you could have the potential of the high of winning or the low of getting smashed, I missed that adrenaline.

I came back again, but the hip was no good, and I retired again in 2019. I was told that I needed to stop training, stop running or else my hip joint could snap. I kept running and had to take a phone with me in case it snapped, and I needed to call someone.

I have had an operation and the hip feels great and to have the opportunity to fight again, I feel elated, I'm so happy! It's given me another purpose to strive to be the best I can possibly be again.

My family are really supportive, they wouldn't want it any other way. They could see how depressed and sad I was.

As an example, if I was fighting in 8 weeks, for 8 weeks every single day you are thinking about the game plan, trying to push yourself in training, you have a purpose but without the date I was lost. There was a massive void.

How have you dealt with this depression over the years?

Always trying to keep as busy as I can, busy in the gym, making sure I was doing all of my training classes and PT sessions, basically distracting myself from thinking about not having a fight to look forward to.

It was always my dream from a really young age to train and fight and all of a sudden, the hand brake was on. I only retired because of my hip, it wasn't my decision, it was my body saying, "Stop, you've had enough, the wheels are coming off." Now that the hip is fine, there is no pain.

I went to a funeral about six months ago, and I saw the coffin of the person and I realized, "That's it, they're done. Once I'm in the box, it doesn't matter. I might as well go out and have as much fun as I can now and keep doing what I love for as long as I can."

If I'm in that box, that's the end of the road. Keep going until you can't do what you love doing.

Everyone has different opinions, I heard them all. I got to the stage where I said I don't care about their opinions, they can either come along for the ride or they can talk shit, either way I'm going to do what I want to do. You're either with me or you're not, it doesn't matter, I'm doing it for myself.

My family understand that this is my life, I'm going to keep doing what I do, and I have everyone's support.

I still feel like I'm at a really high level, I'm still sparring, training and kicking just as hard as I was before the operation and I'm still sparring great, I'm not losing rounds, I still feel I'm at the standard I was prior to all the injuries.

With the opportunity to fight for a championship again, it's such a massive show and even though I have achieved everything I could in the sport, I get the chance to fight with this company and the whole world is watching.

I want to keep inspiring people; I want to show young kids that martial arts is a great way for the mind, body and soul to interconnect. There is no better feeling than feeling healthy, strong and feeling

confident with yourself knowing that you have done the work in the gym.

Going into surgery, I decided to treat my rehab like a fight. The aim was to get back to 100 percent health as fast as I could. I made sure I was active throughout the rehab period, if I had sat on the couch and felt sorry for myself, I dare say it would have taken a lot longer.

Once I recovered, I was offered an opportunity to fight again and as the old man in the sport, I didn't think I would get that opportunity again.

For the promoters to approach me and say they would love me to come back, it made me feel wanted again. When you reach a certain age and your body is broken, you can feel discarded, so to have the promoters want me back fighting is great because I didn't want the journey to end.

I invented the sport of Caged Muay Thai in 2012. It's in the cage, MMA gloves, Muay Thai rules where if you fall over, you stop, stand back up and start fighting again. If you get knocked down, you still get an 8 count like boxing.

So, ONE Championship has taken my idea and they are doing it on a world stage. It's so humbling for me to see that taking a risk back in 2012 was worth it, and to see it now grow to such a standard where the best of the best are fighting and putting on a show is surreal.

I remember when I first bought it out, I copped so much criticism, "How dare you, you're bastardizing the sport and out of all the people to do this, I can't believe you're doing it."

Someone even wrote to me and said, "The only reason you are doing this is to make money." Yes, that's correct, funnily enough it is. Everyone needs to make money somehow and you have to think outside the box. So, to see it now growing and going ahead in leaps and bounds, I'm so happy to be part of the show.

LIFE PURPOSE AND SUCCESS

What do you ultimately strive for?

My ultimate goal is to leave a legacy that can hopefully inspire other people to travel to Thailand and learn the sport, learn the art and language.

I want to be the Australian version of Ramon Dekkers - he was the first guy to go and fight in Thailand. I was the first to go and live in Thailand on a long-term basis and live and learn the Thai ways. I lived there for four years full time and lived on the circuit.

I want to be able to inspire my children also and show them that by hard work you can achieve success and especially through my hobby. If you can turn your hobby into a profession, it's a great outcome. Through doing the work and being determined, you can live your dream. It doesn't have to be working a 9 to 5 job doing something that you hate, go and do something that you love, every day is then a blessing.

OVERCOMING CHALLENGES

Have there been any key challenges that you have had to face in your life? How have you faced them?

When I was growing up, I went to 11 different schools – I was always the new kid and I learnt how to blend in really fast, like a chameleon. I was a small child too, so I could easily have become a victim. You figure out who the cool guys are, and you start hanging out with them.

Martial arts became one of my passions very early on, so I started training at the age of 11. Every time we moved home the first priority would be to find a new gym because that was my happy place.

Martial arts was my form of keeping focused so I wouldn't get led astray by the bad influences in life. Muay Thai kept me sane and kept me on the straight and narrow and gave me the desire to one day be the best.

I could easily have been led down a different path, definitely. But I always wanted to do martial arts since I was about 4. We lived in country towns and were always moving. Living on farms, there was nothing close by. Then we moved to the city and I started training and from thereon in, there was no stopping me.

I wanted to not only become great, but to leave a legacy. I know I am not going to be on the earth forever, but when I pass, I want people to remember me, and to draw inspiration from watching my videos.

How has failure, or apparent failure, set you up for later success? Do you have a "favorite failure" of yours?

Yes – I got deported from America in 2002 – I overstepped my visa by two days. I met my wife, I got married over there. We only had a marriage certificate; we didn't have proper government paperwork filled out.

I came back to Australia for a fight – I picked up $5000 for it – and then flew back to America and got stopped in LA by immigration. They asked, "When was the last time you were here?" and I said, "About 3 weeks ago." They asked, "How long were you here for?" and I said, "About 3 months."

They said, "What? You can't be here for 3 months – you're only allowed to stay here for 90 days! You were 2 days over your visa. I'm going to put you on the next plane back to Australia."

At that stage, Muay Thai and martial arts wasn't very big in America at all, so I was teaching in a boxing gym, I was just getting by, there were no fights on the horizon. It was hard to do anything.

The moment I got deported, my career exploded in Australia! I started fighting overseas with a company called Super League in Europe and I got picked up by the K-1 Max in Japan, and then I made the Contender Asia reality TV show.

At the time I got deported, it was the worst day of my life - because my wife was seven months pregnant, I wasn't allowed to see her, I had no money. I was just lost. But the moment I got back to Australia, everything just happened in a positive way.

Looking back – it sucked at the time but getting deported was the greatest thing that could ever happen to me.

If there is one piece of advice you can give young people, what would it be?

Looking back, don't give up because you can achieve it. I'm proof of that - I was a lonely kid on a farm who had a passion of one day becoming somebody. There are highs and lows – and it's true that it's not about the destination, it's about the journey. Try to have fun while you're climbing the ladder, and don't lose focus on who you want to be. You can achieve anything if you don't give up.

EMOTIONS

What makes you truly happy?

Family. I've got three kids – two girls and one boy, and my wife.

How do you express anger? What do you do to release frustration?

I'm very lucky – I don't get angry that often. I'm one of those guys where the glass is half-full. If something doesn't go my way, I use it as a way to learn. If the car breaks down, there's no point getting angry, you may as well just fix it. I think I'm pretty hard to piss off.

Every now and then you might get an idiot that comes into the gym and wants to start beating up on the students. That annoys me. All it takes is one sparring session to make them quickly become humble. They either become humble or they leave, either way they don't beat up my students anymore.

The gym and my students are my family – so there's no one coming in on my watch. I take full responsibility for making sure everyone has fun. You want to walk out the same way you walked in – if you're leaving with black eyes and blood noses and you've got a limp, you're going in too hard. If you're not having fun, you're doing something wrong.

What does strength look like to you?

For me, it's having the mindset where you can't let anything get in the way of your destiny. For me, my destiny has always been being world champion, ever since I was 5 years old. I knew I wanted to be a fighter, I just didn't know what style it would be – wrestling was really big with Hulk Hogan, and there were movies like Karate Kid and Rocky. I started with

Taekwondo and then moved onto kick boxing for a little bit.

Having that mindset that nothing was going to stop me – whether that be girls or work – I know where I've got to be, and if you're going to get in my way, I don't want you in my life.

Because I lived on farms, and I was an only child, I had to dictate my direction. I had friends for 6 months and then we would move to a new house. So, everything was self-driven, I didn't have anyone to help me.

My parents worked in the horse-racing industry, so they would leave for work at 4am. I would wake up and there would be $2 on the table and that was money for lunch. I would come back from school, and they wouldn't finish work until 6.30pm. They would come home, have dinner and be in bed by 7.30pm.

So, I'm used to being a loner. I think that's what helped in my career – I don't want to have anyone tell me what to do, but I know where I want to be. I was my own motivation.

Do you talk with anyone, or have a group of friends you can talk to, about how you feel when things are happening in your life, or do you keep these thoughts internalized?

Mainly myself – every now and then I go through a rough patch and I just need to snap myself out of it. There's two ways to think – either let it get the better of you or just snap yourself out of it and find a positive in other things.

I try to put a smile on everything – I can get pissed off and break things, or I can get on with it. I've got too many things I want to accomplish, and I don't want to be burdened.

SPIRITUALITY AND MINDFULNESS

What role does religion or spirituality play for you?

After being in Thailand for so long, I came back to Australia and my sponsor gave me a call. Every male Thai person becomes a monk once in their life – whether it be 7 days, 1 month, 6 months, 1 year. My sponsor is Thai, and his two boys were going to become monks and he said, "Do you want to join them? You speak Thai, you live like a Thai, you fight like a Thai, this is the last thing on the list." And I said I would love to.

I had my head and eyebrows shaved and ended up being a monk for seven days, which was very enlightening. You didn't have any possessions, you just had your robe, and you were given a bowl. Every morning, we would walk the streets, and people would give us food offerings and that's what we would eat that day. If there was no one there, we wouldn't eat that day. We would do Buddhist studies twice a day, morning and evening.

After seven days, I realized that so long as you have a roof over your head and food in your tummy, life's not that bad.

When we strip everything back – it's not hard to find happiness, but we drown ourselves in all these problems that at the end of the day don't matter all that much.

So long as you're a good person, you create good karma and good karma comes back to you. If you're a dickhead, hang on, because life is going to get pretty rough and you are going to have a rocky ride.

If you're nice to people, people are nice back. It's amazing what doors you can open just by being polite.

RELATIONSHIPS AND FAMILY

Who has been the most important role model in your life? Has there been someone who has led by example?

Definitely my parents – but I moved out of home at 18 and moved to the Gold Coast and Richard Vell became very important. I lived 15 minutes-walk from his restaurant and so every day I would walk down and as Richard was preparing food, I would sit on a chair or on top of the fridge and we would sit there and talk for hours. He would give me life advice on how to be a man.

I was infatuated by this magical place called Thailand, and when I moved there, my skill at being a chameleon from moving around so much was really important, and I was really good at learning another culture and another language and blending in and staying out of trouble.

That gave me an advantage over other people – I would watch other Westerners come and they would get homesick and they would start missing their friends and family and I would look at them and think, "You're a wuss!"

For me, it was just another day and I knew where I wanted to be and if that meant living in Thailand long-term, I was happy to do it to become a champ.

Muay Thai was the only thing that mattered and when the opportunity came to go to Thailand and learn from the best – Richard would tell me all these stories about how they would sleep on the floor, training hours upon hours on end – it never deterred me. If I had to sleep on the dirt to become world champion, I was happy to do that.

What was your relationship like with your mother and father?

With Dad, it was pretty tough – I would only see him for an hour or so each day because they were always working. Looking back, it was a pretty rough childhood. It was a very weird upbringing – it's only now that I'm older and I look at my kids and I think, "How the hell did you just leave me like that?" But it is what it is.

It wasn't until I got back from Thailand that me and Dad became best friends. As soon as I came back, we were no longer just father and son, but he became a friend and a fan. Wherever he would go, he would make them watch my fights and he would tell them stories about what I was up to... it became really cool. He even came to Japan once to watch me fight. It was very special when we had that bond.

I'm thankful for my childhood – if I didn't have those experiences, I wouldn't be where I am now.

Mom was working crazy hours – and she would sacrifice a lot – she would drive me to training, sit in the car till I was done, drive me home. She probably fell asleep in the car waiting while I was training in the gym. She knew the direction I wanted to go, and she helped drive that passion.

Dad passed away in 2008, but Mom is still with me which is great.

What qualities are most important for you in being a father?

Hopefully I show my kids that whatever you put your mind to, you can achieve – if you work hard enough. Hopefully them watching me fight, and all the sacrifices and training to give them a better life, they can feed off it. No-one's going to give them anything in life, they have to work for it.

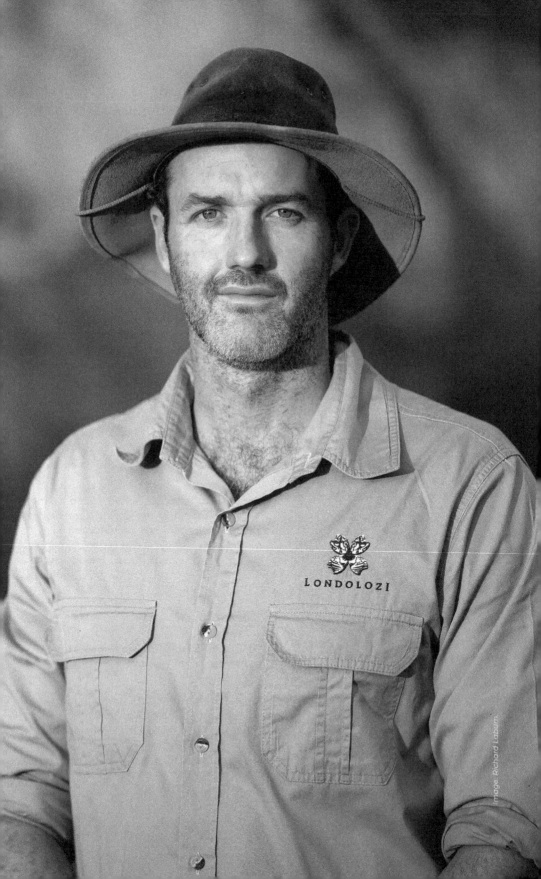

BOYD VARTY

AUTHOR AND WILDLIFE ACTIVIST

 @boyd_varty   @boydvarty   Boyd Varty

The wildlife and literacy activist Boyd Varty, author of the memoir *Cathedral of the Wild*, had an unconventional upbringing.

Born to a family of conservationists, Boyd grew up on Londolozi Game Reserve in the South African wilderness, a place where man and nature strive for balance.

Founded more than 90 years ago as a hunting ground, Londolozi was transformed into a nature reserve beginning in 1973 by Varty's father and uncle, visionaries of the restoration movement. But it wasn't just a sanctuary for the animals; it was also a place for ravaged land to flourish again and for the human spirit to be restored. When Nelson Mandela was released after 27 years of imprisonment, he came to the reserve to recover.

Boyd survived a harrowing black mamba encounter, a debilitating bout with malaria, even a vicious crocodile attack, but his biggest challenge was a personal crisis of purpose. As a university student, he studied psychology and ecology, supplementing his education by learning martial arts in Thailand, hiking through the jungles of the Amazon, and apprenticing to a renowned tracker from the Shangaan tribe deepening his intimate knowledge of the natural world.

What is one personal quality that you are most proud of?

The willingness and ability to feel.

My desire is to serve and build work that allows me to consistently support and serve.

I can feel what has energy in it, I can feel what I feel called to, it's not a rational strategic plan it's almost like I can feel what is calling and that's what I pay attention too and the willingness to be dynamically creating with life.

The best I have heard it explained is by a guy called Otto Shram who runs the Presencing Institute at MIT, and he refers to it as "Leading from the emergent future". The idea is you can feel what wants to happen by being present and you can feel what needs to happen next.

What are the issues - whether social, environmental, political or economic - that you feel are most pressing and for which you feel the greatest personal concern and responsibility?

Right now, what I am most concerned with is the transformation of human consciousness. My deepest love is for the natural world and I am aware that the protection of wild places must begin with a transformation in humanity's relationship with nature.

We are in need of a great remembering of how closely tied we are to nature and we need to imagine new systems for living. New systems for living for me refers to many people finding new ways to live that are far simpler, more connected to nature. New systems for living will rely on literally reimagining how we live.

LIFE PURPOSE AND SUCCESS

What do you ultimately strive for? What is your mission in life?

My mission is to be a voice for nature, create healing in the world and help transform the consciousness of humanity. My mission is to be present. Discovering and serving meaningful work is never static.

How do you define success? At what point did you identify as being "successful"?

Success to me is presence. Success is doing what you feel called to do. Success is the courage to discover your own unique gifts and share them. Success is freedom. Success is having enough to pursue your art.

Success has been learning to go inward. Discover what truly brings me to life and then consistently take small steps toward that feeling without fear.

What makes you feel fulfilled and energized?

I am energized by doing the work I am meant to do. Serving, practicing, and stepping towards the goals I have set for myself. For me any time I am involved in an act of healing or awakening or joy or laughter I am energized. Life is quite simple.

Where did your internal drive come from?

From my uncle, father and mother I got a wild sense of belief. They built the Londolozi Reserve from nothing and they built it on belief and they were willing to go without knowing, almost like their modus operandi was "We will just start". I definitely absorbed some of that and then I was profoundly affected by watching the land come back to life as they built the reserve.

I thought I would be a conservationist, I thought that that would be where you might put me but watching the land heal and then later going through my own healing process, I really found that all my work was around the idea of restoration: how a landscape can heal, how a wild place can return, life's impulse towards itself and equally how we are all a part of that process. I feel like I absorbed that into my body in a way that is very masculine, I was in that energy field of wildness and restoration and life!

"Nothing you achieve in the outer world will count as enough if you don't understand what drives you, motivates you, hurts you or makes you feel truly alive. Let simplicity be a guide. Learn your own unique way inward to your own being."

They say in men's work, the masculine body absorbs the presence of other men and the lessons you get from other men are very rarely what they say to you, instead it comes out of presence. When you are with them a lot, you feel their way, you absorb how they are and as I grew up around trackers and people who were a little bit wild, the inclination was always there was possibility. We could go out into the bush and track a leopard and find something in this restored landscape and that's where I absorbed the sense of possibility.

One of the things about a person that really heals, as it becomes our most authentic self, unguarded, undefended and in touch with what I call our truest nature, which is intelligent like nature, one of the primary overwhelming feelings is "enough".

For people who touch the authentic life, the true self, true nature, they don't want stuff to make them feel good. It's like an antidote to a consumerist culture, you stop wanting external things and people like this are inclined back towards nature and people who touch that have a natural affiliation towards silence and the natural world, they have an immediate sense and desire to live more simply, they become interested in the experience of a becoming creative and to serve in something meaningful. It's not like they are trying to do it, it just flows out of them when they become more humane again, more themselves.

You spent some time with Nelson Mandela when he was released from prison in 1990 and stayed on the Londolozi Game Reserve, what did you learn from him?

I used to take him breakfast in bed and what was definitive for me was that I was aware of a very strong, quiet presence. It was not a presence that was outwardly calling attention to himself - there was a stillness to him.

And then I would see these images of him on the TV where he was commanding this incredible transformation in front of millions of people crowded around him on his release. That's when I started to understand that it's not the loudest person in the room but the person whose presence is deepest, the person who is most themselves and all of the paradoxes of presence, the more present you are the more you are yourself, the less you are your small self. When you are really present, something greater is coming through you and simultaneously you are the most yourself and something much bigger.

I am now also aware of his capacity to humanize the moment, I wasn't aware of it at the time, but he had a way of humanizing every moment and what I saw him do time and time again was instead of going to what the social of the moment would have gone for, he went for what the relationship needed in the moment.

As an example, when he recovered, he and my uncle had a ritual of having breakfast together every morning and it was just the two of them.

My uncle used to sit at the head of the table and Mandela would sit on his left and they would converse over the morning's activities out there in the bush; it was very personal, very private.

There was a moment where there was a gathering at the camp and what had happened was there was members from the party who had become the senior leadership in the government of the country, this was right at the time of change, they had come for a lunch and, in a rare moment of tact, my uncle said to Mandela, "Mr Mandela this is a very official gathering, and you must sit at the head of the table." At this point Mandela said, "Oh no, JV, I would never take your seat at the head of the table."

This was a big gathering but there was something private, human and personal between these two men and what was alive in the relationship between them transcended how it should have looked in the moment and that's what he consistently did.

He had a total connection to the person first and that was the biggest lesson and what I continue to work with.

He had a profound impact on my life. I did a TED Talk and he passed away 15 minutes prior to me starting.

I was sitting there listening to the people at the TED Talk who are incredible experts in their fields and I'm a campfire story-teller from South Africa. I was getting consistently more nervous through the day and then it was my turn to talk and as I found out he had died it was like this incredible energy came over me and it was like, "This is not about me, it's about his presence," and this amazing calmness came over me.

That TED Talk has travelled to classrooms all over the world and into people's lives and it's almost like that energy was with me at that moment, in the moment.

OVERCOMING CHALLENGES

Have there been any key challenges that you have had to face in your life? How have you faced them?

The one thing that immediately comes to mind was when I had a period of time just as I was turning 20, where two incidents occurred.

One was the very unstable time in South Africa's history and myself and my mother and sister and a tutor who we had at the time, so there were three women and myself were held up in a home invasion in Johannesburg, South Africa.

It was a terrifying experience to see the women you love, your family tied up around you at gunpoint and one of the challenges I had to overcome at that point was a very South African mentality, "We're not dead, okay, so everyone get on with it."

But I couldn't sleep, I couldn't rest, I was super vigilant, but I couldn't relax, and I felt an incredible sense of responsibility in the relationships and I felt I was always on guard.

Eventually I understood that this was a form of PTSD and then the journey of healing began, and I think I was lucky to meet some people along the way who understood the healing process and for me it was actually learning to feel my feelings in some respect.

Learning to feel them and acknowledge what's there and then to create a different outcome for myself. Part of what happens when you have been traumatized is you become frozen in a certain respect. So, the first thing I needed to realize was that I wasn't feeling my feelings, I had a numbness.

The next thing was to recognize that the numbness is actually a feeling where I feel almost unmoved by the world so what do I need to start to be able to move through that?

So that was a process of okay, number one, work out what you need to heal; number two, being able to actually get the support you need; three, be willing to let myself be honest about what happened; and four, allowing yourself to be witness in the fact that I was terrified and uncertain and that I don't know how to process it.

Through this process I was able to say when this happened, I was scared and being able to talk about it and acknowledge it became the doorway back into feeling.

On this journey there were some women who were very helpful to me and there were some men who were also very helpful to me and I had to learn who I could trust and start opening up to the people who I could trust so I could let it go.

Relationships became very important and working out what I could share in those spaces became very important. Letting myself feel what was going on including the feelings that felt weak like I'm jumpy, I'm scared, and I don't know how to move forward. The feeling of being depressed.

It's kind of a depressing thing to be a depressed person, so I had to say, "I'm not feeling much at the moment" and be willing to be in that feeling for a while so

that you can move forward. The artform for me is learning to go down and feel the things you need to feel so you can move through them into a different identity.

I was very lucky to have both masculine and feminine healers come into my life and in a way, they provided certain archetypal support. From the women I received warmth and comfort and a holding that said, "It's okay, you're safe, you can feel your feelings."

From the men I received a certain masculine presence which says, "I'm here for you, you are strong, you can find your way through this."

From the masculine, it's much more direct, there is a presence of support, it's not warm and fuzzy. It's like, you can find what you need to heal but you have to be courageous about actually feeling what's there. The support is, "I won't do this for you, you will find your way through this, but I will be beside you."

I was lucky to get both sides of the coin and together I think it integrated a very whole healing where I could both feel my feelings, acknowledge what happened and at the appropriate moment take action. Obviously, the danger is when either the masculine or feminine healing dynamic energy is out of balance, you just keep trying to do things to feel better, you don't actually let yourself.

In the masculine it's, "I just keep going and I won't have to feel any of this, we can push through."

In the feminine the expression that's out of balance is by always feeling my pain, "I'm a victim and I'm really hurt."

So, you need to be able to feel it, take action. Take action but feel it!

That to me is the masculine and feminine integrated healing process.

What was the point where you feel you were back to being normal and could get to another level?

I would say it was about a three-year process, it wasn't a quick process.

However, a few months after that I was attacked by a crocodile and my leg was very badly mangled, so I was in a secondary process as well, coming through a physical trauma.

The willingness to become someone who has healed has helped and anyone who has come through a healing process becomes someone that has something to offer.

So, I'm incredibly grateful for it now and what I would say is that anything that you can overcome, you will become a guide for people within that area of life that you are overcoming.

Part of the willingness to be in it is for yourself but there is also a higher purpose that you can attach it to especially when you are really in pain, when you are really lost and shut down and if I get through this, I will have a map for other people and I think that's really valuable.

How has failure, or apparent failure, set you up for later success? Do you have a "favorite failure" of yours?

My life has different areas, but one story is with the first book I wrote.

I had a very strange experience with it - in some ways it looked like it would be a great success. The publishers advanced me a large amount of money and they were very excited about it and then the publishing kind of died.

It was at a time when publishing was very uncertain and so on a certain level, that first book, you could look at it through a lot of different lenses, you could say it was financially a success, but it was a failure commercially.

Yet I learnt so much out of that book and although it didn't do anything great in terms of numbers, I wasn't overly disappointed because for a period of time I still received letters and the letters would be like, "I'm sitting beside my husband's bedside and he is on chemotherapy as we speak and I'm reading this book to him and we are so grateful to be out in the wilderness with you".

Out of that experience I got an incredible sense of how your own narrative makes you a success or a failure.

I could have told myself I was a great success because of the advance or a great failure because of the sluggish sales.

I was a success when I received that letter and others, I was a failure when the book was criticized by some of the marketing team of the publishing house and that's when I realized, "I've done my part."

Part of creativity is, you do your part, then you let go. Your 50 percent that you were responsible for which is bringing it to the world is done. The next 50 percent of the book is what the world does with it.

I don't know if this is my defining failure, but it's a place where I have succeeded and failed and learnt a lot.

I would also say that some of the early groups I ran were pretty bad. I would say that I failed with some of these for sure. It's an awkward thing when you try to run a personal development group and it's bad.

Everyone in the group knows it's bad, and they are all looking at you, thinking, "This is bad, and this guy is bad at it." At the same time, I was so committed to get that work going that I started when I was young. I started by supporting other people's groups and by the time I was 26 to 27, I was putting my own groups together.

Who wants to come to a group about learning how to live your life run by a 26-year-old?

It was gutsy and some of it was bad, but it's bloody good now!

What I learnt through this is that there is a certain authenticity and people in the groups could see it was bad but they could see that I was authentically committed to it and I learnt that I had to get better, I had to be the sort of person who iterates.

At the end of every single retreat, I want to sit down with my team and say, "How can we be better?" I want to be in a feedback-fit environment, and I want to be the sort of person that, without being self-critical, is self-evaluating.

I want to create a growth environment around me where I have to grow, my team has to grow and in building an environment where we can fail well and then grow, at the same time I know that if we are authentic, people will feel it which can also include when we can say we don't know what to do.

BEING A MAN

What does "being a man" mean to you?

Being a man to me is an evolving journey towards, presence, courage, mastery and authenticity. Being a man is the cultivation of the bravery and sensitivity to pursue what life is asking of you.

Being a man is a constant becoming. It is the willingness to grow and generate but it is also the willingness to learn how to let go of our identity so that we can allow for wisdom.

To me the greatest quality a man can develop is integrity with his own being. Integrity means to be "undivided," when what you say and do and believe is aligned.

If there was a single piece of advice that you could give every young man in this world, what would it be?

I would offer that learning to go inward and be in touch with your inner life is as important as developing your outer expression into the world. As the old eastern saying goes, "If you don't go within you will go without".

Nothing you achieve in the outer world will count as enough if you don't understand what drives you, motivates you, hurts you or makes you feel truly alive. Let simplicity be a guide. Learn your own unique way inward to your own being.

How do you see yourself and your message to the world?

I would say it falls into three categories, the first, almost the most primary and you might say I have a Buddhist view on this, is that I have to continually improve and do my work to let go of illusionary thoughts that I'm believing.

I have to be aware when I am behaving out of a pattern of personality. I know if I commit to that work inside myself, it translates later. The Buddhist idea of the greater service you can do is attend to your own enlightenment, so I believe my work in the world is making sure that I cultivate my presence, my mindfulness, my gentleness and kindness and the strength that comes with that.

Secondly, I am very interested in what I call trying to accelerate awakening in the world. I don't mean awakening in some sort of spiritual insight, I mean it towards simplicity, stillness and connection to nature.

People who are awake to these are more committed to those things so I would say that my work is in restoration and accelerated awakening, and all of that comes out of telling stories and creating narratives that people can imagine, and creating transformational spaces in which people remember how to live again. So my work in the world is to grow the number of people I can bring into a transformational space in which they can get in touch with their gift and their medicine you might say.

EMOTIONS

What makes you truly happy?

I am truly happy when working on my craft as a tracker. Tracking is an ancient art form and a practice. It is the place I learn about nature, mastery and myself. Learning to serve my practice has made me truly happy.

How do you express anger? What do you do to release frustration?

As John O'Donohue says, "Anger is a sacred emotion that restores boundaries."

When I am angry I turn to myself to discover why something has made me angry there is usually a deeper reason than the surface issue. I then bring that up for discussion when I have cooled off and am able to talk and - more importantly - listen.

I also don't underestimate that small frustrations just build up and challenging my body physically can help create perspective.

What does strength look like to you?

Strength is staying in your own integrity and taking responsibility for your mistakes.

Strength is trusting the voice inside you in the face of a confusing and often ambiguous world.

What does vulnerability mean to you?

Vulnerability means you are willing to feel your emotions. Share your heart. Step forward towards love and feel how profoundly fragile that makes you. Vulnerability is the willingness to feel rather than fix.

How do you deal with conflict and diffusing difficult situations?

I try to develop personal power by noticing if after speaking with someone I held something back to avoid conflict. If the answer is yes I go back and say what I held back.

I find that this kind of honesty actually diffuses a lot of conflict and also helps to create clarity and stamp out resentment. It's difficult but it can be a practice that builds trust and personal power and honesty.

Do you talk with anyone about how you feel when things are happening in your life, or do you keep these thoughts internalized?

I have developed a group of close people who I trust and get counsel from. This has been revolutionary for me. We all need perspective. We all need people we can trust.

SPIRITUALITY AND MINDFULNESS

What role does religion or spirituality play for you?

My spirituality is critical to every aspect of my life. My connection to my work, loved ones and nature is born of a deep state of presence. This presence is the great mystery manifest simply in a moment in my life and the most valuable gift.

What pastime or practice enables you to relax and connect with your inner self?

I have had to learn to intentionally rest. I find it important to balance solitude with time with loved ones.

The ocean is a great friend in issues of relaxing.

RELATIONSHIPS AND FAMILY

Who has been the most important role model in your life? Has there been someone who has led by example?

My parents have had a huge impact on me. They created a powerful model for restoration and a space of transformation called Londolozi game reserve. They showed me the power of having a dream and the willingness to take small daily practical steps towards it.

In what ways have the women in your life influenced the man you have become?

My sister and my mother have been powerful guides. They taught me to honor the wisdom and power of the feminine impulse and they showed how much power you can give a person by simply believing in them.

STEPHEN MANDERSON

RAPPER

 @professorgreen   @professorgreen   Stephen Manderson

Stephen Manderson, better known by his stage name Professor Green or simply Pro Green, is an English rapper, songwriter and television personality.

Growing up on a council estate in East London, Stephen went on to become a multi-platinum artist, with 3.5 million combined sales in the UK. He has had a string of hit songs such as Just Be Good To Green, Lullaby and I Need You Tonight as well as the UK Official Singles Chart Number 1 Read All About It in collaboration with Emeli Sande.

Stephen was raised by his grandmother, great-grandmother and uncles in a two bedroom flat on the Northwold housing estate in Clapton, Hackney, London, in a home which he describes as chaotic. Stephen's great-grandmother Edie taught him to read and fed his intellectual curiosity as a child.

He sold cannabis and smoked it on a daily basis between the ages of 16 and 24.

When Stephen was 24 years old his father died by suicide. He stopped using any drugs from that point to allow himself to process the death fully.

Stephen is the patron of the anti-suicide charity CALM.

Do you have a favorite quote or philosophy you live by?

"Don't be shit!"

There's a lot of quotes around like, do your best, be the best and all of that... just "Don't be shit!" It started as a joke and then it ended up on the back of our tracksuits when we were sponsored by Puma on tour. It was what I used to say to the band before we went on stage. None of the band were really religious so we didn't pray or anything beforehand, it was just a case of "Okay, have a good one and don't be shit."

It doesn't come with undue pressure like "Be your best." Just "Don't be shit."

Who inspires you?

It's weird because there are so many people who have done so many brilliant things. Someone asked me recently, what advice would I give to the next generation or the youngest generation? My response was that I probably wouldn't give any advice, I would probably take advice from them.

The problem with trying to bring about change is the older you get, the less comfortable you are with change because change is scary whereas for the younger generations, the world is somewhat more malleable and they see room to improve and they have the energy to make the changes, they're not so stuck in their ways.

So, who inspires me? Probably the younger generation, the young voices that have a different perspective.

What is one personal quality you are most proud of?

Improvement, I guess. There are still things I want to work on, I still have behavioral issues, I can still revert to a child in some instances – I'm not beyond being triggered but I'm definitely getting closer.

I'm not Zen Level 10 yet – I'm like Zen 1.5... but I'm creeping up.

LIFE PURPOSE AND SUCCESS

What do you ultimately strive for? What is your mission in life?

I haven't worked that out yet. Things that I have worried about have largely been around unpredictability and unknowns and not being able to see what's around the corner, so my belief is to stop worrying what's around the corner. It's not conducive to a happy life or being present. If you're too far forward or too far back, you're never going to be where you're at currently.

So as far as my mission, I kind of take things as they come, opportunities present themselves, there are openings that I see.

I made one documentary because of the situation with my father, I never had a clue that I would then build a career as a documentarian. There was the opportunity there and half is seeing the opportunity and the other half is the hard work that's involved in taking an opportunity and making it work. I think there is something to be said for winging it.

I met a group of people a while ago and between the group they were all hugely successful - much more financially stable than I was, some of them were married, some were divorced, some separated, some had kids and from the outside you look at any of those people in the group and think that they've twigged it, they've got life, they must have right?

That evening, in the conversations that we had, I realized in an epiphany for me, that everyone is just winging it, things change and there are so many variables in life, and you don't ever "get it"!

It's like where you think there's a point where you become an adult, there's a point where we try to become adults, mine was when I was in my twenties which I wouldn't re-live if you paid me.

I'm in my thirties now and I have comfort in my skin in realizing that being an adult is about opening the bills and paying them, taking care of your responsibilities but you still should be able to find joy in the things that you did when you were younger without letting go of childish endeavors.

Someone explained to me that the feeling in your stomach, your gut feeling is really your younger self. How do you take care of that child, how do you fulfill that child that you carry around with you? I thought that was a really beautiful way to explain things. I've carried a lot of tension which suggests that my inner child has been quite unhappy with a lot of the things that I've done.

Some of the things I've put that child through, Jesus Christ!

So, my mission is to wing it until I can wing it some more.

Collaboration with other artists in your music seems to be something you just love to do. How important is it to your success?

Well, I can't sing! I'm a bloody good writer but I can't always sing what I write.

Adele doesn't need to work with anyone to make her albums – she is an incredible writer, but I imagine for her, it's the same thing – it would be boring. If you throw a tennis ball at a wall, you know where it's coming back so if you are in the studio with someone that you're throwing the tennis ball to, you never know where that tennis ball is coming back – you have to move and adapt.

Chemistry is really important in music – it's a bad analogy – but it's kind of like sex. I've had some of the worst sex with some of the most beautiful women – and I take full responsibility! But I've had some terrible studio sessions with some amazing artists and producers but sometimes it just doesn't click.

I'm strong enough in my own artistry to go, "You know, we don't need to force it just so we have a record together. I still

love what you do, and I hope you have the same appreciation for me." But then there's other people who I always have the same magic with – Naughty Boy, Mojam, Gold Fingers – when we're in the studio something just goes. Chris Loco – he and I have maybe done about three sessions - and out of it we got the songs "Photographs" and "Lullaby", which are two of the most important songs I've ever written because they were so personal.

When you find that with people, you're incredibly lucky.

OVERCOMING CHALLENGES

How has failure, or apparent failure, set you up for later success? Do you have a "favorite failure" of yours?

Yeah, man. I wouldn't say I've failed at anything really, but there's been a lot of false-starts, and I'm not a good finisher, I never saw things through. That was my problem. I was very, very bright, I could have done very well academically. By 13, I was in a pupil referral unit. I can blame a multitude of people or reasons for that but, ultimately, I didn't see it through.

My recording career – Jesus Christ – the amount of times that it was "nearly there" and then it wasn't for many, many reasons.

But if I was to pick a favorite failure, it would probably be not releasing my first album under Mike Skinner's label. He signed me when I was 21 but there's two reasons as to why that album didn't come out. The first is that I didn't work hard enough in the time I was signed so the album was never ready in time. The second is because, just as we were getting somewhere with the music, Mike and I were having disagreements on the sound of things. He wanted me to be more like him, and I definitely didn't want to be. Just as we were working it out, Warner pulled the financing from his record label and from all subsidiaries because Napster streaming had begun and record labels were pulling the purse strings tight. I never released my album, and I was back, selling drugs.

But I didn't stop – when everyone around me was saying, "Bro, come on man, you've got to find something else to do. This music thing is just a pipe-dream." I just said, "Is it? Okay" and I carried on, and I carried on, and I carried on, and then in 2009 after nearly losing my bloody life, I got signed by Virgin and I put a single out – we didn't put much out, we just wanted to test the waters and I charted at Number 3 with a single off the first album.

People always say, "Why did you carry on?" and I don't know – but stopping is just not something that I was going to do. It really, really wasn't.

My life changed exponentially, but I didn't catch up, you know. I didn't change as quickly as my life did. What a 10 years...

EMOTIONS

What makes you truly happy?

There are two things.

Nothing makes me happier than writing a lyric that makes me shake my hands. When I write something or come up with something like the last line of a chorus, it hits me. If I'm ever stuck on a line, I go to the loo, and I'm literally standing there with my dick in my hands and I'm like, "Got it!"

It's that feeling, I get my hands shaking with excitement, you've nailed it, you know it's right.

When I made my documentary, the rewards were so different. It was so difficult to film, there was a lot of sadness and I took a lot of that on, you know, you can't empathize and not.

The documentaries were rewarding but not in a way that made me happy.

Music is the outlet for me and that lights up my life.

There are other little things also like exercise, it isn't something I'm happy about doing – ever - but I definitely feel happier afterwards. Walking my dogs, these are the things that lead to happiness, if not in the moment, then afterwards. No matter how shit I feel of a morning, whether that's due to where I'm at, or because of stress or because I'm hungover – I always feel better when I get home after walking the dogs than when I did when I left the house. That makes me happy.

My partner makes me happy, most of the time! My friends, anything that nourishes you like making good decisions. The nights when I've gone home early, and called it when everyone else hasn't, and I've woken up the next morning, feeling smug as you like – that definitely makes me happy!

Good decisions beget good decisions in the same way that bad decisions tend to beget bad decisions.

Happiness isn't something that should be sought after as a constant, a better baseline is content, nor should happiness be pinned on moving targets, "I'll be happy if only…" or "I'll be happy when I…", it's never ending; bear in mind people tend to move a lot too so I wouldn't advise pinning your happiness on a person either.

You have had your share of trauma throughout your life, do you forgive easily?

Yeah, I do.

I don't like repetition, as far as learning is involved, repetition is important, but I don't like re-runs. By my own doing, I have welcomed some of that into my life, some by me making the same mistakes and doing the same things and not learning from things I've encountered and on the other hand inviting people into my life who are the same person in a different body who have bought me the same trauma.

I think when you encounter certain things as a child you learn to love in a really weird way, or you don't learn love, so you take the trauma and friction as feelings and that's what you seek.

I always thought that I sought calm, but it was impossible for me to find calm when the chaos was in me.

As far as forgiving, I find it impossible to hold a grudge maybe even to my detriment. I'm not sure it's healthy. I don't think holding onto it makes anyone unhappier than you.

To get to a point in life where you recognize something in someone that you don't like. It's like in a romantic relationship, it's incredibly difficult to find someone that you love 90 percent but know that the remaining 10 percent is intolerable. It's 10 percent that you can't fix because it's not your job. Your job is to manage yourself, not someone else, and you know that 10 percent means that you cannot be together. That's what an educated and emotionally intelligent person is capable of doing.

How do you express anger? What do you do to release frustration?

Anger is something that I have been working on a lot. In my younger life there was a lot of shouting and swearing, a lot of screaming, crying and upset and hurt and to protect myself you learn tools to survive. You don't necessarily need those tools in later life and in situations that you find yourself in. They were tools for survival then.

Anger, for me, normally stems from being fearful or upset and they are two things that as men, as people, we don't like being.

Since I have stopped responding angrily to things, I have had to deal with being more upset and feeling more vulnerable which is not pleasant.

They are not pleasant feelings and the only thing that I can hope for is that in situations where someone does upsets me or makes me feel vulnerable and I'm vocal about it, they have the decency to take that onboard.

Problems arise when you don't talk about those things and they build up and up and the person has no idea because you didn't say anything the first time they did it, and on the eighth time you respond in anger and you respond disproportionately. When we talk about men and emotions, there's really just one emotion and its anger, that's what's associated with men which is terribly unhealthy.

You need to be strong enough in the first instance if someone is pissing you off, you need to do it passively and say, "Hey, that really upset me" or "Hey, that makes me uncomfortable."

If you allow someone to continually do something that hurts or offends you and you don't make them aware, telling them later on is almost like trying to change the small print in a contract after it's been signed.

Situations are much easier when you don't respond in anger – but it's difficult to take that breath, or take that day, or take that sleep or take that walk - it's really difficult when you're in the eye of that storm to take yourself out of it but that's the only place you can ever really be if you want to respond rationally.

Where does this inner calm come from? It wasn't always there – you've obviously spent a lot of time studying your own emotions.

Exhaustion! I'm still a work in progress, we all are – don't ever expect that one day it's all sorted. I've learned that's not how life works. No-one is completely together, all of the time. It's maintenance, constant maintenance. Anything that has moving parts needs oiling.

What does vulnerability mean to you?

The most beautiful thing in the world is to be vulnerable. You look at relationships, if you can't come home and be vulnerable with your partner, then you're in the wrong place because you're holding up a façade and having to wear a mask.

We all wear masks – no matter who you are. We all have days where we feel like shit and we have to get stuff done, and we have to put that mask on. But if you can't come home and be vulnerable with your partner or your best friend, then that's not your partner or best friend – or you're deceiving them as well as yourself in holding up that mask, and that's tiring.

If someone leverages your vulnerabilities or makes you feel bad for being honest for how you feel, then get rid of them.

You put a lot of yourself out through your music and your words – do you ever find you get negative feedback and how do you deal with that?

The power of negative is stronger than the power of positive – it's just about perspective. I think we should have some understanding of our time of day. For me, I'm probably most vulnerable in the morning, so I try not to look at my phone or watch the news as soon as I wake up. I try to do something to gather my faculties and compose myself and ready myself for the day, so I walk the dogs, or I exercise and do something that wakes me up and takes me out of my most vulnerable state.

You don't have to be aware of what everyone says, and you don't have to inform your decisions based on the opinions of people who should be completely irrelevant to you. If one of my friends says, "Stephen, you're acting like an absolute knob" I'm going to take that on board but if someone drives by in a car and yells, "Hey Professor Green, you're a knob!" I say, "Thanks mate, have a nice day. Sorry for what's going on in your life but I'm having a good day and I'm not going to let you ruin it."

I don't seek validation from people who aren't relevant or prominent figures in my life. I think it's really unhealthy, and unfortunately, we live in an age where people do.

I was successful because I had a talent not because I wanted to be famous. The fame was, at times, completely unwelcome but it was something that people wanted to be. Now you can be an idiot on a reality TV show and become famous, and people don't understand what they're getting themselves into. I started rapping when I was 18 and I didn't start selling records until

I was 27 – that's a long time to grow up and cut my teeth. This shit doesn't come with a manual – be careful what you ask for.

You've spoken in the past about the importance of talking through your problems with people, and getting it off your chest - do you still do that? Do you have a group of people that you can talk to, or do you find your writing and music is your way of getting your thoughts out?

I think my writing is incredibly cathartic, although I haven't been doing as much as I would like lately.

For me, therapy is the healthiest approach because I don't want to blur lines and include people in relationships that they really shouldn't be in between. So, for me therapy is the most important way for me to understand and talk about things. If I want to talk about something that may be happening in my romantic relationship, I don't want to talk to my friends about it because their perspective is skewed by wherever they are in their life at that time. So, if they're unhappy in their relationship, they're probably not going to give me much positive advice.

It's the same with friends as well – I don't want to talk about one friend with another friend. I think it's really nice to have someone who's unbiased and who's away from everyone else.

Therapy is amazing because it doesn't just help you understand what's going on in yourself, but it also gives you the tools to be able to communicate and convey how you feel about something and to do so in a rational manner.

In life we learn resilience through suffering, experiencing trauma and surviving, entering into a difficult period and coming

out of the other side, the only rational way to build mental resilience is to use therapy when not at a point of crisis, to gather the tools you need to better navigate life and be better equipped for anything you may encounter. Being resilient of one of the most important things we can be.

The most important thing is to try to remain still, right? Equilibrium is really, really important and that's difficult to keep in the heat of the moment.

Some of my friends are quite calming but for the most part, a lot of people will have some emotional involvement. So, if someone's done you wrong, they're going to be like, "Someone's done what? He's done what??" Then, all of a sudden, you're being gas-lighted and the worst part of you is being encouraged.

This is something I'm learning as I'm growing up – you don't want other people coming between something that's going on with you and one other. So, for me, my sounding board is my therapist.

I want to touch on suicide – and your exploration of suicide. You have experienced tragedy with the suicide of your father, and you have gone on to explore suicide and to try to de-stigmatize suicide as being "weak".

It's a really difficult one to touch on. If I was talking to you about my Dad's suicide and I was saying to you, my Dad's problems were weaknesses that he perhaps didn't work on. So, this is then the turn of phrase I would use – how did he find the strength to hang himself?

I can't say that out loud too often because then that's implying that suicide was a strong decision – that to me is dangerous because people could read that and think to themselves, "This is a noble act I can do because this is me taking power back into my own hands. This is the only choice I can make – it's finite and I'm making it because I don't want to live anymore. I didn't ask to live, I don't want to live, this is my decision."

That's not someone in a well state. We have innate desire to survive – suicide ideation is not a normal thing. We've all had that moment where we might be standing on a train platform and had that weird second of "What if?" and then the "Whoa" and the snapping out of it. I think that's probably occurred in all of us, and it doesn't equal suicidal ideation.

It's such a tough one – because I couldn't figure out how Dad found the "strength" to do that because it's such a finite decision. I really wanted to understand how he could have done what he did. I couldn't – and I realized that the only way I could understand was if I was in the exact same situation, which I will never be.

SPIRITUALITY AND MINDFULNESS

What role does religion or spirituality play for you?

Tequila is my spirit, and the honey badger is my spirit animal! I'm an animal on spirits... sorry, that's the rapper in me.

It's weird – I think everyone prays during turbulence, but I believe in energy. I think we are quite distracted from how intuitive we are. If you pick up the phone, you can tell in the first word that someone's tired or angry – that's intuition. I think we come unstuck when we question ourselves too much.

As someone like me, who's quite obsessive-compulsive, if I am in a bad place I over-think and over-analyze and – at worse – over-catastrophize. Even understanding all of this, I can still find myself in a place where I do that.

I'm definitely more on the spiritual side than the religious side, I think. I think religion is inclusive if you buy into it, but it excludes you if you don't, and I'm not a fan of exclusion. From society, to school, to religion, I think exclusion is a really bad thing and causes a hell of a lot of problems in people.

BEING A MAN

Have your concepts of masculinity/ being a man changed over time? Is it significantly different from when you were a teen?

Growing up with mostly women around me, I didn't know what to do – I didn't know how to be a man. That was a great insecurity, looking back, because I just didn't know. When Nan told me to walk away from a fight, I did, up until the point where I felt like such a f*cking coward! And so, then I responded disproportionately.

It felt HORRIBLE for having hit someone or the times I've said horrible things to people, which was something I learnt quite young, because of what was going on in my household and how people spoke to each other. I was never taught how to shave or learn any of those things. I didn't really know what it is to be a man, when I was younger.

There's a little bit more of an understanding of what it is to be a man now. I understand what it is to be a man biologically and I understand that there are differences between genders, biologically. Beyond that, the problem we find in ourselves, a lot of the problems around gender come from applying behaviors to a gender.

The phrase "Why are you being a girl?" is offensive to me, not because you're calling me a girl, but because the women in my family didn't run away, the men did. So, the women in my family were stronger than the men.

What does "being a man" mean to you now?

Whoever I am on any given day, which I hope is becoming more and more consistent. I don't feel the pressures of the macho side of things, I don't buy into it anymore. I understand I can talk about my vulnerabilities and not be looked upon as weak. People who aren't aware of their weaknesses are the most in danger because they can have those leveraged.

RELATIONSHIPS AND FAMILY

Who has been the most important role model in your life? Has there been someone who has led by example?

Different people at different points, to be fair. I don't think there's been one person. My Nan for her work ethic and for the fact that she took me in, and I didn't end up in a care home. My great grandmother for her humility, her kindness, her wit, and her willingness to nurture me. Mike Skinner gave me some great advice when I was signed to his label. Ged, my manager, has been a huge influence. There's been so many people, at different points, who have helped me to see things. I feel really fortunate in that.

Dad – irrespective how little time I spent with him – was a huge, huge influence in my life, probably bigger than any other one person.

In what ways have the women in your life influenced the man you have become?

My grandmother, Nanny Pat, was out working three jobs a day so when I was at home for the most part, I spent my time with my great-grandmother Nanny Edie.

She taught me to read and write and numeracy, I was so ahead before I went to school because of the time I spent with her and she made learning fun. So, when I went into school, I sought validation in better places than some of my friends because they were seeking attention by acting up because they didn't get the attention that they needed at home which I think is what happens in a lot of single parent families. It's really difficult when you need to make a decision to work so you have money or have time with your children and they both present problems.

I didn't grow up in a single parent home because I had my great grandmother until I was thirteen when she passed.

My Nan had an incredible work ethic. She got up at 4am to get picked up by a governor to go and clean the bank - I used to go and clean with her sometimes. It was hard graft; she was on her hands and knees. Then she would work in a bakery and in the afternoon, then she would clean houses for members of the Jewish community in Stamford Hill.

She worked three jobs a day which meant that when she came home, she wasn't always in the best mood, but I took her work ethic from her.

There's loads of working-class values that I still have, like keep your doorstep tidy, leave a place how you found it, your pleases and thankyous, and that your life is not dictated by what's in your wallet or your bank account, it's how you treat people.

DACRE MONTGOMERY

ACTOR

 @dacremontgomery   @dacremontgomery

Dacre Montgomery is best known for his role as "Billy Hargrove" in season 2 and 3 of Netflix's hit series *Stranger Things*.

In addition to his film and television work, Dacre also wrote and produced beat poetry podcast, DKMH. The podcast features his spoken word poetry with accompanying music from various musicians and is a meditative, confronting and relatable depiction of what drives him and how his experiences have shaped him.

In 2017, Dacre made his big screen debut starring in Power Rangers as Jason Lee Scott, the Red Ranger.

An Australian native, Dacre graduated from the Western Australia Academy of Performing Arts at Edith Cowan University in 2015 with his degree in acting. He currently resides in Sydney, Australia.

Do you have a favorite quote or philosophy you live by?

It's a great question.

My mom said when I was growing up, "You never know what's around the corner." I've actually placed a lot of weight on those words, particularly in the past five years where I've been lucky enough to be working professionally.

I was always pursuing a career in the entertainment industry, but it didn't come to fruition until a decade after I started. Whenever I was feeling down and out, Mom would always give me a nudge on the shoulder and say, "You never know what's around the corner."

I remember at a couple of points being so frustrated in my adolescent years and saying, "What do you mean? What do you mean 'what's around the corner? You have no idea what's around the corner!"

And she would say, "You're right but I have a certain level of optimism for you and your life and I guess I'm manifesting that for you."

My mom is not a spiritual or religious woman, so it was always interesting that she gave me this piece of advice which was a bit esoterical about the world and about existence.

Even when I challenged her in my younger years, she would smile and say, "You've just got to wait and see what happens."

I think because of that, through my manifestation of what I wanted to do with my life, I placed a level of optimism that despite whatever happens to you, you're never sure about what's around the corner.

I still use that at the moment because, especially being a freelancer in the entertainment industry, I could be moving to Toronto tomorrow or you could be knocked back on five jobs next week. It's a constant ebb and flow and I think having that piece of advice that I have taken into my adult life has been extremely valuable.

My mom had a lot of that stuff when I was growing up – she was super supportive of me.

That's a great insight into the uncertainty of being an actor – how have you found living in such an uncertain time with COVID-19, career-wise?

This time has been really nice to actually force myself to relax and appreciate a few things that I didn't beforehand, to be honest with you.

When COVID first started my partner and I spent time in Perth with our families – and we had a big period of time where we didn't have all the outlets that I survive on in my downtime, like yoga and a whole lot of fitness-style components and going to the cinema. So, I got big into running and riding my bike and things I haven't done since I was younger, and having movie nights at home, instead of going to the cinema.

There was also finding in myself some sort of creative, internalized component coming out – what I mean by that is I've just finished a short film, which is pretty esoterical. I've just finished the filming and post-production in Sydney. I'm going to use this as an anecdote to answer your question, being that basically I used this piece of Shakespearean text which I haven't revisited since drama school to do some mask work and shadow work – exploring shadow self and how our shadow self is built. The concept of shadow work is that as we grow up, based on any bad or traumatic experiences we have, a version of ourselves is repressed.

So, say for example, you're growing up and your parents say to you when you're 15-years-old, "You can't do this" or you have a really shitty experience in school, and someone says to you that you're a bad person, or they do something to you, or something happens – that's kind of a facet of yourself that you repress. Then – when you're older – let's say you're angry with your partner, or your kid, or a workmate, the school of thought is that that's part of your shadow-self coming out.

For me, the biggest thing was to use a piece of this text from Hamlet and to basically use it as a piece of removing mask work/shadow work for myself, and then ultimately perform it on camera, which is what we've just done.

I spent a lot of time in this break unpacking myself and my childhood, traumatic experiences and really used it as a time to confront a lot of 'stuff' rather than just coast in isolation.

So that's a weird, wanker-y, actor way of answering your question!

You mention your mentor – who was this?

The first film I worked on was a reboot of Power Rangers, and the screenwriter and producer of the film is a prolific screenwriter called John Gatins, and he basically has become a bit of a second-father to me.

Every time I'm in the States, he opens his home to me and my partner and has provided me with lots of great advice.

What are the issues - whether social, environmental, political or economic - that you feel are most pressing and for which you feel the greatest personal concern and responsibility?

My mom created the first program in Western Australia for women suffering postnatal depression, and I've always been interested in mental health – that's been a big thing for me. That's something that, in the future, I want to become a big advocate for, particularly for younger people.

Childhood and adolescence are the hardest bloody time to get through in the world, and I think helping kids get through it is really important. Letting them know that there's a light at the end of the tunnel after high school – that it's not everything. Also, this traditional system of going to university and everything is quite black and white – but it's not exactly the way you have to do it.

Who inspires you?

Everyone is a human being and I think it's less about being well-known and more about energy, less about success and more

about how you act in that success. I think I'm more interested in people who are able to achieve longevity in their industry than those who have a momentary spark. I think I'm interested in those who have had tougher journeys, rather than those who have been given gratification.

For me, with someone who's considered famous – if I don't know their story intimately from them, I'm not connected; but as soon as I do, I'm completely connected. That's why it could be anyone – someone on the street – they become the people who inspire me, because there's a level of truth that they have in anonymity that some people in public life lose without their anonymity.

I went to university with hundreds of better actors than I am – it's just a matter of timing and preparation, and then to achieve longevity, how do you behave when you are given the luck? For me, I learnt so many things from these individuals who don't have the limelight.

LIFE PURPOSE AND SUCCESS

Have you identified your mission in life?

No, I don't think so yet. I think I'm still growing, and I just want to spend many, many more years learning new lessons and new skills, and travelling and experiencing new things.

I think I know my mission for the moment, which is to continue to grow, and it's a cliché – but every day I wake up I want to learn something new and try something different.

Keep going and keep discovering new things.

OVERCOMING CHALLENGES

How has failure, or apparent failure, set you up for later success? Do you have a "favorite failure" of yours?

Yes – it was just before the "rise" – it was at the end of university and I had lost my job and I got dumped, and people in my class were getting roles and my mental health was just shot and I was really struggling. But I think it gives you an appreciation for the color that you see in your life after that, when you're on a high. I think it also gives you an appreciation for the strength you had to have to push through. That time was an amalgamation of things other than what I just mentioned – and it was a time where you don't think you're going to make it through.

Again, you just never know what's around the corner. That constant optimism for the unknown keeps you pushing forward, even threw the shittiest times.

But through it, you grow, and in retrospect or hindsight you look at those experiences and you think, "I don't regret a single failure in my whole entire life because it built me into who I am right now – and that person I want to be. That person has been built through mistakes and I wouldn't be the same person if I hadn't had those experiences."

You've been quite open and public about your anxiety and growing up, being bullied at school and body image challenges that you've had. Is acting a tool that you utilize to overcome over that?

Definitely, if you allow yourself to be emotional, you can find stuff. And if you're in a safe space, in a good role, it allows you the opportunity to be able to explore those things. I have been quite public about

those things, and being in the industry for a short couple of years, now what are the choices I really want to make? What are the characters I really want to dance with? Doing a lot of writing and a lot of reading and coming up with worlds that I want to take part in and going for it head-on.

If you could have a conversation with yourself as a teenager, what would that conversation look like?

"You never know what's around the corner. The experiences are tough, but they build you and they build your strength for when you really need it. Secondly - live in the moment while you're a kid. There's no tougher period of time, but there is no freer period of time, where you're not thinking about responsibilities. Make the most of this time. Don't take this as seriously as you do."

That's definitely a common thread among all the men I've spoken with...

Definitely. Even when I met my mentor, John, who's had a great career and he said, "I think this whole time I was just chasing contentment." When I heard this three or four years ago, I literally thought "Stuff contentment! Why would you ever want to be content? Shoot for the stars, and you just keep going – the sky isn't the limit – you can keep going and keep pushing."

Now I know what he means – it's such a valuable lesson of wanting to be content. And I think in order to do that, you have to not take things so seriously.

EMOTIONS

What makes you truly happy?

Watching films – that's a big one. When the cinemas are open, we go every Thursday.

"I've also found a lot of peace in exercising – that's been a big thing since I left school. Yoga or boxing or running or whatever it be, I seem to find a deep level of peace in those experiences."

On set, there's nothing like the adrenaline rush of working 17 hours a day with a crew that's like a family, day in and day out for months on end. I love it!

Being at home – I've always been big into interior design and creating spaces, and thankfully I've met someone who feels the same and she's very interested in creating and building spaces.

I've also found a lot of peace in exercising – that's been a big thing since I left school. Yoga or boxing or running or whatever it be, I seem to find a deep level of peace in those experiences.

How do you express anger? What do you do to release frustration?

My stepfather, who has been a great role model and mentor for me, carried a lot of anger throughout his life. He had this particular individual in his life that he didn't confront till he was three marriages deep and in his 40s. He left it until he was in his 40s to confront this person.

Two years ago, I wanted to confront a person in my life that I felt that I carried their anger – and I found that anger very hard to control. So, I spoke to my step-dad

and I said, "Why did you wait until you were 40?" and he said, "Because I was scared. I was scared of confronting this person and what it meant and how it would end up."

So, I asked him, "What happened?" and he said, "Well I met your mom and that's that – there's no 4th or 5th marriage."

He was able to be a very strong partner, father and stepfather.

When I met my partner, I didn't want to carry someone else's anger, so I confronted that person at 22 rather than in my 40s, and it was one of the scariest and hardest experiences of my life, but I felt like I dropped a lot of weight, both in emotional baggage and anger.

Ultimately, I felt a much stronger connection to that side of myself and an ability to control my anger a lot more than I used to because of it.

I remember talking to some friends afterwards about it and saying how much freer I felt. I was so scared, don't get me wrong – it's one of the scariest things you'll ever have to do. But then that person and that experience no longer has the control over you, so it's completely freeing.

Even if the other person doesn't want to have the conversation, at least you can put it to bed that you've tried to vocalize what you needed to.

Is vulnerability something that you welcome into your life?

Definitely – and in all the characters I play. Finding sensitivity even in the worst human beings that you play on screen. Again, I have to thank my parents for encouraging me to be who I was. I'm a strange individual – I have a lot of OCD tendencies and growing up was pretty tough, I suffered a lot from anxiety and to be honest with you the only way I got through it was talking.

I don't think I would have gotten through my childhood and my teenage years if I wasn't allowed to talk about what I was going through. There's a lot of different cultures and people's experiences where they have parents who don't really encourage a dialogue about what's going on with you.

I've taken that into my adulthood and my relationships now, and I'm really trying to foster communication – whether it's a personal relationship or a business relationship and have a level of transparency and then embed it into my moral compass or code, moving forward.

That translates into acting with characters and having a really open dialogue. In the role of Billy in *Stranger Things*, who's this archetypal villain, but they've had a journey, they've had a past, they've had a world that exists, and they are a sensitive human being, so finding that sensitivity in every character is so important.

I think it's also good seeing a man on screen being sensitive and vulnerable. I think that's really important for young people.

"You just never know what's around the corner. That constant optimism for the unknown keeps you pushing forward, even through the shittiest times."

SPIRITUALITY AND MINDFULNESS

Do you have a mindfulness practice you use?

A big one that really helped me during my toughest time is a super simple exercise of breathing all the way out, so you have no air in your lungs, and then you breathe in. Through my hardest periods, when I woke up I would do it 12 times – it gives you a sense of being in the present. It really did help me.

I discovered yoga in the second year of university – that's been a massive thing for me. The practice is often built in heat – I love the warmth and that it's not narcissistic and based on your image. Then by the end of the class you are so bloody exhausted you have a level of enlightenment when you leave.

RELATIONSHIPS AND FAMILY

Who has been the most important role model in your life? Has there been someone who has led by example?

My mom has been a big one – just by everything I've talked about in terms of the emotional support.

John Gatins from a career point of view has really helped me.

I've had some amazing friends along the way who I have a lot in common with, but who have just been great. We're all dreamers – particularly in the film industry – and a lot of my friends are actors and there have been many, many nights sitting around dreaming, "This is the dream, this is the goal we want to get to" and I've had a lot of support and encouragement from those people.

Also, oddly, my anxiety. My anxiety has pushed me far further and far greater than anything else because that's been my drug of force to get out of bed and push myself to work harder in every capacity of my life.

That's probably an odd answer to your question, but I definitely think that that's an element that I would pay tribute to for getting me to where I am.

You've mentioned your mom and your partner, Liv. In what ways have the women in your life influenced the man you have become?

Huge! I think the sensitivity component has come through my mom and then obviously my partner, Liv. Liv has also encouraged me to calm down a bit.

When I met her, I was functioning on 200 per cent all the time, letting my OCD control me, always living in the future or the past, never the present. Liv has helped me live in the present a lot more, which has been a really powerful tool because you can center yourself, and if you are centered, you can make better decisions that are more cognitively processed, thought-out, life decisions.

Mom – my support in growing up and getting through those really tough years. It was a combination of people, but mom was definitely at the fore-front of that for me.

Then my mom's mom – my grandmother – played a big role in my life. Growing up, both of my parents were in the film industry, so I spent a lot of time with my grandparents. My grandmother was definitely the matriarch of the family – she was the one that kept everything together. For my mom's siblings, she was the glue. She had a huge impact on me because she was soft and sensitive and encouraging. She passed away at the very beginning of 2012.

Talking about women in my life – strong women that have had an impact on me, I would put her in that category.

I have a younger sister, who is 12 years younger than me, who's home with my family. There are things you can learn from the younger generation, and she's just now figuring out who she is – life is new. I can teach her things, and she teaches me things.

AARON "WHEELZ" FOTHERINGHAM

WHEELCHAIR STUNT CHAMPION

 @aaronwheelz   @wcmx4life

Aaron WHEELZ Fotheringham is a WCMX athlete from Las Vegas, Nevada.

Aaron was born with Spina Bifida, a birth defect of the spinal cord which resulted in him having no use of his legs. He is the third of six children, all adopted.

Aaron has never let anything stop him - even as a baby and small child, he did everything anyone else his age could do; he just had to figure out how to make it work for him.

Aaron started riding at skateparks at the age of 8 when his older brother Brian, a BMXer, said he should drop in. He had been going to the park with Brian and their dad for weeks, but Aaron would just watch from behind the fence. The first time was scary, and he fell hard, but he was never one to give up just because it wasn't easy.

So, he tried again and from then on, he was hooked.

At the beginning of his career, Aaron entered and won a few BMX Freestyle competitions, including the legendary 2005 Vegas AmJam BMX Finals, but for Aaron that was always secondary to the joy of riding and hanging out with friends at all the skateparks in Las Vegas.

Over the years, Aaron has challenged himself to pioneer even more difficult stunts. In 2005, he perfected a mid-air 180-degree turn. Then in 2006 he landed the first wheelchair backflip. In 2010 he landed the first ever double backflip and has gone on to perform live on tour with the Nitro Circus.

He is a 5-time winner of the WCMX World Championships and has recently executed the first Wheelchair Flair/backflip 180.

Do you have a favorite quote or philosophy you live by?

"I have wheels stuck to my butt. How can that not be fun!"

This is the one I use the most – just because it expresses gratitude. Gratitude in a tough situation can transform it into something else.

I had a pretty rough start to life – I was adopted after being abandoned in the hospital and thankfully I was rescued by my parents.

I had lots of surgeries, so it started off pretty rough, but then there was so much to be grateful for.

What is the personal quality that you are most proud of?

My hair! Ha-ha.

It's a tough question – probably my big heart, whether it's compassion or wanting to help and having an impact on people.

What are the issues - whether social, environmental, political or economic - that you feel are most pressing and for which you feel the greatest personal concern and responsibility?

I feel great responsibility towards changing how people see wheelchairs and other disabilities. Many people view the wheelchair as strictly a medical device that impedes any kind of independence, as well as any kind of quality of life. My vision is to help people see these things as less of a ball and chain and more as something that can be leveraged towards success and growth.

"I would say a battle I'm constantly battling is my mind. I always think – if only people knew – my chair is not my disability. I feel like my wheelchair has been a blessing, if anything."

Who inspires you?

I get a lot of inspiration from other extreme athletes but mostly I get my inspiration from my dad on everything.

Especially right before I am about to make a bad decision, I just have these echoes of my dad in my head, and I reflect on what he would do or what he would say.

When I was younger, he would always go to the skatepark with me and be like, "Drop in on this one dude!" And I was like, "I'm not ready for that yet!"

BEING A MAN

What does "being a man" mean to you?

I feel like one of the biggest ones is humility – I feel like for me, that's the biggest one. It takes a lot to admit when you're wrong – that's the hardest thing.

Just really being honest – it's hard for me to put into words. I feel like all the great men that I have looked up to or been inspired by have a lot of humility and they're really honest.

Have your concepts of masculinity/being a man changed over time?

That's a hard freakin' question!

I think it's completely different to what I thought when I was younger. When I was younger, being a man was all about maybe doing the biggest, scariest trick or something. That was my main focus – the next big trick – that was my purpose.

I feel like as I've progressed through life, I've realized that my personal progression is important, but I learned that it's more than just riding – what I'm doing has a bigger purpose to inspire and help people.

That has changed my vision of what a man is from doing the biggest, baddest tricks to trying to help others.

If there was a single piece of advice that you could give every young man in this world, what would it be?

I would say that a lot of time, when we are faced with a trial or struggle, or if it's just a goal we have – at the beginning it feels completely impossible – don't let the failures stop you. Just go for it.

My dream, ever since I was little, has been to build my own wheelchair – but it's felt like a huge dream. I was landing all these tricks and stuff, but building my own wheelchair felt impossible to me and within the last 3 – 4 months, I've really progressed that more. I just dove in, and I started to run some of the machines I got, and I just kind of went for it.

I have a lot of scrap metal that I've messed up on over here – but then just recently I've built my first skatepark wheelchair by myself. I would say that at the beginning, it feels extremely overwhelming and impossible, but I think my advice is to just start and you'll get there.

EMOTIONS

What makes you truly happy?

Landing on my wheels!

Aside from tricks? That's a tricky one! That might be the hardest question here.

I feel I would say progression – whether it's on the skatepark or in the shop. When I feel stagnant, I go down dark roads, and get depressed.

When I'm busy, and learning, and doing stuff – that's when I'm the happiest.

Whew – I thought I was going to fail that question!

How do you express anger? What do you do to release frustration?

That's my problem! I struggle a lot with anger. I get pretty pissed. The way I should deal with my anger is to go to the skatepark. That's how I usually overcome a lot of my anger – instead of chucking a wrench across the shop or something. I'm working on becoming more mindful and noticing when I am starting to get to my breaking point.

And when I get there – I try to do it before I get there – but go do something I enjoy. I sound like a boring person but go to the skatepark or go to the shop or go for a drive, because I'm quite an emotional person.

Anger can be a positive emotion – it's like a driving force – if you don't get angry, you won't make any movement. It compels you to take action to do something.

How do you deal with conflict and diffusing difficult situations?

My wife! I feel like in a lot of situations, it's nice to rely on my wife. A lot of time I'll get in my head about something, and it really helps me a lot to go to my wife and get a second opinion and let her point of view in.

A lot of the time I'm like, "Go away! I don't want your opinion" but when I'm really struggling it's really nice to have her there.

Do you talk with anyone about how you feel when things are happening in your life, or do you keep these thoughts internalized?

I'm pretty open when it comes to talking about my emotions to people. Sometimes I feel like I should reel it in a little bit, because I'm too open, and then I could feel shame or regret it or something.

If it's not my wife, it's my dad or my mom or friends or people I look up to and call them up and get their professional opinion.

LIFE PURPOSE AND SUCCESS

What do you ultimately strive for? What is your mission in life?

Continued happiness. It feels so fleeting. I feel like that's my mission in life.

Career-wise, I want to be on top and land all these big tricks and keep pushing the limits of that stuff and help grow the sport and get more people around the world who are on wheelchairs into skateparks.

What's your next trick? Are you working on anything at the moment? Are you working on a triple??

I over-rotated a couple of double backflips recently so it's definitely doable!! I want to be the one to do it.

My next trick I would like to land is a double front flip. I've got the double back, but the double front is difficult.

How do you define success? At what point did you identify as being "successful"?

I define success as dealing with momentary failures by learning from them, making adjustments and continuing on your path towards a certain goal. I think I identified as being successful when I was 18 and landed the first double backflip on a wheelchair.

It was a full year of crashing and injuring myself, as well as destroying my wheelchair in the process.

After reaching a low point where I felt failure was the only constant, I told myself, "Two more tries" and on my second try I landed it. It was at that moment I learned that success was usually only obtained after many failed attempts.

What do you think was your main quality that led you to your success?

My main driving thing towards my success is going back to my anger.

When I fail, especially when I am trying a trick, I get this real burning anger inside of me. Sometimes it worries me – like maybe I have a problem.

Recently I was trying to land a double backflip and I was worried that I was not okay, and that maybe I was dysfunctional

because I am literally beating the shit out of myself. I was like, "Maybe I should stop". I eventually took a break for a couple of hours, and I had a clearer mind, and I was able to just do it and land it, 3 tries later.

I think what helps me a lot with my success is that drive to just keep going and keep getting up after a crash. I want to succeed more than I want oxygen. But it also has to be a balance.

It sounds so bad that anger led me to my success - maybe anger is a side-effect. Having pushed through lots of difficulties and come out on top with several different tricks I feel like it shows me what is possible and if I can persist through these struggles, I can make it happen.

Anger is part of it, but what drives me is the feeling I get when I think something is impossible.

OVERCOMING CHALLENGES

Have there been any key challenges that you have had to face in your life? How have you faced them?

I would say a battle I'm constantly battling is my mind. I always think – if only people knew my chair is not my disability. I feel like my wheelchair has been a blessing, if anything.

What I really struggle with is my mind and negative thoughts, and fear and I'm probably the most anxious, paranoid, depressed person ever. Well maybe not ever, but I feel like I always struggle with those things.

How do I face them? It depends on the day. Some days I just lay on the couch and not do anything, and some days it's just like pushing through it.

Going back to the need to always progress – I feel like if I am struggling with depression, I'm going to read some books. I like to read a lot of different things – I feel like the knowledge helps. I feel like if I am struggling with something, I can find another point of view and do everything I can by educating myself.

How has failure, or apparent failure, set you up for later success? Do you have a "favorite failure" of yours?

The first thing that comes to my mind is my disability – but that's not really a failure. That's just natural causes, and that's just being.

Probably my favorite failure was my first drop-in on a wheelchair – because I pretty much just face-planted.

If I had just rolled away from it, who knows if I would have been turned onto it in the same way. Me getting up on this quarter pipe as an 8-year-old kid and being terrified and then just wiping out completely. I was there watching my older brother and he suggested I give it a shot – I think he was trying to kill me!

> *"I think what helps me a lot with my success is that drive to just keep going and keep getting up after a crash. I want to succeed more than I want oxygen. But it also has to be a balance."*

I had to get back up and try it again, and I crashed again – I think I crashed 4 or 5 times before rolling away from it, and that was what really drew me to it – just that anger again.

SPIRITUALITY AND MINDFULNESS

What role does religion or spirituality play for you?

Huge – I feel like in everything I do is spiritualistic. I'm a member of the Church of Jesus Christ of Latter-day Saints. My faith has helped me and guided me through my life and different decisions.

Where I am and the people I've met have all been through my faith.

What pastime or practice enables you time to connect with your inner self?

For me, a big part is in the skatepark or just welding and metal fabrication because you're so focused on what you're doing, and your mind is not wandering too much. You feel like you're one.

I like to wake up at 5am with the sun – that sets me up for a better day. I feel like a hippy now!

What do you do to relax?

Food! I like to do stuff around the house – home improvement stuff or yard work. It's so rewarding doing stuff around the house.

RELATIONSHIPS AND FAMILY

Who has been the most important role model in your life? Has there been someone who has led by example?

I would say my parents – and I look up a lot to my wife because she's got a solid mind and she's inspired me a lot. Our wives put up with a lot!

In what ways have the women in your life influenced the man you have become?

I would say love. My mom, my wife, my grandma. They've always shown me this unconditional love. That has shown me how to truly love and be more kind to people.

Love, love, love.

JORDAN LIBERTY
MAKEUP ARTIST AND PHOTOGRAPHER

 @jordanliberty   Jordan Liberty

Jordan Liberty is an LA-based makeup artist, photographer, and creative director. In addition to producing beauty campaigns and content for top brands like Urban Decay, MAC, Sigma, and NARS, his work in consulting and product development have made him the secret weapon behind the success of many well-known products.

Respected in the industry for his professional approach to education, Jordan continues teaching pro-level workshops and makeup masterclasses around the globe.

Do you have a favorite quote or philosophy you live by?

"Move towards fear." If something scares the shit out of me, I feel like it's probably worth trying.

Every amazing thing that's happened in my life is the direct result of an attempt at something that previously intimidated me. For example, I had a big fear of sharks growing up – and now you can't pry me out of the water! On my most recent adventure, I free-dived with hammerheads in the Galapagos, which was absolutely incredible. I owe that experience, along with so many others, to that first terrifying decision to get into the water.

My debilitating fear of public speaking was something I thought I'd never get

over, and I've now spoken on stage in 22 countries and no longer suffer from any stage fright at all.

Just like my fear of taking the plunge, taking the stage was something I had to force myself through as well. The first time I got an offer to keynote in New York I said "Yes," hung up the phone, had a complete meltdown, and didn't sleep for the entire month leading up to the day. I trembled stepping up onto the stage, but it only took one round of applause to confirm that I had made the right choice. Suddenly I was getting booked in Toronto, Orlando, LA - and then it became Dubai, Reykjavik, and New Delhi. I blurted out "YES" when I received that first offer because I knew that it would open a lot of doors for me, and it did. Fear has become my best motivator.

What is one personal quality that you are most proud of?

I think, especially with what's going on politically in the world right now and socially, with toxic masculinity, and all these issues coming to a head, particularly in the past few years – I think empathy is something that I'm most proud of.

I've always been an empath, and when I was younger, that made me feel pretty insecure – like I should be tougher, and I shouldn't be as attuned towards others and now I realize that it's absolutely a rare quality and one that I value most about myself.

What are the issues - whether social, environmental, political or economic - that you feel are most pressing and for which you feel the greatest personal concern and responsibility?

Selfishness. There is a massive lack of empathy and understanding towards people who are different, there's a lack of empathy towards people who are suffering, and victims of bigotry and systemic racism are constantly fighting just to be validated. There's a lack of empathy for the planet. I think we're all pretty overwhelmed right now.

I've learned that I can't carry the full weight of every issue on my shoulders, but I can work towards bettering myself every day while being mindful of others. I can educate myself on the lived experiences of black people and commit to being anti-racist. I can be mindful of my own carbon footprint and explore sustainable options when creating products. I can admit when I f*ck up and take the necessary steps to

be better - no matter my motive. I concern myself with and take responsibility for myself because that's all any of us can do.

Who inspires you?

I've always looked up to people who are innovators in whatever they do. Being a makeup artist, I really look up to Francois Nars, the founder of the brand NARS. He's a makeup artist and photographer – and I respect that he created a career path for himself that no one had ever done before. And I've always admired the legacy of Gianni Versace, who imagined completely new types of fabrics and was a really forward-thinking designer - and truly an artist in the 90s.

BEING A MAN

What does "being a man" mean to you?

When I was younger, it was difficult to identify even AS a man, because we're raised in a culture that has a very myopic definition of masculinity – where little boys are taught that emotion or sensitivity is a sign of weakness and that "gay" is an insult because to be gay is seen as degrading.

I think, for me, removing the noise of what other people think has been a struggle – we're social creatures, and no matter how much we say we don't care what other people think – we do a little bit! We all want to fit somewhere, and we all want to feel comfortable when we go out in public, and I spent the majority of my life feeling like a puzzle piece that didn't fit. Hearing relatives and friends make gay jokes, reading news articles that reduced my identity to a statistic, and seeing one-dimensional gay characters in movies and on TV caused me to feel incredible discomfort and self-hatred.

Gay marriage wasn't legal for most of my life – my own country didn't recognize that my love is equal to the next person. That's really, really hard to reconcile for me – I didn't want to be gay growing up.

It wasn't a choice, but I didn't want to be that, because I thought, "That's not what a man is," and if I'm gay I'm something lesser than. It's as though your love isn't real, you're not a real man, and you're nothing more than a label, a caricature - the quippy sidekick in the movie that helps his gal pal get the guy. There are still places in the world that I can't travel to. I've been to countries where it's illegal to be gay. So how can I see myself as a man if I'm still struggling to be seen as a person?

I don't see myself as a thirty-something gay man, I see myself as a thirty-something man. Why do I have to be a "gay" something? Being a man, for me, started with the confidence to embrace my identity without labels and outside opinions. I had to remove the burden of what other people thought of me in order to start appreciating the very three-dimensional man that existed underneath.

I believe being a man means doing what is right, not necessarily what's best for you but for what's best for people around you as well. It's having that maturity, and not modeling yourself after stereotypes of masculinity - having the security to be human.

Real men don't need to harm others to validate their power. Real men aren't threatened or insecure about femininity, feminism, or homosexuality. If you have to constantly prove your manliness through cruelty and intolerance, you're probably pretty insecure with your own masculinity.

Have your concepts of masculinity/being a man changed over time?

They absolutely have! Growing up I was taught the same as everybody else – boys don't cry, and I thought that meant you weren't supposed to feel anything. We're taught that being a man means ignoring and suppressing everything that makes you a human being. It's bullshit. We're all complex creatures with a full spectrum of emotions, and I think young men who embrace that truth early on grow up to be exemplary leaders and praiseworthy fathers.

If there was a single piece of advice that you could give every young man in this world, what would it be?

Leave people better than you found them - it's much easier to be cruel than it is to be kind.

Kindness and tolerance are qualities that aren't always imprinted on young men, but they're qualities that we desperately need more of in the world right now.

EMOTIONS

What makes you truly happy?

Happiness has always been elusive to me. Severe depression led me to suicidal thoughts by middle school - thoughts that would come and go every few years until I finally surrendered and sought help. That wasn't too long ago either, so I'm still in the process of discovering what truly makes me happy.

Creativity has been a long-time friend and probably my only constant source of joy. Art was my only method of escape growing up, and I still find so much peace when I'm being expressive. Turning my creativity into a career really saved my life, and now I'm working outwards to find joy in everything else.

You mention you were suicidal in your teens and you have had a battle with cancer in the past few years. Is mental health something that you're open to talking about?

Oh sure. It's a constant journey – it's been a struggle. I've wrestled with severe depression and anxiety since I was very, very young. I remember having my first suicidal thoughts at the age of eleven. I was hospitalized for panic attacks in my early twenties and for a while it was so intense, I couldn't even drive a car.

I've worked diligently to put myself at the center of my own recovery. I've had to face the ugliness that broke me in my formative years, confront my own thought patterns – essentially, I'm rewiring my own brain.

Recovery hasn't progressed without obstacles, the largest being my own comfort with the sickness that was killing me. I was content with suffering, as so many are, because I didn't feel worthy of happiness - and what would I find if I opened Pandora's box, you know? So instead of getting better, I just survived as best I could.

I suffered in silence while building my career, never stopping long enough to hear my own thoughts; and as I was rapidly accumulating hundreds of thousands of followers and subscribers, the ground was giving way beneath me. I learned to hide my depression really well, and even when it became apparent to close friends that I was in trouble, I still couldn't fully commit to recovery because part of me didn't believe I could recover.

Cancer halted all of the momentum that had aided my avoidance. I had all this time

to ponder my mortality and ask myself some pretty big questions about what I really wanted to get out of life and just how serious my situation had become. I was fighting for my life, simultaneously, in body and mind.

I had cancer twice. From the moment I discovered a strange lump until that last ride home from chemotherapy a year and a half later, I still can't tell you how I did it. I look back at my withering body, the horror-show of tubes and needles sprouting from my arms, and midnight races to the emergency room and it feels like it all happened to someone else - that it couldn't have been me.

The strangest part of that disbelief was my eventual realization that cancer was the easier battle. Mental illness will be a lifelong journey for me. It's not a chapter of my life that I can look back on - with a beginning, a middle, and an end, you know? But I'm a thousand times better than I was a year ago, and a million times better than I was a decade ago. I'm grateful for it, really.

Do you embrace the challenge of fear?

Like I said, fear is my best motivator. I find the best thing to do is to stare at it straight in the face, whatever it is that scares you. You might not want to do it – it's like ripping off a band-aid – but that when you do, it's done and it's good.

In business and in life and in love, you can't have success without a little courage. Seize opportunities, and if they aren't there, make them for yourself. I didn't sit around and hope someone would see what I had to offer, I had to prove it. I never took the safe route in any aspect of my life and I didn't take advice from people whose lives I didn't want, either.

"When I was younger, it was difficult to identify even AS a man, because we're raised in a culture that has a very myopic definition of masculinity – where little boys are taught that emotion or sensitivity is a sign of weakness and that "gay" is an insult because to be gay is seen as degrading."

I had to make a lot of risky choices because I wanted something bigger for myself, even if it meant looking foolish when I would sometimes fail.

How do you express anger? What do you do to release frustration?

This is a tough one to answer because I have a complicated relationship with anger.

I used to be explosive – I'd go from zero to a hundred really fast. I've never hurt someone physically, but good lord this mouth of mine! I was so reactive. I expressed anger through words, words I didn't even mean - because I was unhealthy.

I'm not proud of it, but I'm sharing this because I think it's important to understand how this tied in with my depression and how it ties in with the bigger conversation we're having. As boys, we're taught that being "tough" is the best way to deal with negative emotions. Boys

don't cry, right? Aggression is normalized. So, when I would feel hurt by something someone did, instead of walking away and putting it into perspective or handling it delicately, I'd fire back with both barrels.

This isn't to say that I walked around on a rampage. By nature, I'm a lover, not a fighter, and most people know me as goofy and sweet. That's what made my anger so toxic - to myself. If I snapped back at someone who harmed me, even if I was justified, I'd recoil afterwards into a spiral of shame and regret.

Recognizing anger was definitely the first step, and now finding ways to distance myself from it in the moment, that's really what I focus on. I'm far better at managing my triggers now, but there are still times where I can feel overwhelmed.

I love cars – and my best release is to just disappear for a while. I get behind the wheel and drive up the Pacific Coast Highway if I have time just to help me regain perspective on the situation. Again, that's not always possible with LA traffic but I do try to take drives at least once or twice a week, even in the middle of the night. You're out with people, but you're alone – and it's sort of a gift.

It all goes back to that rewiring process for me - unlearning all of the things I was taught as a kid that don't serve me now.

LIFE PURPOSE AND SUCCESS

What do you ultimately strive for? What is your mission in life?

That's a really great question. You know when you're a kid, and you get a birthday cake, and you make a wish? I never wished to be rich or famous – I wished for happiness. It's kind of a weird thing –

but our definition of happiness changes over time, and I somehow knew that even when I was really little.

Happiness and freedom are things I really strive for – I've created a career where I work for myself, I'm responsible for myself and I get to do what I love every day.

I'm in this position where I've created my ultimate career and my ultimate dream and I'm living it – and now I have to figure out what's next.

For me, it's about being better than I was the day before and not comparing myself to anyone else because, especially in a world of social media, we tend to compare ourselves and want to keep up with the Jones'. I'm thinking about my legacy now more than ever, and how I can contribute, how I can be part of something bigger than myself.

That wish to be happy as a child – was that a difficult thing to achieve when you were younger?

I had a difficult relationship with family – I have not always had the support I should have had, and I sometimes wish I knew then what I know now; it would have made those years so much better. But I don't wallow in self-pity. Everything I've done, I've had to figure out on my own, which has been a good thing for me.

I had a dad who rubbed my nose in my failures, and who is not a part of my life at all, and who didn't even reach out to me when I was going through chemo. But the advantage of having a father who never really validated me was it made me an overachiever.

I have to be careful that it doesn't burn me out, because I'm never satisfied – it can definitely be an endless cycle that

is never fulfilling. I think I'm learning to appreciate where I am, right now, and what I've created.

Do you define yourself as a successful person?

Yes. If I died tomorrow, I think I would die fulfilled. The places that I've been, the people I've met and the things I've seen, it's been really, really wild.

For a long time, when I was speaking at events, people would ask when I knew I made it, and I would say, "I'm still waiting." I have a much better story now.

There's a makeup artist that I really look up to, his name is Billy B, who I should have identified as one of my role models, because he is so incredible. He did all the music videos in the 90s – TLC, Destiny's Child, Pink – he's done like every Pink video – and I remember I got invited to an event in his honor when I moved to LA.

It's such a small thing, but I got invited to this event where he was releasing a product and it was a collaboration with a cosmetic brand. So, I called one of my girlfriends and I said, "You wanna go to this event with me?" and she goes, "Do you even know this guy?" and I said, "No, I don't know him, so let's just go and drink champagne, get a swag bag and get out of there in 30 minutes. We'll show some support."

So, we go to this event in a fancy hotel in West Hollywood, we take the elevator up to the rooftop and open the doors and he's all the way in the back of the room, but I spotted him immediately. Somebody he's talking to, who's facing me, sort of acknowledges that I've walked through the door, and Billy turns around and goes,

"Oh my god, you came!" and he runs up to me, and he's running across the room and my friend said, "I thought you said you didn't know him?!" and I was like, "Just roll with it!"

He comes up and he gives me the biggest hug, and I'm doing that thing over his shoulder like "WTF?" to my friend, and he goes, "You want to come hang out with me and RuPaul?"

I was like, "What is HAPPENING??"

So, it was one of those things where someone I thought was so amazing, that I idolized, that was the moment where I thought "I think I've made it now." I got my seat at the big kid's table.

I thought "I don't think he knows that he's a way bigger deal than me!" but he kept saying, "I think we should work together, I would be so nervous to work with you!" and I'm thinking "WHAT?"

I'm not going to lie – I was sitting there thinking "This is such an inconvenient time to have, like, a full stroke."

OVERCOMING CHALLENGES

How has failure, or apparent failure, set you up for later success? Do you have a "favorite failure" of yours?

Hahaha – how much time do you have?

I shared that I went through cancer two times – I had it back-to-back – I was cured, and then on the one-year anniversary of my surgery to remove my cancer, I was re-diagnosed... it had come back.

It was awful, because as an adult the chemo nearly bankrupted me, and it was the first time in a long time I had to ask for help.

It was a very vulnerable time for me, and I was actually more public about it than anything I've ever been.

When I came out of it, I started my first world tour, and that started only two months after I finished chemo. We hit nine destinations in seven countries that I taught in, starting in Australia and then throughout Asia.

I really wanted to get a tattoo when I was in Japan and my translator said to me, "I followed your journey, not only personally but professionally of course, and there's a quote I think you would really love."

In Japan, it's very common to have quotes of 4 kanji or 4 characters, and this one was "7 falls, 8 rises." In the professional world, you fail more than you succeed, and for me having cancer for a second time, and having a lot going on in my personal life in my 20s, it was also very personal to me. It's a much more eloquent way of saying 'persevere' or 'persist'.

It's not really answering the question, but my point is that failure is so important to my success, I had it permanently tattooed on me.

My favorite failure though – there's so many... My favorite one was when I was 19 and I got an apartment on my own in Philadelphia. I thought I was grown, and I got an apartment with someone I had only been dating for a few months and, of course, we broke up like a month after moving in together. It was an apartment I couldn't afford on my own and I eventually fell flat on my ass and had to move back in with my mom in Ohio, and it was awful. I basically spent that whole year getting drunk and feeling sorry for myself, and not feeling motivated at all.

Then, finally one day I said, "This is not my life, this is not what I want to do – I had my moment, it's over!" and I packed my shit in the car, moved back to Philadelphia on my own, and I've thrived ever since.

I think I needed to have that moment where I – and I don't want to sound corny – but it really was a crossroads, where I could have stayed there and drank myself into a coma and said "I failed. I tried it and it didn't work out," and stayed in Ohio with my regrets and humiliation.

"Happiness has always been elusive to me. Severe depression led me to suicidal thoughts by middle school - thoughts that would come and go every few years until I finally surrendered and sought help. That wasn't too long ago either, so I'm still in the process of discovering what truly makes me happy."

I had fallen flat on my ass, but I knew that I had to move back to Philadelphia to build a life for myself - one that I wanted. It was the failure that taught me the value of failing, and it gave me confidence.

RELATIONSHIPS AND FAMILY

Who has been the most important role model in your life? Has there been someone who has led by example?

I was very influenced by the father figures in my life, but I didn't really have a positive male role model growing up.

My birth father is a creative guy and a fantastic artist. It's not something he did for a living; he chose a corporate life and chased after money instead, and that didn't make him very available to us as kids. As an adult, he has absolutely nothing to do with my life. He is one of those people, I have never heard him say that he's genuinely sorry. He taught me everything I didn't want to be.

I've never told this story publicly before, but on our home videos as a kid – we took this trip to Florida – and you can hear my mom and my sister and me in the background on the beach, but the camera isn't on us, my dad is zooming in on half-naked women on the beach - on our f*cking home movies! I was six-years-old. That was my dad, and it's audacious shit like that that unraveled our family and drove the wedge between us.

After my parents divorced my mom met my stepfather, who had issues with alcohol. We lived in the Midwest, and he came from a family with 3 brothers and was a self-proclaimed redneck – so having a new stepson who's gay, he didn't understand me at all. He projected a lot of his ideas of what kind of man I was supposed to be and that put a lot of weight on my shoulders. I had 2 father figures at 8 years old but neither of them were able to be there for me to guide me.

I have a much closer relationship with my stepfather now and we've got great respect for each other – at the end of the day, he did apologize to me in private for how he treated me. Our relationship continued to improve – we had our ups and downs – but I do consider him my dad and he's so much more open-minded and supportive now. But it took a lot of time and patience to get here.

I can't make my birth father give a shit. I can't change what happened in the past with my stepfather. I've made peace with a lot of it, but it's still a work in progress. I know that didn't really answer your question, but I guess I learned more about who I wanted to be by seeing all the things I didn't, if that makes sense. I think that, even if you're lacking role models, you're not doomed to fail or repeat the mistakes of the adults who raised you. I chose a new path for myself, and the dad that matters is the one who earned my respect by eventually becoming the father I needed him to be.

In what ways have the women in your life influenced the man you have become?

My relationship with my mother is fantastic – she's who I want to be like – she's a good person, she doesn't have an evil bone in her body.

She's always taught me to be kind, she's taught me to be a gentleman, she's always taught me to do the right thing. She's black and white in that way, and I think I get that from her too. I see things as being right or wrong. I've always thought that if I have poor behavior, just because other people are doing the same, I'm still accountable for my actions. I think that's

helped me to always own my faults and take responsibility for myself.

Mom's a caring person, and she always made sure we were taken care of growing up. She gave up everything to marry my dad – that was their generation. When they divorced, she really had nothing and still somehow made it all work for us.

I think that's why it's hard for me to see cruelty out in the world – I don't know who said it, but there's a saying that "you see the world as you see yourself." I always see people as trustworthy and good and kind and empathetic because that's how I see myself – so I get soooo disappointed when people aren't that, and I think a lot of that comes from her. I want to think better of things, and people, than sometimes they really are.

What are the values you bring into a relationship?

I was a serial monogamist when I was in my twenties – I really sought out security in my relationships.

Now I'm in a space where there is someone I care very deeply about – and I'm in a position where I am very, very comfortable in my own skin in a way I've never been before. I no longer feel that need to rush into anything.

Honesty and transparency are more important than security in my thirties because those are qualities I admire in others and qualities I bring into any relationship myself. I'm not perfect, but I'm honest about my mistakes and shortcomings and I expect the same. It's a matter of integrity. You can't have intimacy or trust without that raw honesty.

MING TSAI

CHEF AND TELEVISION HOST

 @mingtsai   @mingtsai   SimplyMing

Ming Tsai is the James Beard Award-winning chef/owner of Blue Dragon in Massachusetts. An Emmy Award-winner, Ming hosts PBS-TV's *Simply Ming*, now in its seventeenth season. Ming is the author of five cookbooks: *Blue Ginger: East Meets West Cooking with Ming Tsai, Simply Ming, Ming's Master Recipes, Simply Ming One-Pot Meals* and *Simply Ming In Your Kitchen*. Ming supports many charities including Family Reach, a non-profit whose mission is to provide financial relief and support to families fighting cancer, of which he is currently the President of the National Advisory Board. For more visit www.ming.com.

Do you have a favorite quote or philosophy you live by?

In two words – be kind. You just have to be kind and that applies to everyone at all times. If everyone in the world were just kind, oh my god, you would have a much better place.

More specifically to my career – the old adage is "You are what you eat" – I have morphed that into "Food IS your medicine" and I have spent a lot of time living a life of "You are what you eat". We don't reach for drugs or antibiotics until we've made sure we've tried everything else first. Ideally, if you eat smart, you actually won't get sick. So, it's about how do you prevent diseases? Pharmaceuticals are about curing diseases, I'm about food is your medicine, so eat smart.

That grew from a Chinese expression which is "*Hao Ren, Hao Bao.*" That was my grandfather's expression, which means "Good people who have good fortune; good people finish first."

I've been blessed with a very strong lineage in my Chinese culture and my Dad always talks about his great-great-grandfather who brought in 16 orphan daughters, because back in the day in China if you had a daughter, they were "useless" because they couldn't be good farm hands etc so he would

get babies left at his doorstep, with a note saying, "Please take good care of my daughter."

That's probably where it started – it started before that too – but he lived a great life.

I'm humbled and fascinated, and just so honored that I can say this - I am the 100th generation Tsai. We discovered this because of a guy called Henry Lewis Gates, a Harvard Professor who has a PBS show called *Finding Your Roots*. He started doing Oprah and Denzel and other Hollywood stars and athletes and did 3 chefs.

We already knew we were 34 generations old, but long story short, we found out that we went back to 2700 BC. One of the first Tsais was Qong Di, one of the first Emperors of China, who invented the Chinese language, among other things.

The reason I am telling this story is that it inherently splays into the pride, but also pressure, of doing really well. I've got 2700 years of Tsais watching!

I grew up with food, shelter and parents that loved me and that are still loving each other. I was never abused. My wife laughs, she says, "I've never met a kid that had a perfect childhood." But I did – the worst thing that ever happened was maybe I missed one meal and that was rare.

What is one personal quality that you are most proud of?

Hmmm – that's interesting. It's about being kind – *Hao Ren, Hao Bao* – good people finish first. Everything else matters too, but the baseline is being kind. If you're kind, you're going to get off okay.

What are the issues - whether social, environmental, political or economic - that you feel are most pressing and for which you feel the greatest personal concern and responsibility?

I think the biggest concern for future generations is leaving the world a better place compared to when I was born.

According to many scientists, we only have a few decades before we cross a point of no return. The fact this point exists, it's absurd. It is not only responsibility; it is our duty to not destroy the world we live in.

When my youngest son did the Earth Day March, he was interviewed why he did it, and he said, "I kind of like the world we live in now. I like air and water."

That is incredibly sad that he even has to think of the world like this today.

Who inspires you?

World Central Kitchen, which is José Andrés' charity. He is the one who was in Haiti and Puerto Rico after the hurricanes, and he went in and made 3.4 million meals and basically helped save the island. He is one of my heroes and one of my greatest friends. He deserves all the props – he was nominated for a Nobel Peace Prize, and he's a chef, so think about that.

Proudly, I was in the Bahamas two days after the hurricane and he had already set up shop, and we were doing 20 – 25,000 meals per day. I was the thankful one – to see these people just smile a little bit just fills your heart that you could be there to help.

Other than that, who inspires me today is probably my father. My Dad is 90 years old, works full-time, still goes to both Asia and Europe once a year, is one of the leading graphite material designers in the world.

"It's about being kind – Hao Ren, Hao Bao – good people finish first. Everything else matters too, but the baseline is being kind. If you're kind, you're going to get off okay."

He has been preaching this for 70 years.

Dad works with composite graphite materials, and to this day works tirelessly, full-time, at Stanford. He's now working with Airbus to do the prototype. It's just unbelievable. He's 90!

He's truly one of the very few geniuses I've ever met. I've seen him draw on a cocktail napkin like "Oh, that's how I do the rocket," and I'm like "Really??"

But more important than that – he's a lover of living life and that to, us, being Chinese, like French, Italian, Spanish and all these cultures... food is the center. That was always our priority – we would drive from Point A to Point B – wherever this was, but if there was a Chinatown Point C, we would go there. We would cross the Canadian border and take 30 pink boxes of dim sum from Toronto to get back to Dayton, Ohio.

Customs would always stop us and ask what was in the boxes, and my mom would feed them! It was always food, food, food – and always taking care of your people.

I have so many lessons my father taught me. He would always invite whoever was from out of town to our home, we were always hosting, always cooking. All the decisions and all the family stuff,

everything would happen at the dinner table – that was the glue.

That's something that's sorely missing in many households around the country because people are busy. There's squash and ballet, there's meetings, travel and work. It's so hard to have a meal together.

Literally we sat down at 5.30pm – no later – every day to have a meal together.

He taught me not to worry about what your superiors think of you, what matters is what the people who work for you think of you. Because the ones above, if you fall, they're not going to do anything but the people below, if you don't take care of them, if you're falling, they're not catching you – they're going to let you drop.

BEING A MAN

What does "being a man" mean to you?

I think being a man is you have to lead by example, you have to be the strength of the family, you have to set the bar because you can't expect your kids or anyone in your family to do something if your bar is really low. You need to set a high bar. Of course, with that comes expectation and hard work.

You try not to ever appear weak, especially in front of your kids. You try to not crack. But I've cried in front of my kids, I've cried in front of my wife – I am a big believer in you have to let that stuff go, you have to let the emotions come out and laugh and cry and scream and do what needs to be done.

I am not a doctor, but I know stress kills more people than probably anything else and holding things inside is stress on steroids. You have to let it out.

I don't hold on to stuff – if something bothers me, I will do it discreetly. I am not going to chastise a cook on the line, but I will take him downstairs and if it's the third time he's doing it, it's like "Dude, you're not listening to me!" and I will rip him a new one, but not on the line in front of everyone. You have to be respectful. I think that DNA of leadership is paramount for being a male.

EMOTIONS

What makes you truly happy?

Family, food, friends. When you're with family and friends and there's food, you're sharing. That's by far the happiest. You're hopefully grateful that everyone's healthy around the table and you can be there. My father is in his 90s – my fortune teller told me he will live till he's 104. Hopefully he's right. I just can't fathom not having him here.

How do you express anger? What do you do to release frustration?

I'm a very physical guy – I play pro squash and played in college and played soccer, tennis. Working out and/or cycling, or hitting the crap out of a squash ball. If it's been something that's really been bothering me, that's a great release. I try to do Bikram Yoga to not even get to that point.

I've done Bikram for 28 years… I don't do it in golf season, because I am a huge golfer, but now there's a chill in the air, I've gone back to it two or three times a week. That has saved me. If you believe, which I do, that you have chakras, you have to stimulate them to keep them healthy.

It's so much more than just stretching your muscles which was my ignorant opinion 30 years ago. It works your organs, it's a great workout, it's 104 degrees, it's an hour and half, it's as tiring as hell but more importantly it makes your mind relax, because it's so hot and so hard you can't think about anything else but breathing.

Ideally that helps prevent you from ever getting angry, but of course we live in a world with a lot of stupid people – and they're usually the ones that get me angry because of some idiotic move or statement.

What does vulnerability mean to you?

You have to be true to yourself. I honestly don't give a flying hoot about what other people think of me. Does my ego like being praised? Of course! Do I like having people talk about how great my food is? Of course, who wouldn't?

For me I grew thick skin – if you listen to the noise of other people, you're either going to be an alcoholic or dead, or both. You can't. I have put myself out there, by design. I enjoy it! I love teaching on TV and in person.

As long as my kids and my wife think my food is still good, that's all that matters. For the record, the best food in the world is someone else's – always.

Do you talk with anyone about how you feel when things are happening in your life, or do you keep these thoughts internalized?

It depends on what it's about – if it's business, I speak to my partner. We've been buds for 20 years and we golf together. He's an all-round great guy, and very smart.

My wife – we don't talk business – but if there's personnel issues, she is my sounding board.

Life decisions or a decision to open a restaurant – it's my brother and my father. They both have a great perspective on business, and they know me well, and they're honest with me, like "You don't want to do that dude, the next two years of your life will be miserable," or the opposite, "Totally do that, that will be a higher quality of life and not taking too much time away from your kids."

That's my inner circle.

LIFE PURPOSE AND SUCCESS

What do you ultimately strive for? What is your mission in life?

It is to leave a legacy for the Tsai name. I feel like I need to, probably have to, but - most importantly - want to.

Admittedly, it wasn't until I was in a head role – when I started running restaurants - that the charity work really started. Once I started getting asked, and started doing it, it became willingly a second job. Especially early in my career, I would almost never say no. There are so many great causes.

There are probably 500 great chefs in this country – the chefs that do all this work together, and we get asked to do so many events. It's a privilege to be asked. We have the skill set and we can raise $1 million for a charity. It's great!

The key that made it doable in the long-run was focusing on one – I still do other ones – but focusing on one means it becomes a lot easier to say "no" and I don't feel the guilt. If I can't do it, I can't

feel guilty that I can't help them out. I'm asked five times a day to do stuff, which goes back to having a thick skin and knowing I can't help everyone out.

I'm not going to the grave thinking I should have helped more people – it might be I wish I could have helped more people – but it's not because I didn't try, that I know for sure.

How do you define success? At what point did you identify as being "successful"?

When I got to the leadership role, that's when I realized I could really mold where I want to go with this good of cooking for other people.

I'm trying to raise $1 million for a charity at the moment – I am doing a dinner for 20 couples only, $50k per couple, which is a huge amount of money. But for people who have $500 million, it's not a lot of money.

We get a lot of great people, great musicians and chefs who contribute to the dinner and we raise the money. That jazzes me. That's success.

I feel so grateful and so blessed that I can do something like that to bring these people together and have a great experience.

Because by the way, you better f*cking have fun! There is one way in life and you're on it. Don't start enjoying it when you're 65 and retiring – no, you blew it! Enjoy it now. When you can combine all your love and do good and have fun, that's success.

It's not a dollar amount, it's not how many cars, it's not the toys – it's the impact you have on people, that's success.

How important is collaboration and teamwork to achieving success?

You have to collaborate and you have to delegate, and you have to trust because if you try to do it yourself, you'll either burn out or fail or both. Life's too hard that way.

I do believe good people attract good people. My wife always says, if someone quits, "You know what? Good people stay, you know that."

I had Blue Ginger for 19 years, and some of my team were there in year one, and the hardest thing I ever did was announce we were closing. Three months out, I told the team we were closing; I had to announce it to the press... you wouldn't believe how busy you become when you're closing after a 19-year run! 80 lobsters a night – it was ridiculous.

I said, "Look guys, you all have families, so you know I am closing in three months, so if you have to move on and get a new job, please do." But everyone stayed. That was so touching. But of course, they had to drink all the good champagne too!

What role does religion or spirituality play in your life?

I'm not really religious – meaning I am certainly not Catholic. But I follow the philosophy of Taoism which in a nutshell is "Go with the way, go with the flow." You can't fight the turbulent waters going that way – so it's how you deal with the water. If you fight it, you're going to drown.

That's really my philosophy in life in general – we all have turbulent waters; we all have problems and issues. Sometimes it's physical, or mental, or financial, or kids or whatever. It's how you deal with it. It's not the problem that becomes the issue, it's how you dealt with the problem that becomes the issue.

OVERCOMING CHALLENGES

Have there been any key challenges that you have had to face in your life? How have you faced them?

I have to be my own boss – I kept getting fired, and not because I was bad and stupid and stole booze or did anything like that.

My first restaurant when I left the Ming Oriental in San Francisco was Ginger Glove, and I worked for this guy, set up the whole deal, was his Managing Director, had shares in it, and the plan was to make like $10 - $20 million from it, which sounded pretty good to me.

Set the whole thing up, and I injured my back, so now I am on workers comp and this is after working 38 days straight. So, my back goes because I didn't do yoga for 38 days straight, so there you go... and he fires me!

He said, "You've done a great job, thanks for setting it up, we don't need you anymore." And I said, "What are you talking about? First of all, I'm injured, so that's illegal and secondly, you're a moron."

You know how much of a moron he was? He sent me a fax that night, on paper, that threatened me and said, "If you say anything about me, I will blackball you from the industry, I will ruin your career."

I go right to the chairman of the board, and I hand him the letter, and he reads it and looks at me and says, "What do you need? Please don't sue." I was like "Dude, give me three month's severance, I'm not suing."

I moved to this café in Santa Fey and I got it to a 27/30 Zagat rating and I did the first James Beard dinner in New Mexico with great chefs. I got their luster back. They loaned me money to buy my home, with zero percent interest because they wanted me there a long time, and nearly two years later we meet in the lawyers' office and they're like, "Hey Ming, you've done a great job, but we can't afford you anymore."

My wife basically said to me, "You have to become a chef-owner, because we can't keep moving every two years." So that is now my secret – I'm my own boss.

How has failure, or apparent failure, set you up for later success? Do you have a "favorite failure" of yours?

I've been very blessed – I've never had any physical challenges – never a disease or anything like that, and I don't take that for granted. We've all been touched by cancer in some way. I've dodged a bullet in that I have good health.

By the way, I do take good care of myself – 14 pills a day – herbs, fish oil, stuff that you know is good for you, and I work out.

Both of the firings I've had were idiots firing me – I didn't fail – they bluntly failed.

I have challenges all the time – the biggest challenge of my life was getting my wife to finally date me after chasing her for 10 years. So that was a huge challenge!

Polly - my wife - her brother is David Talbott, who 40 years ago was my squash coach at Yale. Polly was studying Chinese at Colorado University in Boulder. She came to visit David at Yale in 1983... we met, but she literally didn't want anything to do with me. But it was love at first sight for me – in the back of my head, I was thinking "There's my wife." it was crazy.

She was living with her boyfriend in China. For ten years, I was sending her care packages and writing her postcards saying, "I miss you."

Ten years of this we end up in San Francisco together and – I can't believe I am telling you this, but it goes to the heart of masculinity and vulnerability... I literally said to her, "If I leave my girlfriend, will you go out with me?" because I wanted that reassurance. I kind of knew she would, but I just wanted to hear it. I just had to cover my bases; I didn't want to be dangling! She said yes, and I broke up with my girlfriend the next day.

Now, 40 years later, David is still the squash coach at Yale and he's coaching my son this year, which is so cool.

She was my biggest challenge.

Professionally, it was opening Blue Ginger, my first restaurant. In 1997 we started this project. We moved to Boston, this is just after I got fired from Santa Fey, and my wife said, "We are not moving from a desert to a desert" so that meant we weren't moving to Vegas which was a hotspot. I completely agreed – to raise kids and stay married, that would have been impossible.

So, we went to Boston – my brother and friends lived there, it was still up-and-coming, it didn't have great restaurants like New York.

After 8 months of trying to get a loan, get a liquor license, and a lease – the bank said, "Look, we will approve you for a $250,000 loan but you need to show you have a liquor license" and the ABC Liquor License said, "We will issue a liquor license but you need to show you have a lease signed" and the land-lord is like, "Oh we will definitely give you a lease but you have to show me you have a bank loan."

So – this all has to happen at the same time, on the same day? Honestly, I had to fib, and said, "I got it, I got it, I got it" and then all of a sudden, I had it, and it worked.

But literally for a week, I was like, "How is this supposed to possibly happen?"

The challenge too was the enormous pressure – my wife quit her really good nursing job. She quit it to help run the restaurant because she did not want us to lose our house because our house was mortgaged, both our cars were mortgaged, our dog was mortgaged – literally our entire life was on the line for this restaurant to succeed.

That's a lot of pressure!

We didn't have kids – and that's one of my pieces of advice; don't have kids until you're set. Kids are so hard period, but my god if you have to worry about the financial part of it too – that's too much stress.

She came along for the ride – it was timing, thank god it was the right lease and location, I was doing the right kind of food, I have or had some game, I wasn't a shitty cook so that helps, right?

Once it opened, we were busy literally from the get-go – and then a year later I go on TV and the rest is history.

It was lucky I got to go on TV – *The Food Network* came to Santa Fey and shot me for five minutes and from that I got my gig, so thank god for the Santa Fey job, even though I got fired.

I do believe in fate, that was predestined, that was all supposed to happen that way, you just have to believe.

Going back to the Taoist approach – you just have to believe – just go with the water. It's been going for thousands of years – you can't fight it, so just go but go hard. You can't be lazy.

> *"You try not to ever appear weak, especially in front of your kids. You try to not crack. But I've cried in front of my kids, I've cried in front of my wife – I am a big believer in you have to let that stuff go, you have to let the emotions come out and laugh and cry and scream and do what needs to be done."*

RELATIONSHIPS AND FAMILY

In what ways have the women in your life influenced the man you have become?

There are three women – my wife, my mom and my mom's mom Lau-Lau.

Lau-Lau lived with us later in her life and was the manager of the Mandarin Kitchen, mom's kitchen which was the kitchen I started cooking at professionally at age 14. She was awesome – she used to be the head dietician at a hospital in Iowa City and so she didn't really care about the good taste in food, she cared about the nutrition, which for her was low-fat, low-salt, which wasn't really our focus at the restaurant!

We spent a lot of time together because she would close the restaurant at 7pm and for about 8 years, she was living with us. She would rinse the Mongolian beef, left-overs from the restaurant, in a strainer with warm water to rinse off all the fat and salt and flavor off it, and I would make so much fun of her and ask "Why?" and she would say, "It's so much healthier for you, son" and I was like, "I don't care! I eat for enjoyment." We would always argue about that.

But she was part of my foundation – she was so stable and so constant and always unequivocal, never-judging love. I could do no wrong in her eyes and she loved me for who I was. I think that was great to learn because to have unequivocal love is non-judging and that was key.

Mom was definitely my biggest influence growing up. She would hit me with her hairbrush when I did something wrong – you can't do that nowadays – but the hairbrush would break on me and then she would get really mad and then eventually go to long-cooking bamboo chopsticks that never broke. For the record, I didn't get beat-up by my parents, but I did get whacked when I did something stupid.

She would always say, "Wait until Dad comes home" and then Dad would come home and in four minutes, he would be laughing in my bedroom, which would make Mom even madder.

Mom was the driving force of work hard and play hard. She would have us get to the restaurant at 7am even though we didn't open till noon, but someone needs to put the rice on, and the janitor work etc.

I loved it. It was a job, but I got to cook, I got to be in a kitchen – I got the restaurant bug because of Mom. I got to see that if you make people happy through food, at a reasonable price, those people come back.

The creative process of cooking, without sounding too woo-woo, is truly the only art-form that uses every sense because you can't eat music and you can't smell most art, but food is everything.

My wife I give a lot of the credit of enjoying life with – she definitely was the reason I have two amazing sons. She's my best friend and she completes me. She's the reason that my life is so good. A lease is the most important thing in a restaurant, a partner is the most important thing in life. If you choose wrong, I can't imagine how bad that must be. We've always been on the same page together. She's my life.

How do you maintain balance in your life between work and family?

I said it earlier – I do take care of myself. I eat smart, I workout, I get acupuncture twice a month, I do yoga. And I realized at 45 that you just got to say "no" because I just can't do it all. And if I get sick, or over-worked or over-stressed, everyone suffers in my family and my restaurants. I'm not embarrassed or guilty to say I selfishly take care of myself – no one else is going to take better care of you than you.

SEAN YORO
CONTEMPORARY ARTIST

 @the_hula

Sean Yoro, known professionally as HULA, is a self-taught contemporary artist, most known for his murals positioned near or in large bodies of water. He has developed a distinct style merging fine art, street art and nature.

In 2015 HULA became widely known and publicized for his viral iceberg murals, which sparked a larger environmental discussion. The Hawaiian native has been known for his delicate portraits of half-submerged women's faces on icebergs across the worlds such as the Arctic Circle and Iceland in order to raise awareness of climate change and the effects on the environment.

Do you have a favorite quote or philosophy you live by?

When I first made the move from Hawaii out to New York, I had a whole wall dedicated in my studio to a ton of different quotes and I love the one from Kahlil Gibran that was "Move in Passion, Rest in Reason."

It's always the game of not burning out while still trying to find your passion and shoot towards it.

So many times, I was so burnt out and it always made me realize that it's just part of the process of the dream - you have no idea what the end goal is going to be but I'm just shooting for it and that has been my motto.

In the beginning for me it was always the black and white of getting out of your comfort zone, because I was always in Hawaii living a very comfortable life and not wanting much more than the standard life.

My end goal then was to be a lifeguard for the rest of my life, I thought that was such a respectable life and it still is. Lifeguards in Hawaii are extremely respected.

I had never seen artists from Hawaii in the fine art scene and I just stumbled upon this passion of mine. I literally had one elective course in my 3rd year of college and I just chose a charcoal drawing class and I immediately fell in love with it.

It was a naive dream of mine to go to New York with $800 and try to make it in the art world with no plan and no idea how I was going to make it.

I think about the naivety of it - if I had known how many times I was going to burn out and hate everything about the path I was on, I wouldn't have left Hawaii. But I'm glad I had this naïve dream that was so miscalculated from the beginning - I'm so glad that I stuck with it and was able to deal with the personal growth and pushing my own limits and then it slowly changed to pushing the limits physically and mentally with my heart itself.

But that first process of dealing with personal growth was definitely the key to how I developed my overall art.

What is one personal quality that you are most proud of?

I want to say grit and the endurance part of sticking to my idea because I had never put my whole self into an idea besides this art idea of mine.

I've been doing this since 2011. For my whole life I was not committed to one idea, I was spread out and very distracted and I think that every time it came down to it, I could have taken it easy.

I always had a plane ticket back to Hawaii and the easy comfortable life, but it took me down to the depths of what made me "me" in New York and it was about finding out exactly how much I can stand.

What are the issues - whether social, environmental, political or economic - that you feel are most pressing and for which you feel the greatest personal concern and responsibility?

An issue I noticed immediately when moving to New York, was the general lack of individual responsibility to take care of the environment around us. In Hawaii, we have a phrase "*Malama Ka Aina*" - meaning to care for and live in harmony with the land.

I was fortunate to be able to see how much of a difference your community can make when everybody pitches in and that's how Hawaii is, everyone goes to the beach and it's not uncommon for people to be picking up trash at the beach. It was so normal for me but in New York it's different and it's not their focus, I was fortunate to be raised with this value and just have it.

When I got the platform and the success with my art it was a no brainer to use the platform for greater good and that was my calling.

Not only that but also the deeper messages... during the concept stage of every project I really hone all this energy that the project will bring and put it to something that could be of greater use and sustainability.

Who inspires you?

There's been a lot... my first art teacher at community college in Hawaii, Snowden Hodges. He saw the spark and light in me and without his guidance from the beginning. I thought I was terrible - I look back at the things I was creating in that first class and they were hideous from a technical and creative stand-point.

I have no idea what he saw but he saw something enough to even lend me some money in order to go up to New York and it was that one key support and I thought, "Maybe I do have something!"

"Life is such a simple equation that doesn't need to be overcomplicated, and it's such a simple equation for me, "Don't complicate your dreams and your ideas."

The unconfident artist in me at that time did just flip the switch and once I got to New York there were a lot of people who helped me along the way.

On a broader level, I am inspired by the many people who lead their industries through innovation and dedication. The most consistent inspirational person like this would be Elon Musk. Not only for his non-traditional approaches to solving problems, but just the never-ending drive to not settle on smaller ideas and always be willing to risk everything time and time again if you need to for your vision.

It seems far too common these days to become comfortable after one or two successes and opt for a smaller, but safer path of goals or ideas. It really helps me to check in on these types of people when I'm low on overall energy or motivation in order to get reinvigorated.

LIFE PURPOSE AND SUCCESS

What do you ultimately strive for? What is your mission in life?

The one mission for me is to go all out on whatever idea or passion. I always go back and think, what if I didn't do that class, what if something else happened?

In my head I would have gone all in on something else and who knows where that would have taken me?

Who knows if there's another career up ahead that might pop up and I become passionate about.

My mission and goal in life is to be willing and not get back into that comfortable mentality in life where you play it safe.

How do you define success? At what point did you identify as being "successful"?

I talked about this recently and I have always struggled with the imposter syndrome where you think you're not good enough with what you are doing...like they're going to find out that I'm not who I think I am, I'm just this kid from Hawaii.

I'm fortunate to have these milestones that reassure your success and I always keep that in mind but at the same time I love the unconfident feeling of needing to always do better and keep working on things and always feeling like you're still in second place.

How important do you think collaboration and teamwork is to achieving success?

The camaraderie you get with people and other creators and see their process and kind of create something together... there is always something to be learned from other people's mediums and crafts that I take back into my own work. It's great to work together on a project and be successful and then all share this one project where we can look back and say, yeah, we adapted so well and it's those relationships that build genuine moments together.

When I'm looking to create something with another artist, there's a lot of collaboration where you can tell it feels forced and I have turned down a lot of projects as it has to make sense for both people, for both artists. It's not a logistics thing and I love it when collaborations happen with musicians or other artists where they are able to find something that completely shines for both and compliments both rather than just mashing two mediums together and seeing what happens.

OVERCOMING CHALLENGES

Have there been any key challenges that you have had to face in your life? How have you faced them?

By far my biggest challenge was making it out of New York City.

I initially moved to the city from Hawaii when I was 21 years old and naively thought $800 would be able to support me until my dreams of being a successful artist came true.

To make a very long story short, I ran out of money and started living illegally in a tiny office space in Brooklyn. For more than three years, I would shower at a gym and have to ration my meals heavily, sometimes having only an egg or two a day. Finally, my art took off in what seemed like overnight, but I'll never forget those years and challenges.

For me it was "How much do I want this?" as I could have easily taken that ticket back home and my family is back there and always telling me to come back and don't worry about it, they would take care of me and get me back on my feet. For me it was so crucial to find out har far I was willing to take this idea.

"To make a very long story short, I ran out of money and started living illegally in a tiny office space in Brooklyn. For more than three years, I would shower at a gym and have to ration my meals heavily, sometimes having only an egg or two a day. Finally, my art took off in what seemed like overnight, but I'll never forget those years and challenges."

It's something I would never have imagined and if I had known all this when I left Hawaii, I would never have stepped foot on that plane, I would have gladly stayed and been so afraid of that idea and to face all those things. It's always surprised me how much you can actually withstand.

I was 20 years old when I stumbled into art class but right before that happened, I actually had a bad surfing accident. I was surfing out of the North Shore of Oahu, the waves were huge as usual, and I was so scared to break my board because I had broken all my boards the previous time.

I was borrowing my friend's board that day and I didn't have any money to pay him back if I were to break his board, so I was playing it cautiously. I ended up paddling in because I thought I would break the board and on my way in a huge set came in and held me down and I almost drowned and the board ended up breaking anyway and I had to fight for my life for like 40 minutes out there.

I finally got in and was completely exhausted, but the epiphany was, for me, I should have just caught a wave of my life, because it was probably the best day I've ever seen out there.

It was so clear in my 20-year-old brain that I was so afraid to leave Hawaii. As dramatic as it was that day because of how close I came to drowning – I realized life is so finite and if I am going to do something, why am I playing it safe by doing what I know? I know Hawaii and I'm so comfortable there so why not find something and go all out. The next month I stumbled into an art class and I knew I had no idea what I was doing but this is what I was asking for... something to throw everything into.

How has failure, or apparent failure, set you up for later success? Do you have a "favorite failure" of yours?

I have had seven or eight different concepts that have become full series, whether it's the free diving or the surfboard murals or the ones we did in the forests, with every concept I always brainstorm it and it never gets old because they all have one or two huge fails in the beginning where I throw all this money into it putting the concept together, pulling the team together and you can have a complete failure onsite or something happens prior to that.

It's a weird relationship when I'm starting out. I have to always accept it, it's always fresh and it still hurts, and I think if I didn't have these I wouldn't really put as much prep work into it because I know it's coming so why would I even try it?

I have to know it is there, it's part of the process. I'm not afraid to fail but I still get wound up about a failure and I care so much about perfection and fine tuning everything that goes on. It's a weird grey area where to draw the line of how much failure gets me emotionally but of course you learn from it either way, but I still want to get it right the first time.

It's a never-ending game of trying to find that right balance.

BEING A MAN

What does "being a man" mean to you?

Throughout my life, this definition of "being a man" has changed significantly.

Growing up in Hawaii, there is a kind of "warrior" culture that definitely plays a role in defining what society thinks a man should be. These ideas of men needing to be this strong and meathead type beings got into my head as a child. It heavily influenced the direction I had for my life and my first big career goal as a teenager was to become a lifeguard.

I knew lifeguards were heavily respected in the island communities, very similar if not more on than firefighters. I thought this would prove my manliness in society and continued down this path until I was 20 years old. It was then I stumbled upon my love for art and was conflicted about changing career paths. I was still heavily influenced by the island culture and it felt being an artist was nowhere near the value of being a lifeguard in terms of manliness.

When I finally made the decision to change paths, I actually was too embarrassed to tell people I would be moving to New York City to become an artist because I felt it would somehow take away the "manly" traits I had worked hard to achieve at that point. Looking back, it is such a ridiculous way to view things and I was equally overwhelmed and surprised when my art took off from the sheer amount of support I had from the islands and my home communities.

Have your concepts of masculinity/being a man changed over time?

Yes. totally. New York has these totally opposite and unbiased ways for a man to be a man. I went from opposite ends of culture and I loved it. That's one thing I love about New York, everybody expresses themselves and there is so little care for what other people think, there are so many people with such diversity... it's fun to people watch out there.

If there was a single piece of advice that you could give every young person in this world, what would it be?

Life is such a simple equation that doesn't need to be overcomplicated, and it's such a simple equation for me, "Don't complicate your dreams and your ideas."

I realized that life can be simple and if you put in the work, you get the reward. If I had known this earlier, it would have made my younger life so much easier to navigate and stay on track with the dedication.

The one thing I see with many artists and people is they spread themselves too thin and get distracted with the digital age, I see so much talent that gets wasted as a result.

It's something I love seeing in people when they hone-in on something and fine-tune that one thing and take out all the distractions of modern life.

EMOTIONS

What makes you truly happy?

Surfing will always be a comfort zone for me. In New York as soon as I got a board and was able to catch a train out to the beaches out there, it was the same experience as I had back out in Hawaii, it was so comfortable, and I get straight back into this meditative state out in the ocean.

I think also that I have been forced to learn that people and the support of people around me and the genuine relationships and friendships go so far.

When I moved to New York I was alone all the time and I thought it was better to be by myself and I was going to do so much work and it's true, but it disconnects you from what you're really working towards.

It's like the quote, "If you want to go faster go alone, if you want to go further go together."

It's been my biggest hindrance because it feels so comfortable for me to be alone and to do my work and kind of be in a selfish little cocoon, but you can see quickly in your mental state how important it is to have genuine people around you.

To have people care about you and help you and you help them, it's a much more satisfying and rewarding experience.

How do you express anger? What do you do to release frustration?

There are so many different chapters in my life that changed how I would deal with anger. I like to think I am learning new and healthier ways to deal with emotions in general, but I think it will always be evolving with age.

Image supplied.

To me, anger always seemed to be the hardest emotion to control since it seemed to come out of nowhere sometimes with the smallest of mishaps. The biggest solution to this problem for me was being able to identify signs and triggers that would give me a heads up to consciously start being aware of the growing emotion and keep it under control.

I also noticed the greatest overall solution to feel more mentally in control and "stable" with any emotions was daily intense exercise. Personally, it would put me in a state that seemed "clearer" and put any issue into a more consistent perspective without the unnecessary stress and anxiety from things that ultimately did not matter too much.

Over time, I learned some key issues that would play a role in these shorter and shorter anger "fuses". The most prominent issue was by default, I would bottle up a lot of emotion (positive or negative) and it would take a lot from a circumstance to outwardly express any emotion.

From that discovery, I learned to the root of my bottling up emotions was the fear of letting people inside my head, even if for just a glimpse.

What does vulnerability mean to you?

When I was growing up, you didn't show it at all. In Hawaii it's such a warrior culture where guys grow up fighting with Jujitsu and any dispute there was rarely any words, you literally go straight into a fight. Some of the best mixed martial artists have come out of Hawaii.

To go on this path of moving to New York and realizing quickly that everything around you – I was so confident leaving Hawaii and then that confidence was completely broken when you're not even able to buy food.

I remember I had a moment when I was eating canned food and I broke my can opener and I couldn't even open my can of beans that night, and I was starving. It was the middle of winter, and I was outside my office building where I was living, and I had seen a video where you rub a can on the concrete and if you rub it hard enough you can slowly pry it open.

So, there I was, at night in the middle of winter in Brooklyn, rubbing a can on the ground. I looked up and there's a group of people my age – I didn't even realize it was a Saturday night – at a bar just staring at me.

To me, that was the lowest I could go, as far as confidence and ego. I completely broke down and cried that night with the waves of humiliation that came from realizing not only how ridiculous my daily life is, but to top it off I had absolutely nothing to show for it yet except this same idea of "becoming an artist". This was by far the most vulnerable I have felt in my life yet.

Before New York, I was able to control how people viewed me and when that was lost, I had no choice but to face these ideas of myself. For me, just starting the mental journey of being more open and honest about my financial situations felt exponentially better as I got used to it. It could have been as simple as "Hey man, I don't have any money to go grab a beer. I need that 5 bucks for my groceries this week." As insignificant as that phrase seems, it personally was always a battle to say in public to friends, but the initial feelings of vulnerability would slowly go away over time.

How do you deal with conflict and diffusing difficult situations?

In the past, I would go above and beyond to avoid any confrontation at all, even if that meant getting the shorter end of deals. Since then, it has been a slow process of knowing when to diffuse a situation or when to push back and stand my ground. I realized in any situation, the more accurately I can envision the other person's perspective the better I can deal with my responses to them.

Being able to see the other party's perspective first, instead of a knee jerk reaction to my view of things, would then allow me to communicate much more constructively and more often than not find a solution or middle ground to solve the issue. Without this initial step, I would find myself trying to justify reactions that only made sense when looking at the situation from exactly my point of view. This would more often than not lead to further escalation and dissolving of relationships.

SPIRITUALITY AND MINDFULNESS

What role does religion or spirituality play for you?

The universe and its energy have always changed throughout the course of my life and what it has always come down to is an understanding of meditation. It's a way of turning everything else off and getting in touch with the overall universal energy.

What pastime or practice enables you to connect with your inner self?

Mental health is such a common thing to ignore, especially because it's so easy to have this filtered lifestyle and not feel the downs that entrepreneurs have. I have talked to so many people and we all have the same type of issues whenever you're throwing yourself into something or testing yourself.

For me, the process and the path was what really mentally took a toll on me and I needed a ton of help to be able to stabilize myself. When I first moved out to

New York, I was a wreck, all this stuff that got thrown at me and needing to stay balanced and what really helped was a lot of exercise and meditation...it's always been my source of saneness throughout the whole thing.

I always tell people that the best concepts and inspiration have come when I'm on a long five mile run or some workout as I have so much clarity right after that.

I have so much clarity on how my body works with the physical and mental side and I'm able to use it to my advantage towards my goals and projects.

RELATIONSHIPS AND FAMILY

Who has been the most important role model in your life? Has there been someone who has led by example?

Surprisingly I think it's my brother, he's older by ten minutes but he is someone I look up to a lot because we have grown up so close and, as twins, I have always felt that growing up we were completely different but the older we get I realize how similar we are.

We had the same environment growing up, the same variables and the same issues we had to deal with and to see how he deals with things and reflect on how I do and see the subtle habits that we have that are different...we almost have an A and B experiment going on.

I can look at him and see he's doing something good in his life, I'm going to try that too and it gives me a lot of confidence and I can see what he was working on and say, "I'm going to give that a go" and follow in his footsteps.

You use female images in many of your art pieces, where does that inspiration come from?

In the beginning I would go out to these abandoned places on the water and find anything I could paint these murals on, it always looked gloomy and these environments were so lifeless and I loved being able to put a female figure in there to balance it out and give almost a Mother Nature aspect where I could get some soul in there and see the balance of nature and these man-made structures. It has a nice dreamy aesthetic to them, and it grew from there.

I work so much with nature and it's always, how can we humanize these landscapes and environments that I want to bring awareness to. It's the one thing that really drew me to art, it's being able to create these figures and I can bring so much emotion with simple pigment thrown around in a certain way. When I was learning these techniques, it came down to a simple illusion of creating these forms and that's the kind of magic that got me into art.

In what ways have the women in your life influenced the man you have become?

My brother and I grew up living with our mom and she was the backbone to why I knew I could go on this crazy path for art and she has always been so supportive and so nurturing. She gave us the freedom to go for whatever we wanted.

I wanted to prove to her that she did a good job of raising me and she raised good men that could go out and do something in the world.

DR LAYNE NORTON

PHYSIQUE COACH, NATURAL PRO BODYBUILDER AND POWERLIFTER

 @biolayne   @biolayne

Layne Norton is world-renowned entrepreneur, physique coach, bodybuilder, and powerlifter from Tampa, Florida. He holds the world record for squat in the IPF 93 kg weight class.

Alongside his success as a competitor, Layne is also an esteemed scientist and doctor; having a Ph.D. in Nutritional Science. He has helped to develop the Carbon Diet Coach app, a science-based nutrition app.

Layne's fitness journey began in high school, when he started lifting weights to gain muscle and improve his self-esteem.

He has since won 7 bodybuilding and 6 powerlifting titles, and has created a popular supplement line and coaching business.

Do you have a favorite quote or philosophy you live by?

I have many quotes I'm fond of; it would be difficult to put them all together or pick out a favorite. Of all that I've heard, probably *The Man in The Arena* by President Theodore Roosevelt stands out the most to me.

"It is not the critic who counts. Not the man who points out how the strong man stumbles, or where the doer of deeds could have done them better. The credit belongs to the man who is actually in the arena, whose face is marred by dust and sweat and blood. Who strives valiantly, who errs, who comes short again and again, because there is no effort without error and shortcoming; but who does actually strive to do the deeds; who knows great enthusiasms, the great devotions; who spends himself in a worthy cause; who at the best knows in the end the triumph of high achievement, and who at the worst, if he fails, at least fails while daring greatly, so that his place shall never be with those cold and timid souls who neither knew victory nor defeat."

That last sentence always stuck with me for some reason. If I know one thing about myself, it's that whether or not I succeed in my goals or fall flat on my face, the absolute worst thing to live with for me would be never trying.

What is one personal quality that you are most proud of?

I'm most proud of my resiliency. I would not consider myself incredibly gifted, and many sports coaches and teachers told me over the years that I was NOT gifted. What I do have is the ability to endure setbacks and keep moving forward. I've seen many people have great enthusiasm for goals until they came face to face with a soul sucking failure. I have endured many failures like most other people who have attempted big goals. I believe the difference between myself and others is that I continue to move forward no matter what it takes.

What are the issues - whether social, environmental, political or economic - that you feel are most pressing and for which you feel the greatest personal concern and responsibility?

I worry about the generations becoming more and more entitled. I noticed this with my generation. I was born in the early 80s and was the first member of my family ever to attend and graduate from college. I recognized what an enormous opportunity was afforded to me by being able to attend an institution of higher learning, however, when I got to college, I was shocked by the number of students who appeared not to care at all. In fact, many of them complained about going to class and doing the work. When I graduated, I saw these same people complain about difficulties in finding a job and found everyone other than themselves to blame. I believe we have a generational blame game where people no longer believe in being accountable and responsible and expect others to do that for them. I think this is a major problem.

Who inspires you?

Many people inspire me. Anyone who has continued forward towards a goal in spite of obstacles inspires me. The small business owner who pushes through all the roadblocks to turn a profit in spite of the odds inspires me as much as celebrity athletes who push through setbacks to have success. In general, I try not to idolize people, as no one is infallible and we are all flawed, I think idolizing someone can set you up for disappointment. That said, my grandfather, Robert Eiseman, was certainly someone whom I aspired to. He was a member of the greatest generation, endured the great depression, fought for his country in world war II, and later started a successful business. He was funny, caring, hardworking, smart, and an all-around incredible human being.

EMOTIONS

What makes you truly happy?

In the long term, I think having goals and working towards those goals is the most rewarding thing for me. If I didn't have my goals I don't think I would feel a great sense of purpose, which would make life difficult. When you have goals, you have purpose, and when your life has purpose, it has meaning. I've seen so many people who feel like their lives have no meaning and I think that's incredibly sad. Of course, I also enjoy having time with my children, wife, and family.

How do you express anger? What do you do to release frustration?

Some people would say I express it on social media! I would say that if I'm incredibly angry, I simply go to a place by myself and let it out. Whether I scream, punch a bag, lift weights, I do something to release that toxicity out of my body.

What does strength look like to you?

Resiliency. Having the courage to fight through setbacks and do whatever it takes to make it to the other side.

What does vulnerability mean to you?

Being able to admit mistakes, own them, and grow from them. Also, being able to forgive others for their mistakes.

How do you deal with conflict and diffusing difficult situations?

I try to remember that the majority of people are good people, doing the best they can, and sometimes we screw up. If you take that approach with conflict resolution, it usually can turn out pretty well.

Do you talk with anyone, or have a group of friends you can talk to, about how you feel when things are happening in your life, or do you keep these thoughts internalized?

I definitely try not to internalize things. Internalization can lead to anger, resentment, and can slowly erode relationships.

SPIRITUALITY AND MINDFULNESS

What role does religion or spirituality play for you?

Honestly, none. I have no idea if there is a god or not. Regardless, it doesn't change the fact that I want to be a good person and accomplish my goals in an ethical manner. Even if there was no heaven or hell, it doesn't change the fact that I am going to try to do the right thing.

What do you do to relax and connect with your inner self?

Lifting weights is a big one. Training is my 'Zen.' Also, I love getting out on my boat in the ocean and fishing. That is probably the biggest thing that relaxes me and just makes me feel amazing.

LIFE PURPOSE AND SUCCESS

What do you ultimately strive for? What is your mission in life?

My life mission is to help improve people's lives by educating them about nutrition and exercise and cutting through a lot of the BS in the fitness industry which is riddled with snake oil and nonsense.

How do you define success? At what point did you identify as being "successful"?

I think success is when you accomplish major life goals. I think graduating college I felt like a success because I had already taken my education further than anyone in my family. In order to feel truly successful however, I think I want to build a legacy that lasts long after I'm gone.

OVERCOMING CHALLENGES

Have there been any key challenges that you have had to face in your life? How have you faced them?

I've had so many challenges it would be difficult to talk about all of them.

I struggled with attention deficit disorder when I was young, and it made school pretty tough for me. I always did well in school because I took it very seriously, but it did not come easy to me like it did for many of the other kids I went to school with. Studying took me much more time because I would constantly get distracted and struggle with focus.

I also was bullied terribly when I was young, and it really wrecked a lot of havoc on my emotions and psyche for a long time. I had very low self-esteem when I was young and working through that was extremely difficult.

However, those problems aided me later in life when working through setbacks like possible career-ending injuries as well as setbacks in business.

Probably the toughest thing I've ever gone through was late in 2017. I had lost one business due to lack of profit and was kicked out of another very profitable business by my business partners who then frivolously sued me in an attempt to bully me into taking less money than my shares in the business were worth. At the same time, I was going through a divorce and had re-aggravated a serious lower back injury. It was an extremely difficult time for me, but I kept showing up and kept telling myself I would make it through to the other side. Eventually, I did, and things got better and still continue to get better.

At the end of the day, getting kicked out of that very profitable business ended up being the BEST thing that ever happened to me.

It enabled me to be free to pursue my true passions and it unshackled me from toxic people who didn't care about me and only were looking to extrude money from me.

How has failure, or apparent failure, set you up for later success? Do you have a "favorite failure" of yours?

Easily getting kicked out of my previous business by my business partners was the best thing that ever happened to me. It was a very public dismissal and they also bad mouthed me publicly in an attempt to sway public perception to their side. I never really talked poorly about them in public and instead I focused on winning the court battle, which we eventually came out on the better side of the deal in my opinion. Further, it got me free from that company to write books and become innovative again, rather than being under the control of people who simply wanted to tell me how to run every aspect of my life.

RELATIONSHIPS AND FAMILY

Who has been the most important role model in your life? Has there been someone who has led by example?

My parents were both extremely hard workers and good people. My grandfather also left a lasting impression as I discussed previously. If I can come close to matching my parents and my grandparents, I'm a happy man.

In what ways have the women in your life influenced the man you have become?

My mother was a very hard-driving person who could be difficult at times, but I learned a lot of my work ethic and the importance of how you treat other people from her.

My ex-wife, while we didn't work out as a couple, I learned many things from my relationship with her and am forever grateful for that as well as the two beautiful children we share.

My wife Holly, I've probably learned more from than anyone. She taught me how to stand up for myself, how to embrace being uncomfortable and she's also made me tackle many of my insecurities head on. She constantly pushes me outside my comfort zone which I love, even though it drives me crazy at times.

Finally, my daughter Livia has taught me about unconditional love. Whenever she sees me her face lights up and she screams "DADDY!" She doesn't care about my faults, the mistakes I've made in the past, or what I've screwed up, she loves me no matter what and that's an amazing feeling.

How do you maintain balance in your life between work and family?

It's very difficult being driven and having a family. I don't think we ever truly achieve balance at any one time. For example, when I was in grad school, I was unbalanced towards school.

When I first got married, I was unbalanced towards my wife. When I was starting my business, I was unbalanced towards work. When my kids were born, I was unbalanced towards them. It depends on the season where balance goes. But I think overall it's important to have balance on the overall course of your life and not neglect any one area.

Right now, I'm a bit more unbalanced towards work at the moment trying to set up systems in business that will require less of my time in the future so I can be more unbalanced towards family in the future.

Is being a father an important part of your sense of manhood?

Yes, fatherhood has been a huge challenge for me. I had difficulty connecting with my kids at first and when my ex and I separated I struggled with not knowing how to really be a dad. Having to go through that challenge and continue to show up no matter how difficult it was really helped me ENJOY being a father now. The hard times always make the good times that much better.

Has fatherhood changed you?

Of course. I never could have understood the amount of selflessness needed to be a real dad until I had to do that. I also never understood the amount of time that went into being a parent. As I said before, the hard stuff makes the good stuff all that much sweeter.

What qualities are most important for you in being a father?

PATIENCE. LOL. It's so hard to be patient, especially when my brain goes a million miles a minute, but I have to remember to enjoy my time with my kids, even when it's tough because they won't be this age very long.

JEFF RAIDER & ANDY KATZ-MAYFIELD

CO-FOUNDERS, HARRY'S INC

 @jeffreyraider   @jeffreyraider   @andykatzm

Jeff Raider

As Co-Founder of both Harry's and Warby Parker, Jeff Raider aims to build companies and brands that people like more. Harry's aims to create exceptional shaving and personal care products that better meet the needs of modern men. Prior to Harry's, Jeff co-founded Warby Parker, the designer eyewear brand.

Before founding Harry's and Warby Parker, Jeff worked at Charlesbank Capital Partners and Bain & Company. Jeff graduated from The Johns Hopkins University with a BA in International Studies and earned a Masters in International Affairs from The Johns Hopkins School of Advanced International Studies. He also earned an MBA from Wharton Business School. Jeff currently lives in Lower Manhattan with his wife and three children.

Andy Katz-Mayfield

Andy Katz-Mayfield is the Co-Founder and CEO of Harry's Inc., an organization building personal care brands that people like more. Harry's, the company's flagship brand, was founded in 2013 after Andy had a bad experience trying to buy razor blades. Harry's ambition is to create exceptional shaving and personal care products that better meet the needs of modern men.

Formerly, Andy worked at private equity firm Charlesbank Capital Partners and management consultant firm Bain & Company. He graduated from Duke University with a BA in Public Policy and earned an MBA from Stanford Graduate School of Business. Andy currently splits his time between Los Angeles and New York City, where he lives with his wife and daughter.

Do you have a favorite quote or philosophy you live by?

Jeff: My favorite philosophy is to try to make the most of every moment. There's a quote I like in that context by Abraham Lincoln that says, "It's not the years in your life that count, but the life in your years."

Andy: I like to try to live by the golden rule, which is "Do unto others as you would have them do unto you" – treat people the way you would like to be treated, have empathy and be kind.

What is one personal quality that you are most proud of?

Andy: I think I'm proudest of my ability to actually listen to understand. It's something that I've always tried to do well, and it's taken some practice to get it right. I learned it from a business school professor, and it stuck with me because it captures the act of truly listening as opposed to just being quiet and waiting for your turn.

Jeff: I've really enjoyed moments where I've been able to bring people together towards a common goal or objective. At Harry's, I think we've brought an amazing group of people together. I get a lot of my energy from the people around me and I get a lot of energy from our Harry's team.

What are the issues - whether social, environmental, political or economic - that you feel are most pressing and for which you feel the greatest personal concern and responsibility?

Andy: Equality, in the broadest sense, is probably a good descriptor of an issue that I feel is very pressing. From a Harry's brand standpoint, and in our company, the way we've tried to bring it to life is to make sure that the brand is really inclusive and democratic.

Harry's is a brand for *every* man - with "man" being more broadly defined, without any kind of particular archetype or stereotype tied to it. That, infused with our internal culture of being inclusive, appealing to all walks of life, and embracing all backgrounds and thinking, bleeds into Harry's social mission of men's mental health, and body positivity for our Flamingo brand.

At Harry's we have an internal philosophy called "embracing the ands" which means that men can be both strong and vulnerable, and brave and sensitive, which shows that there are lots of ways for "masculinity" to come to life.

Jeff: Andy summed up our joint focus really well – which is on equality and making life more enjoyable for guys. As part of that, we've dedicated our social mission to men's mental health, which is a huge issue for our customers and, for men more broadly today.

To date, we've reached over 645,000 men in need of mental health care, and have given over $5 million to non-profit organizations to achieve that goal.

Who inspires you?

Jeff: My kids provide me with amazing inspiration every day. Getting to see the world through their eyes, and hearing the questions that interest them, gives me such a wonderful perspective.

Andy: There's no one specific individual that pops into my mind, but I really admire people who have a passion for a cause, and who are relentless in the pursuit of that cause - especially in the face of significant obstacles and odds.

LIFE PURPOSE AND SUCCESS

What do you think was your main quality that led you to your success?

Andy: It's probably just fundamental optimism and positivity; I think they both enable a level of risk-taking and thinking about up-side rather than down-side. People are often naturally risk-averse, so the calibration there is sometimes tricky. It's led me astray at times, but overall it has led me to a willingness to take risks and to look at all of the possibilities.

Jeff: Being optimistic and willing to take risks has also been important for me too. To add to that, hard work and persistence are important. That may sound cliché, but setting clear goals that we want to achieve, and then working hard and persistently to overcome roadblocks and achieve those goals has definitely played a role in our success.

OVERCOMING CHALLENGES

How has failure, or apparent failure, set you up for later success? Do you have a "favorite failure" of yours?

Jeff: I like to think of failure as a teacher of valuable lessons. One of our values at Harry's is to "Improve, always," so we don't tend to dwell on the failure itself for very long – we focus on what we learned and how we can move forward.

One failure that I found personally helpful occurred early on when Warby Parker launched. The demand for Warby Parker drastically exceeded our expectations and capability to deliver - we were out of stock for a long time, etc. What we did, in that instance, is we personally took it upon ourselves to reach out to customers, to get to know them, and to apologize for not being able to serve them in the way that we intended. In these conversations, we vowed to do everything we could to make it better for them. We gave away free glasses at that point in time to try to make it right.

What I learned in that moment was that those customers deeply appreciated that we personally went out of our way to serve them and, in turn, we created a lot of loyalty. This is a great example of something that we would have ideally tried to do a bit better, but where we ended up learning a lot and feel like we ended up in a good spot.

I think vulnerability was really important there. Understanding the value of being a hands-on advocate to help fix the problem and being able to personally relate to the people we were serving, was really important and meaningful to me, and to us as a company.

> *"I believe that if you don't see mistakes as failures, and instead see them as learning opportunities, that's a really positive, growth-oriented mindset that will prove to be really useful... I've made thousands of mistakes, but I just try to learn from them and move on."*

_____

"Most things that really trigger you and make you angry in a moment aren't that big a deal. If you can find some peace and serenity and find the root cause of what's making you angry and then productively deal with the root cause rather than the emotion itself, that's usually the best way."

_____

Andy: Similarly, I believe that if you don't see mistakes as failures, and instead see them as learning opportunities, that's a really positive, growth-oriented mindset that will prove to be really useful and comes back to my earlier point of resilience. I fail every single day, if you want to use that word. I've made thousands of mistakes, but I just try to learn from them and move on.

I think that what Jeff and I try to do as leaders of the company is to be transparent about those mistakes, and if we can get up in front of the company and say, "Hey, we screwed this up. Here's why, and here's what we are going to do differently," then it encourages other people to do the same.

An example is when we bought a factory in Germany. We're called Harry's, the factory was called Feintechnik, and in an effort to find some middle ground, we re-named the entire company HF Global. In retrospect, it was an idiotic thing to do – no-one knew what HF was, we were acquiring them, and we actually needed to instill Harry's values and ways of working to continue our growth as a brand. It was originally perceived as a compromise, but in the end, it did nobody any favors. Ultimately, we said, "Okay we can keep defending this, and try to build equity into this thing, or we can admit we were wrong, call the whole thing Harry's, and move on with our lives." So, that's what we did. It was a bad decision, a bad choice, but that's one of 10,000 examples you could pick!

EMOTIONS

What makes you truly happy?

Andy: What makes me happy is being able to be true to my authentic self, and not having to put on any front or mask, whether that's to adhere to some professional standards, social norms, or to impress people.

If I am forced to be someone I'm not, or if it doesn't feel authentic, that conversely leads to dissonance and unhappiness.

Jeff: What makes me happy is being with other people who I know and love, and with whom I feel like I can be myself. I get a lot of energy from other people.

How do you express anger? What do you do to release frustration?

Andy: Interestingly enough, when I was younger, I used to have a pretty significant temper, where anger would explode and boil over. I found, through plenty of experiences, that this was a relatively unproductive way to deal with things.

In time, and through training myself with yoga and meditation, I found ways to - I wouldn't say suppress anger, because I don't think that's productive either - but to put it aside. It helps if you're able to develop some perspective, get some distance, and build some empathy.

Most things that really trigger you and make you angry in a moment aren't that big a deal. If you can find some peace and serenity, you can find the root cause of what's making you angry and then productively deal with the cause rather than the emotion itself.

Jeff: I have two things. One, I try to exercise or do something to try to take my mind off the anger I'm feeling. It helps to dimensionalize it with myself a little bit. And two, I like to talk it out with other people and get their advice and perspective. I rationalize it and figure out how best to bring it forward.

What does vulnerability mean to you?

Andy: My experience is that the fear of being vulnerable - and therefore being perceived as weak, or lacking confidence, or being unsure - can be defeated by just embracing it and calling it out.

If you're afraid of something, and you admit you're afraid, and can talk about it, in many ways it makes it less scary. Ironically, people view you as stronger and more courageous for calling it out. Vulnerability, and embracing your own emotions and concerns can be a very powerful tool in that regard.

In a professional sense, it certainly makes us more relatable to our team, and it makes them feel more assured that we're not just putting a brave face on things, but that we are being honest and truthful about our feelings. It makes it easier for them to be honest and vulnerable if they see us role-model it with others.

Jeff: Echoing Andy, I think people really respect you when they feel like you're being totally open, honest and truthful with them.

Do you talk with anyone, or have a group of friends you can talk to, about how you feel when things are happening in your life, or do you keep these thoughts internalized?

Jeff: I go to Andy a lot – I think that's one of the amazing benefits of having a co-founder. Also, with my Warby Parker co-founders, we talk a lot about those things together. It's just really great to have that support network.

Andy: In a professional context, I think there's something unique about co-founders and shared experiences where because you're going through the same stuff, you can share and get the empathy on the other side. Your co-founder in life is generally your significant other. That shared experience enables empathy, I think.

SPIRITUALITY AND MINDFULNESS
What role does religion or spirituality play for you?

Andy: I would characterize my experience as being more spiritual, it's not religious in any denominational sense. The actual practice of trying to stay centered or grounded, and believing in a greater purpose in terms of having impact, hopefully improving the lives of other people, and leaving a legacy beyond myself is certainly front and center.

Jeff: I similarly feel a spiritual purpose. I was raised Jewish and I do find that some structure of religion does provide time to reflect on spirituality and moral values.

I also walk to work every day – I find walking to be really helpful in giving me time to think, adjust and clear my head.

RELATIONSHIPS AND FAMILY

Who has been the most important role model in your life? Has there been someone who has led by example?

Jeff: One role model in my life is my mom. She raised my brother and me as a single mother, and was an entrepreneur herself. She helped to build a company and was able to instill good values in us. She worked hard to have an amazing impact in the world, and always took time to make sure she was doing the right thing for us as a family, and for the other people in our lives.

I try to shape myself through a lot of different influences, but she was really important. I probably share her natural optimism that things will work out, her penchant for risk-taking (maybe a 'lack of rule-following' is a better way of putting it). I've come to realize as an adult that she doesn't really believe that many rules apply to her! Sometimes I feel like that's helpful in the context of building a company - that is treating rule-breaking as a way to think beyond conventional norms.

Andy: My dad's a huge role model – he is always his authentic self, for better or for worse. It used to make me cringe when I was a kid and he would say embarrassing things. But as I've gotten older, I've grown to appreciate that he is who he is. He lives in the moment, appreciates time, and has a real positivity that's infectious. I've tried to pick up on some of that.

In what ways have the women in your life influenced the man you have become?

Andy: The first that comes to mind is my wife, who I first met when we were 18, so I've known her for some really formative years beyond just my adult life.

Emotional intelligence, empathy, and being mindful of other people's feelings and reactions comes quite naturally to her. To me, it comes a little less naturally – I'm highly rational, not particularly emotional - so I think she's instilled in me an appreciation for the importance for understanding how your actions and behaviors actually impact other people beyond just who's right or wrong, and what the facts are. She's helped me develop a lot in that dimension as a person.

What impact have women brought to your businesses that men don't bring?

Jeff: Diversity and inclusion, in general, is really important to us at Harry's. It is something that we measure empirically in all levels of our company. We measure it in our promotion and hiring processes, and we share all the results with our team to discuss where we stand relative to other companies.

We're also very proud of the fact that as a company that has been focused very much on men as customers, a little over half of our team are women, and we have incredible representation of women on our leadership team. And it's not just about making sure women are key players at Harry's, but about racial, ethnic and cultural diversity, as well.

We have employee resource groups that are geared towards a number of different communities, to help ensure that people really feel welcome. We feel that the more diverse perspectives we have across the board, the better we will be in terms of decisions we make.

Andy: I would add that women bring other women – and that's why it's such an important focus for us at the leadership level. If you have women in leadership who can be role-models for junior women, and who can provide mentorship, it creates a much more welcoming environment. That's true too of all potentially under-represented groups. If you're able to elevate and have them in positions of leadership, it creates a much more welcome environment for more junior folks from similar backgrounds.

JUSTIN LANGER

COACH, AUSTRALIAN MEN'S CRICKET TEAM

Until the announcement of his retirement from test cricket in 2007, Justin Langer was one of Australia's great top-order batsmen. Originally playing at number 3 he moved to opener in 2001 and played 105 test matches scoring 7,696 runs including 23 test centuries.

Justin continued to play domestic cricket for Western Australia in the 2007/08 season and also played English County Cricket as captain of Somerset during the 2007, 2008 and 2009 English summer seasons. Justin also captained Western Australia from 2003 to early 2007. He retired from playing for Western Australia (Western Warriors) in March 2008. In November 2009 he was appointed Batting-Mentoring coach of the Australian test cricket team and in May 2011 was appointed Assistant Coach. In November 2012 Justin achieved a long held dream when he was appointed Coach of Western Australian cricket (Western Warriors and Perth Scorchers).

After six very successful years as Coach of Western Australia, Justin was offered the highest position in Australian cricket in May 2018 when he was appointed Coach of the Australian men's cricket team.

Do you have a favorite quote or philosophy you live by?

Without doubt for me it is, "The pain of discipline is nothing like the pain of disappointment."

I live it with it in everything I do. When I built my house around 20 years ago, I had a little tin shed at the back of the property and in there was my punching bag, a number of books, a meditating cushion and a few permanent marker pens.

Amongst other things, I used to write my favorite quotes on the wall.

When we demolished the old house and built our family home in Perth, we built a more permanent 'tin shed' in the back yard. This tin shed was made of bricks and mortar and is a beautiful part of our property. On the first day we moved in, I took a big marker and wrote on the freshly painted wall, "The pain of discipline is nothing like the pain of disappointment."

My wife was devastated!

After Sue recovered from the initial shock, I have kept adding my favorite quotes to this now quite large and great space and

just as I finished. The room has continued to grow and now these amazing quotes and scriptures all over the walls... it's the best wallpaper in the world!

What is one personal quality that you are most proud of?

Concentration. I started doing martial arts when I was about 16. I was in this sunrise Dojo which meant that we trained at 6am. My sensei, Johnny Andrews, was the toughest and meanest bastard in the world, but I learnt so many lessons from him.

We used to start every morning in a sitting position where you are sitting squat on the back of your heels. It used to kill your feet and you had to sit there with your hands on your knees and he would talk you through the session that we were about to do.

I was certain that he kept us holding this position for so long to teach us the pain. It killed your feet, the ache was mad, but I'm sure he was testing us each day. It took an amazing amount of concentration to deal with this pain and continue to focus on his messages. This has been one of the great lessons of my life which is to stay focused regardless of the distractions.

Who inspires you?

I wouldn't be sitting here now talking with you if I haven't had the unbelievable mentors I have had in my life. My mentors, family and friends inspire me every day.

I have a bookshelf filled with books from and about people who inspire me. Bono from U2; The Rolling Stones - I met Charlie Watts - and I'm inspired by their longevity and their energy at their ages; Nelson

Mandela... I went to Robben Island and was staggered by how Nelson Mandela lived and then came out with forgiveness and love.

Sir Donald Bradman, the greatest cricketer ever.

We took the Australian Cricket team to the Western Front and Gallipoli and what an experience that was! Major General Stephen Day was our host, who is an incredible person and leader. Alan Border, my first Captain, still inspires me and then there is Phil Hughes who was like a little brother to me who passed away after being hit in the neck by a cricket ball...his smile and energy still inspires me.

The list goes on and I am so lucky to have access to all of these people and influencers in my life.

I wouldn't be who I am without some of these men and my dad, he's number one right alongside my mom who died a few years ago with ovarian cancer.

My mom and dad have inspired me throughout my whole life.

In my experience, too many men close themselves off to learning. They might think they already know it, or they are not secure enough to ask for help or advice. If I had a son and could give him some advice, as I do with my daughters, I would say, "Be open, be open to learning, be open to everything. Reach out to people, read books, learn, and ask questions."

The people who have been the toughest and most honest with me in in my life up are now my best friends and greatest mentors. They wouldn't be tough on you unless they care about you.

EMOTIONS

What makes you truly happy?

Time!

Dad recently said to me, "Son, I haven't seen you this happy for 15 or 20 years."

Recently with COVID-19, I have had time with family. It's given me time to do all the things I love to do. I get to take my daughter Gracie to school, I haven't had that opportunity for all of her life.

I see my kids every day because I have more time. People say, "That's what we all do..." I don't. I often spend 300 days of the year away from my family and my home, so the time is really important to me.

How do you express anger? What do you do to release frustration?

I don't get angry very often.

I think that meditation has helped me with that. One of my weaknesses is that I hate losing and when I do, I go incredibly quiet and get very introverted. This probably affects my body language, I'm aware of it and it's something as a coach I am working on.

One thing I have learnt is that men need to be able to talk, you have to be able to talk it out or it becomes like a cancer. I think this happens to a lot of men who let their anger out in different ways because they don't have a release and they let it build and then bang! The sledgehammer hits.

I've learnt from bitter experience that it comes down to talk. Whether it's with my mates, guys I coach or family that I need to talk and if I do get grumpy about something, I will get it out but then I will forget about it two minutes later. It's like therapy for me.

I can't ever remember raising my voice in anger. On the flip side, one of my strengths is my honesty and I just say it in the only way I know and that's to look someone in the eyes and tell them the truth.

When I'm coaching up in the box, I show no emotion to the point my daughters have said, "Dad, how do you stay so calm?"

It's a mask of calm - underneath, my heart's pumping, I'm nervous - but outwardly I'm staying as calm as I can.

In coaching, parenting or leadership, calmness and consistency are really important qualities.

What does vulnerability mean to you?

I know it's like a buzz word at the moment but it's really important to let it happen, honesty is really important and as a man you need to be able to admit that you make mistakes and admit that you're not bulletproof.

I played a game of golf recently with a friend of mine who is in a senior leadership position and it's been really tough for him lately. I sent him a message after the game saying, "Thanks for the game of golf but much more importantly, thanks for being so honest with me." He spoke to me about something that was really difficult and really hard to talk to other people at work and he was really brave.

I have no problem being honest and open and telling people how I feel, but I had to learn this.

Do you talk with anyone, or have a group of friends you can talk to, about how you feel when things are happening in your life, or do you keep these thoughts internalized?

I remember in 2001 where I had been

dropped from the Ashes Tour team and I walked off the ground in Sussex England. Steve Waugh, the Australian Captain, had torn his calf muscle and I'm thinking there is a chance that I can get back in the team. I was trying so hard, I'm 31 at this stage, still living and learning, and I got out for a duck in the second innings.

As I'm walking off, I wanted the ground to open up and swallow me alive. I walked into the change rooms and grabbed Adam Gilchrist by the throat and said, "Look what you f*ckers have done to me!"

I had been training like a machine, that was my way, train, train, train. I was so fit, I hit a million balls in training, but I didn't talk. I was still so emotional about getting dropped and that was a real switch point.

That night, after grabbing Adam around the throat we jumped on a bus to get back to the hotel and John Buchanan, the Australian coach at the time said, "Come on, let's grab a beer."

I said, "No, I don't want a beer, I'll work it out myself" - which was obviously working well for me! But I went and grabbed a beer and sat with the guys and we chatted for a few hours and it was like spewing cancer out. I was sad, I was angry, but I got it out.

After that as I was walking up this grand stairway, I got to the top and John Buchanan and I met, it was like almost having your first kiss. John dropped his bag and looked at me, I dropped my bag, and he gave me this massive hug and he said to me, "I've been wanting to do this for weeks, but the moment hasn't been right." John is a father of five kids, so he gets it. He said to me, "Hang in there, I'm feeling for you and it will work out."

That night I also rang my wife and my mom and dad and my best mate and everyone was worried about me. My wife jumped on a plane and flew over the next day from Perth to London with my little three-month-old baby.

The next night I went out for dinner with Steve Waugh and told him how I had been feeling and we talked it out which was unbelievable and at that point I thought, "Okay, If I never play for Australia again, at least I have these people around me, life won't be that bad."

One week later, I was about to head back to Perth, I was thinking about quitting from Australian cricket; I was thinking about retiring and getting on a plane to go home, I was so flat and Steve Waugh rings me and tells me, "Mate, I'm letting you know that you are opening the batting for Australia tomorrow."

I said, "What do you mean? I'm batting as bad as the f*cking phone in my hand!" and he said, "No, I reckon you would be a good opener."

So, I opened the batting, scored a century, scored four 100s in a row and opened with Matty Hayden for the rest of my career.

The point is if you hang in there, take the lessons that come your way, take the lessons from adversity it's amazing what can happen. A lot of people quit; they don't take the lessons from life. My philosophy is that in the toughest times you have two choices; you either quit or you learn and get better. Pretty simple. I also understand that you can rarely get through the toughest times by yourself. You need good people around you.

Emotion then really became part of my game especially with Matty Hayden, we hugged a lot and still do. Every time I see Gilly (Adam Gilchrist) now, we hug each other, every time I see Punter (Ricky Ponting), we hug each other. These guys are like my brothers...Steve Waugh doesn't like to hug as much but I force it on him a bit!

LIFE PURPOSE AND SUCCESS

What do you ultimately strive for? What is your mission in life?

When I started out in this job as the Australian coach, I understood that you must have a higher vision if you like and have a really strong vision for what you want to achieve.

It's like what do you want people to say at your eulogy?

My vision right now is to make Australians proud of the Australian cricket team again. I've said those words every day for two years.

It's another thing about leadership, you need to be consistent, consistent with your people, consistent with your messaging and behaviors and consistent with the public if that's the role you are in.

When I was 16 years old, I went on a school-boys tour to England, missed a month of school while I was doing Year 12 - probably not a good thing - but I scored a 100 at Lords and I rang my mom and dad and said, "How good was that? 100 at Lords!" I will never forget how proud my mom and dad were of me.

From that day on I spoke to my mom and dad every day until the day my mom died a couple of years ago.

So, my legacy has always been and still is to make my family proud of me. Now that I have kids, that drives me – to make my family proud of me.

Another important purpose for me is that I want people to know that I really care for

people. Compassion, empathy, humility and care are vital traits of leadership, in my opinion.

I've always said that I will know if I'm a great coach, not by how many trophies, but by the number of wedding and christening invitations I get. That's how I measure it because it means that in a really tough business, I've earned people's respect and built strong relationships. They wouldn't invite me if they didn't think I cared about them.

It goes back to my mentors...they were tough on me but they are still my best friends and there the people I talk most fondly about because they cared about me and at the end of the day, if people can say I cared about things and cared about people, then that's how I would like to be remembered.

If you could give your younger self some advice, what would it be?

Don't worry so much!

I used to say to my beautiful nana, "Nan, I'm really worried about something and she would say, "Is there anything you can do about it darling? No, so don't worry about it." If I could do something about it, she would still say, "Don't worry about it!"

I used to worry so much...what if I don't get runs on the board, what if I fail, what will everyone think? I'd worry about what everyone was thinking.

If you worry too much it creates stress and stress means you're not in flow, you don't smile much under stress and, as a sportsman, if you are stressed it manifests itself in your body as well.

You tighten up, your feet don't move, and if your feet don't dance, you're dead!

What do you think was your main quality that led you to your success?

Well concentration in my opinion is everything. I remember that I wrote Sir Donald Bradman a letter in 1995. One of the amazing things to come out his reply was the first line of his that said, "I'm flattered that you believe an octogenarian like myself can help you with your cricket."

What humility. This is Sir Donald Bradman, the greatest batsmen ever!

The second line that I always recall is, "Always trust your instinct, and never become a slave to coaching."

Like a lot of young athletes, I had a lot of self-doubt when I was younger, I was always trying too hard and I now know the harder you try, the worse it gets.

I had to learn how to deal with this and it was all about concentration, concentration, concentration.

It basically allows you to give 100% attention to the next task you are going to face, and you can only give 100% if you have the strategies to get rid of the distractions. Whether it's the ball before, the day before or the week before or worry about what could happen in two minutes time or an hours' time or a weeks' time. I learnt this from tough experiences, and I wasn't great at it, but I learnt that if I wasn't living for the moment and concentrating on living in the moment, you get penalized for it.

You mentioned your writings - can you tell me what writing your thoughts down gives you?

When I was at school in Year 12, I did English and English Literature and I actually won the English Literature award.

I often ask myself is it the writing that helps my storytelling or is it the storytelling that helps my writing?

I did a public speaking course when I was 19 and I remember the guy saying, "Know what your point is, let's say the point is concentration, make the point about it and then tell a story about it.

It's like when you are a little kid, what do you remember? It's the stories every night when you go to bed, we love stories.

In one way, writing is good therapy, but it also helps me in other areas of my life. It helps me remember moments and I can bring them to life.

I write in my journal every single night about my day's thoughts and I meditate every morning, it's just my thing.

In 1988, I was 18 years old and as a family we did a time capsule that we were going to open in 2000. As an 18-year-old kid, I wrote about ten pages of thoughts and one of them about being at the crossroads of my life - I'm 18!

I had written about Sue, should I go to university, not sure about cricket...all these thoughts. But I had also written that if I had a contract to play cricket for Australia for the rest of my life, I would be the happiest person in the world.

I'm sitting here now at 50, I have played for Australia, and I'm still involved in Australian cricket.

I wrote all of this down when I was 18 years old and by writing it down, it brings it to life.

I'm not sure of the science behind it, but gee, it's powerful.

How important is collaboration and teamwork to achieving success?

I describe it like this. If you see your brother involved in a punch-up in the school yard, you're going to jump in and help him.

Cricket is like going to a school yard brawl. It happened every time we walked out onto the pitch in England, it was brilliant. The camaraderie within the group is like the glue that keeps everything together particularly when the pressure came on which it did, we loved it.

As a team, we knew the recipe for success, we were confident and went and played our roles. We had each other's back. I remember a game in New Zealand, Australia were five wickets down for 60 runs, not going well at all. I'm there panicking, Steve Waugh turns to me and says, "Don't worry, someone will pull us out of it, don't worry about it!"

That was the confidence of the captain and it happened all the time.

OVERCOMING CHALLENGES

Have there been any key challenges that you have had to face in your life? How have you faced them?

In my 100th Test match for Australia, I was knocked out first ball. Here I am living my dream of making 100 tests and it's been my dream forever. The very first ball of a 5-day game, I was knocked out flat. Not the best start.

My batting coach, Noddy Holder, picked me up in the car not long after and he said to me, "It's time to retire mate, I don't want to see you keep getting hit." He was like old Mickey from Rocky throwing in the towel. I could almost hear the Rocky music playing in the background!

I told him that I wasn't ready and that after we lost the Ashes in 2005, we promised each other in the team that we would win the Ashes back together, I couldn't quit as I had made a promise to my teammates.

So, he says to me, "Okay, I respect your decision, but we have some work to do." I put myself in the most uncomfortable situations for the rest of my career. I knew that I had to find a strategy to deal with my batting technique.

When we talk about being a man, I was literally petrified every single ball I faced after that. I'm meant to be the tough guy, the opening batsmen, I was scared every ball I faced but I knew that I had to find strategies to deal with it.

We all get scared in life, right? Scared of different things and what I have learned is that you must find ways of dealing with it. You must face it front on and you have to deal with it, otherwise you will fade away as you can't keep facing up.

After we lost the Ashes in 2005, we promised each other in the team that we would win the Ashes back together. Thankfully we did and retired in the last Test match after we beat England 5-0 in the series. I am glad I put in the work so that I could enjoy the fairytale end to my career. Very few sportsman get that opportunity.

How has failure, or apparent failure, set you up for later success? Do you have a "favorite failure" of yours?

In 1993, getting dropped from the team, led me to learning about meditation. This in itself has been a life changing endeavor.

At the same time, I went back to the Cricket Academy and met Rod Marsh who then got me back as a scholarship coach as a 24-year-old. That opportunity allowed me to still train to get back into the Australian team, while learning the art of coaching, under his tutelage.

Rod's encouragement as a batsman and a coach has had a huge influence on my life and maybe that wouldn't have happened if I didn't experience the pain of being dropped and losing my dream.

In 2001 I got dropped again and that's where I learnt how important it is to talk to people, to never give up, hanging in there, and then letting go.

From there I opened the batting for Australia for the next 5 years.

When you have "perceived failures" you have two choices. You either quit or you hang in there and take lessons from it. Quit or get better, it's simple. What do you want to do? It's your choice.

A lot of people quit because they don't want to experience that feeling of disappointment or sadness or hurt again.

One thing I have noticed is people only do reviews when they fail...that just doesn't make sense. When things go wrong everyone wants these big reviews, why don't they review when everything's going great? Then you get the right recipe.

What role has luck played for you in your career?

There was a time where I was really unwell with being hit in the head quite a lot and I was getting sick from concussion.

I met billionaire Kerry Packer about six weeks before he died, it was an awesome experience. We went to his house, there were six or seven Australian cricketers who went along to his house. It was the night before a test match after the Ashes tour where Australia played the World XI.

We were sitting around, and Kerry Packer was telling us how important luck was in life which is incredibly important. He was telling us about his great-grandfather and then his dad and he was just about to tell us about his luck in life and all of a sudden, he looks at me and slaps me on the shoulder. He turns to me and says, "You've had a bit of luck in your life haven't you, young fella?" I'm like, "Yes Mr Packer, I'm pretty lucky."

He says, "Lucky they invented helmets, or you'd be f*cking dead!"

Everyone was rolling around in laughter.

At the end of the night, one of the hosts turned to Kerry and said, "What do you reckon Kerry, are the boys ready for the most important piece of advice you can give them?"

Kerry says, "Yeah, I think they're ready."

You can imagine, all us guys are sitting there waiting for this amazing piece of advice he is going to give.

He says to us, "Boys, the most important piece of advice I can give to you is this: if you know who you are and your mates know who you are, the rest can go and get f*cked!"

It's actually really powerful when you think about it. Sadly, the whole world is open to this now with social media - everyone is open to criticism. It's one of the things I hate about the world at the moment, people can just say anything publicly.

RELATIONSHIPS AND FAMILY

Who has been the most important role model in your life? Has there been someone who has led by example?

In 1993, I got selected to play for Australia to play five Test Matches against New Zealand. The Australian selectors were using this series to select the team for the upcoming Ashes Tour to England.

All my life, all I had ever wanted to do was go on an Ashes Tour but unfortunately the last of these tests I got a pair of ducks in both innings and didn't score a single run. I was devastated!

John Wright was the old warhorse opening batter for New Zealand who was a bit of a hippie, a little different, and it was his 100th Test match. He came up to me at the end of the game and we sat and talked over a beer and said to me, "I've been watching you, young fella, and you're trying way too hard. You need to learn how to relax and let go and let things flow. I can see you trying hard and fighting as a tough little bugger but that's not working for you. I would recommend that you learn Transcendental Meditation."

Well, I said, "What! What are you talking about? Transcendental what?"

He told me that he had learnt it and that he recommends that I give it a go, it might help me to relax and concentrate on the moment.

I didn't really think much about it.

I was then dropped for the Ashes Tour which at the time, I was completely devastated. Not long after, I was at home at my mom and dad's place, reading the newspaper and I opened it up to a page and saw this advert for Transcendental Meditation. I will never forget it and I don't normally believe in coincidences, so I rang the guy Derek, spoke to him and signed up.

I went and learnt how to do it and I have been meditating every day since 1993, so it's been a big part of my life.

In what ways have the women in your life influenced the man you have become?

My mom and dad used to be good cop vs bad cop. If I had a bad day dad would say, "Have you got your tail between your legs, son? Do I need to come over and kick your ass?"

My mom would get on and say, "Colin, leave him alone. Are you alright darling?"

She always had a beautiful soft touch.

I know my daughters love their dad, and I would never want to jeopardize that by doing something that upset that. It was always about making my mom and dad proud, now it's about making my wife and kids proud.

I met my wife when I was 14 years old, she gives me perspective, she's been there the whole way and she is a great barometer for me.

Another thing that I learnt was through the Fathering Project and it's really simple:

How I treat my wife is the most important gift I can give to my daughters. If I treat my wife with love and respect and kindness, that's how they will expect to be treated by the men in their life.

TYLER KNOTT GREGSON
POET AND PHOTOGRAPHER

 @tylerknott   @tylerknott

Tyler Knott Gregson is a poet, author and professional photographer based in Helena, Montana. Tyler has accrued fame as a poet on social media platforms such as Tumblr, Instagram and Twitter since 2009. He and his wife photograph weddings, elopements, travel, and lifestyle all over the world, and while home, he writes and posts a "Daily Haiku on Life," and a raw poem from his "Typewriter Series" every day.

Do you have a favorite quote or philosophy you live by?

"To me every hour of the light and dark is a miracle," by Walt Whitman.

As someone, somewhere on the Autism Spectrum, I've always seen the world a little bit differently, always seen little miracles in the mundane things, and reading this quote for the first time made me feel like maybe, just maybe, I wasn't doing it all wrong.

What is one personal quality that you are most proud of?

I am most proud of the love I give, without ever expecting to get anything in return. I love hard, and give whatever I have to give freely to those that wander into my life without expectation or preconceived notion, I just keep giving it out, even and

especially when those who receive it may not deserve it at the time they are getting it. Thoreau once said, "The only remedy for love is to love more," and that's something that's stuck with me for a long, long time. I am proud of how I love, and I am proud of just how wide that love can spread.

What are the issues - whether social, environmental, political or economic - that you feel are most pressing and for which you feel the greatest personal concern and responsibility?

So many issues are pressing, so many that demand our immediate attention and care. This planet is our home, and we're destroying it. If we don't start actively trying to reverse the damage we've done and put into place practices and promises that can prevent it from occurring again, we won't be around much longer.

This, I feel, is the most dominant and pressing issue, the one that must be attended to before all others can be fully addressed, for without this place, all the other issues fall away. On a similarly massive, but more tangible scale, there is still so much hatred, so much prejudice, racism, and fear that must be eradicated.

There is this burning fire in some to prove how different we all are, and how those differences, those fires need to be stoked and grown, and I cannot understand this. We are so nearly one thing, what hurts one of us hurts us all, and I wish more people saw this. I wish I knew the words to make people believe it, make people hold it as truth. I think that's why I keep writing, maybe one day I'll write the right words on the right day, to make some sort of change. Maybe.

Who inspires you?

So many people, in so many places, but I am noticing the longer I'm around, that they all share a single trait, and that is tenderness. The Dalai Lama, a man you're featuring in this very book, has always been a beacon of compassion, grace, and tenderness for me since discovering Buddhism at 12.

His living proof of how to remain not just empathetic and kind in the face of adversity, but joyful despite it, has inspired me in a way I cannot articulate.

On a personal level, my wife, Sarah Linden Gregson, has inspired me in ways I'll never be able to repay her for. Her grace, her daily kindness to everyone she meets, her tenderness in the face of more struggle than anyone should have to endure, have shown me what it is to be human, what it is to be alive, and how valuable both of those things truly are. If you are lucky enough to know her, you'll understand this.

LIFE PURPOSE AND SUCCESS

What do you ultimately strive for? What is your mission in life?

To live a life I can honestly say I did my best for, to give out every drop of love and compassion I have inside me, to leave every person I meet feeling better than when I found them, to take care of every creature in every place I go, to suck as much joy and adventure out of every minute as I possibly can, to swim in every sea I find, to push myself to be better each morning than the day before, to laugh more and cry more and hope more and hate less and complain less and worry less.

To live and say exactly what I mean, always, without need for lie or pretense, without excuse or veil, and to keep trying all I know to write it as I see it, photograph it as it wishes to be, and put out whatever art I end up making, in case someone, somewhere, happens to need it.

How do you define success? At what point did you identify as being "successful"?

I still don't know if I am, as it may sound cliché and trite, but I think success is more about the journey than the destination. I don't think success is something I'll ever arrive at, but something I'll just hopefully feel along the way.

If I close my eyes each night knowing I did my best, I feel successful. If I gave what I had and truthfully expected nothing in return, I feel successful. If I said what I have to say honestly, and for no other reason than to say it as truth, I feel successful. I don't think books sold or money made, or items checked off a bucket list are indicators to this, I think it's something personal and inherent and different for every single person.

What do you think was your main quality that led you to your success?

I absolutely, positively, NEVER give up on something I believe in. I believe in hope, and I believe it's such a vital force. If you have hope, you can do anything. There were so many times I could have given up on so many different things in my life, but hope kept me going forward. Everything I have and am today, I owe to that strange little ember of hope that kept the fire from dying out completely. Hope, it's worth it, always.

What makes you feel fulfilled and energized?

Exercise, adventure, the outdoors, and the pushing of yourself beyond the point you thought you'd break. I think if you don't push yourself beyond your preconceived breaking point, you'll never be able to grow.

"It's BECAUSE of my strange brain and the way it handles the life I live, that I am able to write poetry, that I am able to photograph the world in a different way than someone else. I create the things I create BECAUSE of where I am on the Autism Spectrum, BECAUSE of the overstimulation of my senses."

We have to break ourselves down in order to build back stronger, and I think exercise, adventure, and discovery are such vital ways to do it. Get out, explore, find new places, new people, new cultures, and you'll never feel more alive. There is a time for rest and stillness, and there is a time for motion and travel, and I think finding that sweet spot of balance is so energizing.

How important is collaboration and teamwork to achieving success?

On a professional level, with my writing I work entirely alone 99.9% of the time. In that world, the need for teamwork and collaboration is most generally minimized.

With my photography business, I work with only my wife, and so our collaboration and teamwork are somewhat of a forgone conclusion we take for granted after a decade of orbiting one another as we work. Saying this, I believe the ability to work with others, to empathize and strategize with others, is a fundamental skill that helps drive so much productivity and creativity.

The ability to absorb ideas and inspiration from those around you opens so many doors, and so in that way, I feel as though I am collaborating with people all day, every day. It doesn't have to be traditionally defined as collaboration or teamwork to send out the same benefits.

OVERCOMING CHALLENGES

Have there been any key challenges that you have had to face in your life? How have you faced them?

Living as someone on the Autism Spectrum has presented me with, quite literally, a lifetime of challenges. School was a challenge as I have always learned in very non-traditional ways in an environment and time that didn't recognize and appreciate those ways.

So many of the tallest hurdles I have faced have come in the strange ways my brain absorbs information from my senses, the way the environments I am in can influence that information, and the way that it all changes my reactions to the events, times, and places in my life.

Every moment, every situation, is a new challenge for me, and it's something that people who do not share my mental state can often not understand or appreciate.

I live in a world that feels like 10,000 radios tuned to 10,000 stations at all times, so simply getting through a day can be rough, but I have faced them all in the only way I have ever known how, forward and filled with hope. I always assume someone, somewhere, has it a lot tougher than I do, and so I should feel pretty damn lucky for the life I was given.

How has failure, or apparent failure, set you up for later success? Do you have a "favorite failure" of yours?

Every day I fail in some way, and every challenge I face as I mentioned above, are the exact things I credit for every single drop of creativity I have inside me.

It's BECAUSE of my strange brain and the way it handles the life I live, that I am able to write poetry, that I am able to photograph the world in a different way than someone else. I create the things I create BECAUSE of where I am on the Autism Spectrum, BECAUSE of the overstimulation of my senses.

I quite literally am who I am not despite the challenges I face, but because of them, and to be frank, I wouldn't change a single thing.

EMOTIONS

What makes you truly happy?

Simplicity. I am so drawn to a simple life, to being away from the things of man, to disappearing into the quiet. We live on a mountainside and forget to go into town too often, we choose travel destinations far off the beaten path, we go during the off-seasons, we walk into the woods, swim in the seas, and sit out and revel in the silences.

I am so happy when things are simple, when I have exactly what is needed and nothing more, no excess, no surplus. I am happiest when I am around people who feel the same, who allow for the quirks and oddities and celebrate them as you do. I am truly happy when I am making others feel the same.

How do you express anger? What do you do to release frustration?

I think I'm a strange blend of human sometimes. As a follower of Buddhism for 27 years, with Viking, Scottish, and Irish blood flowing in my veins, there is a clear and certain juxtaposition that takes place. I feel anger from time to time, it flashes up hot and confusing, but it never manifests itself in violence or a lashing out.

I will stand up for what I believe, and I will stand up for those I love fiercely and feverishly, but it takes so very much to make me truly angry. I think of the few times I have ever been truly and unmistakably angry, and it was only in response to some kind of hatred, cruelty, or unkindness being shown to someone else. On small scales, when I do feel frustration or anger bubbling up, I tend to exercise, to sweat out the negativity, or use deep breathing and quiet,

eyes-closed meditation, to bring myself back to a stable and centered point.

What does strength look like to you?

Strength to me has always been tenderness. It takes so much more strength, in my opinion, to be tender and graceful than it takes to be abrasive and rough. It takes strength to cut across the grain of what makes someone a "real" man or woman, and to be kind, and compassionate.

Strength to me is the pushing forward with hope, when all else around you says it's impossible, it's the refusal to respond to unkindness and cruelty with the same, it's the act of forgiveness for those who never earned it. Strength is giving out the love and kindness and compassion, even though you know for fact, it will never be returned the same way.

What does vulnerability mean to you?

To me, vulnerability is the ability to open yourself up to the world despite the fact that you're afraid to do so. Opening without fear is not vulnerability to me, it is not courage if you're not afraid. Vulnerability is opening, always, knowing that the simple act of doing so can always lead to ridicule or exclusion. Vulnerability is choosing tenderness when everything in you wants to show ferocity.

How do you deal with conflict and diffusing difficult situations?

By trying my very best to put myself into their shoes. Everyone you meet is facing their own battles, their own long and curving path they took to get to where they are right then, at that moment of conflict, and if we don't understand and

appreciate that, we'll never get anywhere. It's so easy to apply our own points of view onto everyone we interact with, forgetting that they have their own history that has shaped them into the people they are that day.

Once you jump into their skin, as Atticus Finch more eloquently put it, you realize that there was often innocence where we once saw malice, or indifference.

I find that people struggle to keep a fight going when you're seeing their side as well. Sometimes, however, you have to fight, and fight, and not back down when you are passionate and confident that what you're fighting for is the right thing to be fighting for. Life is all about deciding which moments are which, and that's something I'm still trying really hard to learn.

Do you talk with anyone, or have a group of friends you can talk to, about how you feel when things are happening in your life, or do you keep these thoughts internalized?

Both. I have no filter, I never have, and I never will, a side-effect of the way my brain works, so if I'm feeling it, chances are I am saying it, and saying it exactly when I'm feeling it. So many things, however, are internalized and then leaked out in the form of poetry and art, and that becomes the therapy I need to feel better.

Poetry as pressure release, and truth told, that's the reason I began writing in the first place. I am lucky to have a wonderful wife, a wonderful family, and a very small group of friends that I can count on with, literally, my life. I tend to not share a lot about what I'm going through, but having the knowledge that you always can, changes everything.

SPIRITUALITY AND MINDFULNESS

What role does religion or spirituality play for you?

I found Buddhism when I was 12-years-old, and for me, it rewired me in a million different ways. The lessons in mindfulness, compassion, empathy and love for all living things, and kindness were, and continue to be, shaping forces. The way I see the world, the peace I feel inside, the calm I can grant myself even in turbulent times, are all things I learned from Buddhism, from stunning human beings like the Dalai Lama, and I am forever grateful for that. I would not be who I am today, had I have never found such a fantastic spiritual system.

What do you do to relax and connect with your inner self?

As I said before, I chase a simple life. I chase light all over the planet, I exercise, I drink lots of tea, I listen to lots of music, I create lots of art. By setting my aim at these things, things slow, things calm, and I can see the way forward.

RELATIONSHIPS AND FAMILY

Who has been the most important role model in your life? Has there been someone who has led by example?

Without a doubt, my family.

My wife, for showing me how big life is, how vital it is to get out into the world and see it, to show yourself to it; for showing me how there's never too much kindness to give.

My father, for showing me what perseverance is, what dedication looks like even when it hurts.

My mother, for showing me what strength is, for her ability to endure and absorb and still care with such tenderness.

My sisters for showing me what friendship and family bonds can truly mean.

The few friends I call brothers and sisters, for showing me how rare true connection is.

Every person I love, truly love, shapes me into the human being I am, and I am so beyond lucky to love every single one of them.

In what ways have the women in your life influenced the man you have become?

Without a shadow of a doubt, it's the women in my life, above and beyond all others, that have shown me what it is to be a man. What it is to be a human. How there is no real definition of a real man, at all, that it's always been about what it is to be a real human being on this planet.

It's the women who have defined strength to me, the women that have shown me what compassion should look like, the women that have taught me of patience, of endurance, of grace.

I am who I am because of the women who have loved me, have allowed me to love them, and allowed me to learn from them. I would not be a whisper of a shadow of this, were it not for them. Thank you, to all of them. I so hope you know who you are.

PAUL ROOS

FOOTBALL CHAMPION AND COACH

 @paulroos1    @paulroos1

An imposing key position player, Paul Roos enjoyed a spectacularly successful 17-season career at the top level of the Australian Football League.

During the course of his career, he picked up numerous trophies and accolades including five best and fairest awards, and All Australian captain.

In 2002, Paul became the senior coach of the Sydney Swans Football Club, leading them to a Premiership in 2005, the first the club had won in 72 years.

Paul has since been the coach of the Melbourne Demons Football Club, a performance and management consultant, a media personality and keynote speaker.

Do you have a favorite quote or philosophy you live by?

A lot of people can talk the talk, but can't walk the walk. Particularly being in the football space, and now the corporate space, there are a lot of quotes and a lot of philosophies, but the ability to live your doctrine and walk the walk is something I live by as much as I possibly can.

What is one personal quality that you are most proud of?

It's not so much a characteristic but the connection to family – that's really important to me. Being a father, a husband – the amount of time we spend together and the amount of effort we put in as a family. The most pleasing thing for me at this stage, with all the work I've done, playing football and coaching, is still the ability to spend a lot of time with my family.

EMOTIONS

What makes you truly happy?

I am happiest when I am around family. When the kids get older, we celebrate a lot of success through the kid's success. If they finish school, get a new job – that's

what makes me truly happy. When my wife, Tami, or my boys do something I'm proud of, that's when I'm the happiest.

How do you express anger? What do you do to release frustration?

I don't tolerate things as much as I get older. I extricate myself from situations rather than argue... I let it go as quickly as possible and withdraw from the anger, rather than confront the anger.

I meditate pretty much every day and through that practice, other people say I am very calm and controlled and have an ability to handle most situations. That's been my release for the past 20 years since I started. If I do get angry, I go for a walk or get out of that situation.

Making decisions when you're angry is a really bad idea.

What does strength look like to you?

For me, strength is being consultative. Strength in leadership and strength in adversity is including people in decisions. That's real strength – when you're faced with a difficult situation, that you don't feel like you have to do it yourself.

Strength is in bringing people together and confronting decisions together rather than individually. Whatever that situation might be – a family situation, a work situation – the ability to bring people together and make decisions based on collective discussion is what strength looks like to me.

What does vulnerability mean to you?

Vulnerability, for me, is about showing yourself – not this mask that we often have as a leader. It brings people together but it also helps manage and understand people. Don't be afraid to let people see who you are. It's all about who you are and showing up as yourself.

Do you talk with anyone about how you feel when things are happening in your life, or do you keep these thoughts internalized?

It depends what they are. Still, men in general – and I'll generalize here – probably one of the biggest problems we have is internalizing things. We're not as good as women are at externalizing.

So, it's yes and no – some things I'll talk about, some things I won't.

I still think we incorrectly see strength in dealing with things ourselves – that's a stereotype that is gradually diminishing but it's still there. It's part of who we are as men and it's something we need to look at.

I was really lucky – you take for granted being in a football environment, there's a lot of opportunities to connect.

A lot of my friends are from that era and we connect because we grew up together. There's a bit of a lack of connection for men in the corporate space. Creating a space for men in the corporate space is something I'm passionate about because I saw the value of it in the football club.

I saw a lot of problems solved because, even though we weren't great at it, there was always someone to talk to – either driving home or sitting in a plane going to an away game.

Even in the 1980s, there was a huge connection between the players. Unfortunately, a lot of people don't get that connection, so it's something I want to try to create.

LIFE PURPOSE AND SUCCESS

What do you ultimately strive for? What is your mission in life?

I think about that a lot – Tami asks me that all the time. I think the closer you get to dying, the more you think about what your life purpose is. There's no question about that, and you think to start about "What have I achieved?' and now "How can I help people learn from what I've done?"

I acknowledge I've been really fortunate in the life I've had – when I think about the question, it's about how do I help people through the lessons I've learnt to enjoy a better life? How can I impact as many people and share my experiences with them?

For me, it's stripping back people's lives to really simplify things. One of the things that frustrates me is "work-life balance". What is work-life balance? It's your life – it's not like I go to work and then I come home, and I walk through a vortex of one life to another. It's "life balance" or "life imbalance".

How do you define success? At what point did you identify as being "successful"?

It's really fascinating – you can't put an old head on young shoulders.

When you're a kid and start playing football, you think, "If I play 300 games and win 5 best and fairests, then I'll be successful." When you get to that point, you're proud of what you do, but then you start asking yourself, "What is real success?"

Real success is being happy in what you're doing, having a positive impact on your family, on your friends and your community. Living a life that matters – that's the definition of success.

OVERCOMING CHALLENGES

Have there been any key challenges that you have had to face in your life? How have you faced them?

Challenges great and small... everyone has them. I think there is an awareness that they are going to have them - if you understand that, then you're more able to cope with them.

If you think your life is going to be easy for 365 days of the year, you're kidding yourself. I think there is a certain expectation that challenges are going to come and they're going to go. If you understand that fundamentally and behave true to yourself, they go quicker. But you have to understand that they're going to be there. You've also got to understand that it's not always going to be bad – it's going to be okay again. That's the main philosophy.

When Dad passed away a few years ago, I was still able to think - as hard as the emotion was – what was the practical thing I could do? As hard as it is, try to separate the practical and the emotional.

I couldn't be with Dad when he died due to circumstances – but I was really proud of the way I could acknowledge his passing. Looking back on it, I don't regret it – if I hadn't been as clinical and analytical as well as emotional, I would have been sitting here now, wishing I had been.

That's the biggest piece of advice – there has to be some sort of analytics during your most difficult time for you to get through it as quickly as you possibly can.

And to be able to look back on it, and not regret your behavior.

How has failure, or apparent failure, set you up for later success? Do you have a "favorite failure" of yours?

A lot of failures for me have been around sport – sport is so public – everyone shares in your joys and everyone shares in your successes and failures. I think it helps define you as a person.

Winning the 2005 Grand Final then losing it in 2006... I was the same person after both. I think in the moment, it's understanding what you can control and what you can't control and despite your failures, you are fundamentally the same person that enjoyed your successes.

Experiencing highs and lows are the reality of sport – everyone knows you've had them, and everyone can see what your response is, so treating 2005 and 2006 with the same humility, or pride or dignity, or whatever you want to call it – that's probably more important than isolating success or failure as dramatically different.

I don't think they're dramatically different - you're the same person when they occur, but it's your ability to deal with both and learn from them.

LEADERSHIP AND PERFORMANCE

You came to coach the Sydney Football Club after they had gone 72 years without winning a flag. How did you turn it around to the club winning a Premiership in three years?

Coming into it, the players were aware of the 72 years without winning a

premiership – so my role was identifying the process that was going to break it. If you focus too much on the 72 years, then it becomes too much of a burden. Embracing it is really important. After 72 years, we've got an opportunity, but this is how we're going to have to do it.

There's an interesting example of pragmatism, called the Stockdale Paradox. James Stockdale spent seven years in a POW camp in Vietnam and he attributes his survival to his ability to blend hard pragmatism with an unwavering hope for the future. He wasn't pessimistic, but he would address the situation with brutal facts – he knew he would be tortured, so he had to mentally prepare for that; he knew he had to try to eat as much as he could; and he knew that his focus on surviving each day was critical. The other soldiers who were optimistic would say, "I'll be out next week," and when that didn't happen, they would get depressed.

So, I look at the brutal facts. For the players it means, how can you be your best? Don't drink, don't smoke, don't take drugs, don't be an idiot, and focus on your performance. It's not really that much pressure – it's not like you're operating on someone's brain or putting a man on the moon.

You've said in the past that meditation and visualization played a critical role in winning the Premiership. Can you talk about the impact that had?

When I took over coaching at the Sydney Football Club, a big part of what we did was about empowering players and getting them to think above the shoulders, rather than just below the shoulders through weights and running and skills.

They weren't the most skilled team – and I credit the meditation program, which I ran with Tami, as being a key part of the club winning the Grand Final in 2005.

The ability to bring that into the football club, and for the medical staff, the fitness staff and the senior players to embrace it, was terrific.

There were only minimal gains to be made in the team by doing more running or more weights, but the maximum gain was going to be made through mental improvements. The players who did the meditation and mindfulness program fully embraced it; they genuinely knew the value of it, and they genuinely wanted to be great.

People think when it comes to great athletes, "Oh he was lucky" or "She was naturally talented."

Yes, some of it comes down to talent, but greatness is a choice. When I say greatness, it might not mean getting to the heights of Michael Jordan, but greatness for you is getting the maximum out of yourself.

The Sydney Football Club was committed to greatness in that period.

We also saw incredible improvement in performance through visualization and meditation at the Melbourne Football Club. The ability by the players to take these tools and transition them into action was terrific. We would always meditate before the main training session – Tami was a real pioneer in coming into a football club and implementing mindfulness practices.

It was interesting, some of the players who were a bit more cynical at the start were the ones that got the most out of the program and they became very aware of how it was helping them.

I always just talk about it as clearing the mind and refocusing and the ability to make decisions under pressure. We called it "re-setting" and that was a term Tami brought in. If you've made a mistake, or done something wrong, just re-set. Sometimes, the players would make a mistake and carry it for the rest of the game, and it would negatively impact their performance. It made a huge difference in terms of the number of games we won over a relatively short period of time.

AFL players are regarded as some of the most elite athletes in the world. What makes a top AFL player?

It's interesting, we've done some study on the top draft picks over five years, and – unequivocally – the number one reason players are successful is character. It's really frustrating watching really talented athletes never fulfil their potential – and it always comes down to character; it's about desire, it's about want.

I've spent time researching performance in the US with the Denver Broncos, Chicago Bulls, the 49ers, and the Chicago Bears, and those teams are the same – they said to me, "If we had to choose between two players and there's a marginal difference in athleticism, we will go with character, all the time."

What does character look like? It comes down to, "Am I going to maximize my ability? Am I going to turn up every day and be better than the day before?"

If you've got a talented player who is driven, the sky's the limit.

Self-awareness is really important. If you don't know where you're at, it's hard to know where you can get to.

Who is a man, from any period, that embodies real leadership for you?

I was a keen student of Phil Jackson's and read his books and was really fascinated by his balance of meditation and the way he taught his players. I really enjoyed watching *The Last Dance*. Phil managed all his players individually, which was critically important, and he was a pioneer of mindful management. People don't realize that the Bulls couldn't win anything before Phil got there, as much as Michael Jordan is one of the top two or three greatest athletes of all time. Without Phil, they probably wouldn't have created their legacy.

There's a really key piece in one of the books I read about Phil, where he sat Michael down, and said, "Your challenge is now to make everyone else better. If you make everyone else better, you will win championships and people will think you're better." It was a really interesting way of changing someone's mentality.

Steve Kerr now is probably a disciple of Phil Jackson, and the way he conducts himself is great.

BEING A MAN

What does "being a man" mean to you?

That's a great question. I'm in my 50s now and you consider yourself a man at 18 or 19 – and it's changed dramatically since then. It's probably a harder definition now than what it's ever been. When I watched Dad when I was growing up, going to work every day and coming home and having dinner and being president of the local footy club or tennis club, it was really quite defined. A bit stoic and a bit emotionless.

Being a man now is a bit more real and diverse. It's a lot harder to define.

What are the characteristics you want to live by? Whether you're a man or a woman, I think that's the main thing. Being honest, hard-working and true to your values.

Have your concepts of masculinity/being a man changed over time? Is it significantly different from when you were a teen?

I guess I am fortunate to have been involved in a football club – player welfare has been at the forefront of football clubs. They're somewhat leaders in the notion of what a "real man" is. It's changed dramatically – the focus is on human behavior and what the emotion is at the time and being able to explore that emotion and let it out, rather than the old notion of the guy doesn't cry, the guy doesn't show vulnerability. We now look at human behavior and welfare.

The notion that men don't cry; men don't show emotion – it's not something I'm great at – but it's no longer a stereotype. Men as the breadwinner was a stereotype when I was growing up – that's obviously changed now and is completely inaccurate. The notion of men being the leaders, by extension, is also a stereotype that is no longer relevant.

Most of the stereotypes no longer exist, to be perfectly frank.

RELATIONSHIPS AND FAMILY

Who has been the most important role model in your life? Has there been someone who has led by example?

My mom and dad when I was growing up – they split up when I was 19 or 20, which is something that happens, but I think that a really stable, sporty family was important to me. If we didn't have the lifestyle we had, I wouldn't have been able to do the things that I did.

I look at my parents – they both played tennis and were really active and involved in the tennis club and the community.

Mom would take us to training, and Dad would be there on the weekends and be the team manager... seeing them encouraging us was so important. My son asked me recently if I had a choice, what era would I grow up in? The answer is the era I just grew up in – we were really lucky being outside all the time, with parks and creeks and orchards. That era was just wonderful to grow up in.

I was incredibly fortunate to be surrounded by amazing people when I first started AFL football – being exposed as a 17-year-old to these great people shaped me.

The smartest thing I did was watch and learn and listen, and just try to emulate some of the things they did. That's the biggest thing when I look over my life - those guys had such an enormous impact from the moment I walked in.

Is being a father an important part of your sense of manhood? Has fatherhood changed you?

I always saw having kids as a massive responsibility. It was life-changing, as it is for everyone.

Once it happened, everything was based around my wife and kids – everything we did, we did together... travelling and coaching. It was a huge responsibility – it still is. As they get older, it's how much do you parent, and how much do you pull away and what advice do you give?

I take it incredibly seriously... you've got to be dedicated to it 24 hours a day, 7 days a week. You can't switch being a father off – it's a lifelong commitment that I really enjoy.

How do your family commitments influence your professional life?

What is your job and how can you combine your family and have them part of it?

I don't think you can have a job that is separate – having been a coach, seeing the kids in the rooms after the game and having them sing the team song. That was important. Having breakfast every week with the boys, dropping them off to school. It's about routines and having a connection between the two. If you're trying to separate work and family, it creates more issues.

The boys weren't really happy with me when I started coaching, then by the time I finished, they didn't want me to stop, so we must have got something right in that period because they just enjoyed it so much.

It's different for everyone but your ability to combine your work with your family is extremely important.

ROBBIE MADDISON

FREESTYLE MOTOCROSS RIDER

 @robbiemaddison   @robbiemaddison

Freestyle motocross rider Robbie Maddison has built a career on world records, triumphs against adversity, and mind-boggling daredevil jumps.

Robbie has broken distance records launching over a football field on live television on ESPN. He's soared over the San Diego bay alongside snowmobiler Levi LaValle. He's jumped across an open Tower Bridge in London, incorporating a backflip for good measure. Throughout it all, Robbie has somehow found time to earn medals at X Games and Red Bull X-Fighters.

Then, in 2015, after several years of planning and preparation, he surfed his dirt bike on the legendary Tahitian wave, Teahupo'o. "My goals are to transform what is perceived to be the norm," Robbie says. "I want to take things to new heights and push boundaries."

That boundary-pushing achievement in French Polynesia saw him combine his two major passions – stunt riding and surfing – into his ground-breaking DC Pipe Dream. He'd already conquered riding on land and through the air, but this project involved maneuvering his bike on the waves of the ocean. Yes, he actually managed to ride on water.

Do you have a favorite quote or philosophy you live by?

Face your fears, live your dreams.

What is one characteristic that you are most proud of?

Being a man of my word.

What are the issues - whether social, environmental, political or economic - that you feel are most pressing and for which you feel the greatest personal concern and responsibility?

Mental health, emotional psychology and people's general well-being. I have experienced the highest of highs and

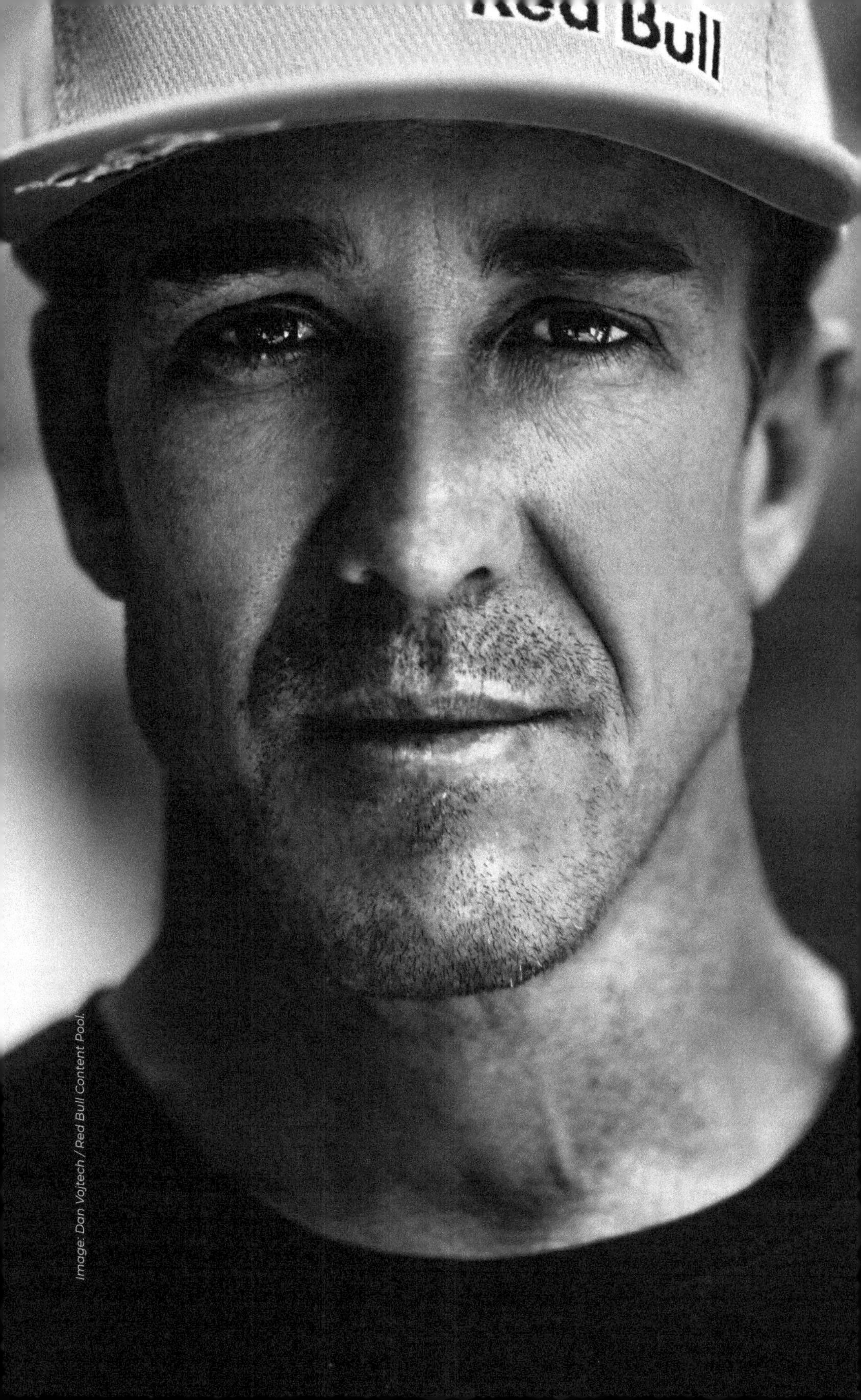

Image: Dan Vojtech / Red Bull Content Pool.

extreme lows, multiple traumatic head injuries have played a huge role in my mental health as well as a viral meningitis infection in my teens that caused brain swelling and stroke-like symptoms that lasted for a long time and took years to fully recover from.

I like to spread awareness on NAD+IV therapy, it literally restored my well-being and eliminated my depression, it restores normal brain function from issues like head injuries which I experienced as well as people who are drug dependent it can erase all cravings and reset the brain's receptors. If anyone is struggling with or you know someone with mental health struggles, please have them look into NAD+IV therapy.

Who inspires you?

Almost everyone at the top of their chosen fields that I become aware of, I appreciate those that grind and push boundaries, who raise the bar of what's possible, from sports, to medicine, discovery, health, psychology and inventors. I'm a man of many interests, I'm fascinated by a lot of things people would generally think I wouldn't have the slightest interest in.

BEING A MAN

What does "being a man" mean to you?

A mature male that has learnt the true values of life and displays them through their actions and words. Being a provider for a family helps in this wisdom, but also exhibiting the traits of being the rock in the family, to one's children, a loyal honest spouse, a gentleman, the more remarkable the person, the more of "a man" he is in my opinion.

Have your concepts of masculinity/ being a man changed over time?

Yeah, for sure. As a kid I looked at all males with facial hair and of age as men, but as I have grown up, I believe being a real man is displaying a certain nature, wisdom and awareness.

Not being a pig but being a gentleman is the type I call a man, those that refrain from conflict yet are willing to remain calm and communicate to reach a peaceful outcome. It's a rare trait, my observation sees so many people quick to get hot headed or not open to the notion of non-confrontational communication.

Walking away is a way of dissolving an issue, but by remaining calm and open to fully dissolve an issue and be apologetic is what a real man in my opinion should do. Walking away and leaving unresolved issues on the table is gutless and toxic for both parties who are having a dispute or not seeing eye to eye.

What qualities are most important to you as a man? Why are they important?

All of your traits are important, the best man exhibits them all, but I feel a great start is to be responsible, honest, courageous, forgiving, loving and kind.

If there was a single piece of advice that you could give every young person in this world, what would it be?

Take on the biggest challenge you can set for yourself, for here you will find the most growth, to become successful you will have to master all the traits and learn all the lessons.

EMOTIONS

What makes you truly happy?

When I feel great inside and I'm mindful enough to appreciate all the beauty around me.

What does strength look like to you?

Strength is both physical and emotional.

Some of the people with the biggest muscles or leanest bodies have the most troubled emotions and are suffering the most.

They are not strong with their words or actions and often try hard to portray an image that they have it all together and avoid those who are onto their issues that most are reluctant to admit or even have a desire to understand and resolve.

What does vulnerability mean to you?

I would say this is someone who is in a position of moving towards a negative situation, it can obviously happen in an almost exponential number of different scenarios.

How do you express anger? What do you do to release frustration?

I try to resolve the issue that has created it, rather than dwelling on it which will only make matters worse.

Sometimes it's best to let the issue play its course but often I set my intentions to a peaceful resolution. Sometimes I find it best to participate in an intense physical activity or a decent exercise, like a surf, or a mountain bike ride or simply tear it up on my motorcycle to release endorphins which help create happiness.

Then I'm in a better, more reasonable state of mind to deal with the issue in a self-controlled manner.

But it's not often these days I get angry, I have let go of all my emotional trauma I have compounded over the years, so most of the time I'm in a situation that would entice most to get angry I simply just focus on the positive of the situation and try to look for the most effective way of resolving the issue.

I don't feel I suffer from an ego and I have worked on and overcome my emotional psychological issues I had from my past experiences.

I have been on a path of self-help and understanding for over 15 years now so what's an easy daily practice for me to avoid a rise in anger and lose control of my temper these days is not a reality to someone who is suffering from their own issues or unrealized areas they need growth in.

How do you deal with conflict and diffusing difficult situations?

This is something I can usually sort out quite quickly just by addressing the situation and using the tools of understanding and compassion, I'm able to accept blame for any situation I have had a hand in, and I take on and accept the other party's observations they make of their perspective.

However, I recently had to stand up for myself against one of the people in my life I love and want to respect the most, who I believe has a real and complicated emotional state.

This situation is painful for me because they are refusing to communicate with me after I was honest to them about my concerns of their behavior. I asked for an opportunity to sit together and have a peaceful, transparent discussion.

This request was not responded to. So, in this situation you have to be able to let go of what you're not in control of. It's painful to know the other party is suffering, but you can only do your best and that you have to be satisfied with.

Do you talk with anyone about how you feel when things are happening in your life, or do you keep these thoughts internalized?

I used to keep them internalized, it's not healthy if you do this and try to keep moving on with a smile. It's hard to talk to your friends because quite frankly not many of them are your real friends that actually would make time for you and even offer to listen or ask how you're doing. If you have some that would, confide in them.

"I speak with my wife daily, it's very nourishing not only for both of us but also our bond and relationship. It's hard at times to talk to your wife or partner about these things. But in my experience, if you avoid this, your relationship can suffer."

I speak with my wife daily, it's very nourishing not only for both of us but also our bond and relationship. It's hard at times to talk to your wife or partner about these things. But in my experience, if you avoid this, your relationship can suffer.

A great practice though is learning the art of mindfulness and meditation, letting go of the internal chatter that you allow to play out in your head is toxic. Set your intentions for the goals you're chasing, smile and don't take things so seriously. Let go of the mental chatter and try to stay "in the moment" aware of the breath in and out, don't let the mind wander in a negative way, because whatever you think you create. So - think positively!

SPIRITUALITY AND MINDFULNESS

What role does religion or spirituality play for you?

It's a big part, I'm not so religious, after what the Catholic priests have shown us they are capable of and the corruption I have noticed.

Yet I'm a big fan of Buddhism and I practice mindfulness, meditation and good health. I'm always reading and progressing on my own spiritual journey. But you won't see me at a bible study group or sitting in church on a Sunday, I don't think you have to go to church to read a Bible, I like to be open minded, but meditating is my source of mental recalibration and it's a path I'm still learning in.

What pastime or practice enables you to connect with your inner self?

I started with guided meditations, then I

went onto falling in love with breathing exercises to lower my internal frequency, after getting super relaxed and mentally doing a full body scan and turning off all my muscles. If I don't fall asleep, I then try to keep my mind still, I focus on my vision of paradise and my mind as a calm flat ocean. When your mind is still, life is sweet, you are your thoughts.

I lay flat on my back, usually with a pillow under my head and I do a series of breathing techniques to lower my heart rate, I then do the body scan from head to toe turning all my muscles off and telling them in groups that they are as heavy as lead and each breath they will continue to relax more and more. It's self-hypnosis.

Once I'm on the brink of an out-of-body experience I just chill and appreciate the peaceful state I'm in. It's something that if you do this every day and stay mindful of positive thoughts coupled with healthy consumption, you will be on the right path.

LIFE PURPOSE AND SUCCESS

What do you ultimately strive for? What is your mission in life?

To make my dreams I had as a child and along the way a reality, to also be content, happy, have healthy balanced relationships and to be respected, loved and appreciated.

How do you define success? At what point did you identify as being "successful"?

It took me a while, I had multiple world records and was still an emotionally broken fragment of a man, I felt successful once I conquered my emotions and state of mind.

What makes you feel fulfilled and energized?

When I take the time to reflect and have some self-reassurance, everyone is worthy of this, no matter where you're at, never compare yourself to anyone else - that is your ego at work.

Embrace all that you are, love yourself, you're at the perfect place at the perfect time for the perfect reason, have faith in your journey and enjoy the highs and lows, don't let the wheels fall off and keep your flag at full mast!

Your thoughts and judgments are just from your current perspective, if you don't like how you perceive a situation try to address it from a different perspective and see if you can look at the same situation and feel differently about it. The cup isn't half-empty, it's half-full type of scenarios.

OVERCOMING CHALLENGES

Have there been any key challenges that you have had to face in your life?

I think my most meaningful one was realizing my dream to ride a wave on my motorcycle. I have faced my challenges with an open mind, I have never not listened or considered anyone's opinions.

How has failure, or apparent failure, set you up for later success? Do you have a "favorite failure" of yours?

Most of my failures have resulted in broken bones or a near-death experience so none of them are jumping out at me as a "favorite failure" but they are all hard lessons learnt and this course has taught me that your failures are due to you getting part of the practice wrong, whether it be technique or timing, as in my case, or a missed step or mistake in order of operations. Regardless of the reason why the failure happened, it's really an opportunity to learn, understand and be better prepared the next time you shoot for success!

What's one of the hardest decisions you've faced?

To leave Australia and move to the USA, I hate leaving Oz every time I'm back, but it's been 15 years now.

My relationships have suffered, my family has suffered and ultimately, I have suffered from it too.

It's been very tough from one perspective, but from a positive one it taught me to "be a man," I don't rely on anyone, I'm self-made from 16 years old, I mortgaged my house I bought when I was 18 when I turned 23 and funded my own career.

I have survived with the incredible support of my wife Amy, and I have been energized every second of it for the fact I was doing life my way, following my dreams, creating my future, dreaming up new ideas and making them happen.

It's been hard work, it's been dangerous, but it's literally been a dream come true, and I wouldn't know any of this without this decision I made.

You have to be willing to make sacrifices at times, you can't have the cake and eat it too.

Think about that and what you really want in life the next time you feel pressured to do anything that's not productive to you and your goals or wellbeing.

RELATIONSHIPS AND FAMILY

Who has been the most important role model in your life?

I'd say my parents, my dad instilled my work ethic and taught me to never give up, my mom taught me to be loving and forgiving, the balance undoubtedly made me who I am.

Has there been someone who has led by example?

Not so much, but it's something I wanted as a personal trait because I was taught of the importance of it, so I have tried to be exactly that.

In what ways have the women in your life influenced the man you have become?

In my opinion women are more inclined to voice their opinion and face an issue rather than walk away from it, those women that have pulled me into line have resonated with me. I don't like to upset people and I hold a big responsibility to myself to be respectful. The women in my life have taught me how to treat them so I appreciate them all, mainly my mom, sister, and wife but also many friends along the way from school to work, socially and professionally.

Is being a father an important part of your sense of manhood? Has fatherhood changed you?

Being a father has changed me profoundly. I'm not as selfish with my time or my actions, it's important to me not to be aggressive to my kids when disciplining them, I don't hit my kids because I have learnt that behavior is unacceptable.

I have learnt to isolate them when I really want to make a point, no access to their favorite materialistic devices and a good stint in the bedroom with the door closed and no TV has worked great for us.

My kids are so well behaved we are complimented daily by outsiders observing their behaviors and traits. If they are playing up there is no yelling and shouting, just a "How would you like to be isolated right now?" and the energy shift is immediate. I'm glad I learnt this through my own short falls, we have a great family bond.

"I had multiple world records and was still an emotionally broken fragment of a man. I felt successful once I conquered my emotions and state of mind."

What advice would you want to pass onto your children?

To always strive to be their best, never quit, have fun, be kind, and keep a healthy mind with positive thoughts... Hopefully I'll be right by their sides guiding them all the way.

How do your family commitments influence your professional life?

We roll together most of the time, they are my life.

We home-school the kids so when they have commitments or want to do certain things, I'm generally able to be flexible and make it happen.

If they went to a traditional school, we would never see each other, and our family wouldn't work. So, I feel blessed we home-school the boys, my wife is a trooper for all she takes on, we all travel together as much as possible.

It's a real treat to be able to give them real life experience and educate them with travel and experiences around the globe as a family.

RICHIE HARDCORE

MUAY THAI CHAMPION AND SOCIAL CAMPAIGNER

 @richiehardcore   @richiehardcore

Richie is an educator, keynote speaker and activist, working in violence prevention, masculinity, mental health and wellness. He is also a retired New Zealand Muay Thai champion and now works as a coach and personal trainer, having helped some of New Zealand's most successful fighters achieve their goals.

You're a heavily tattooed fighter by profession who talks about the experience of masculinity. But when you speak, it's a heartfelt message with a lot of empathy and compassion, it's a really emotional perspective. How does it work?

My full legal name is Richard Hardcore Steward – but no one ever calls me that, just Richie Hardcore. Hardcore is a style of music that originated in New York City out of the punk rock scene, and I fell in love with hardcore as a late teen – I ran a radio show here in Auckland called Viva la Hardcore, that was my first public platform, and I was obsessed with the music.

Hardcore is strong, with an ethical lyrical focus - and when you're 19 or 20-years-old, everyone is super idealistic, so we'd go to these shows that had trestle tables with DIY Fanzines and magazines that highlighted social issues and that's what these bands would sing about and that

whole lifestyle and community were part of who I am.

So, all the work I do now, and my introduction to politics was through that music – so in my mid-20s I changed my name to Richie Hardcore and it became my ring name when I was fighting. And it's funny because I'd been fighting since I was a teenager, and I'd started doing alright, I won a bunch of titles and people were like, "Yo wassup, Richie Hardcore man" and it began forming my identity.

It's an odd juxtaposition from the way I look and my sport and then all the other work that I do. I guess it's all very organic; I never set out to be 'this guy' - it's just evolved. I didn't plan to go on TV and have the byline say 'Richie Hardcore' – that wasn't in the plan! I just liked jumping off stages feet first and screaming along to good songs. And when people ask, "How did you build your brand?" I didn't – I just did my life.

The work around masculinity and alcohol and drugs, it's a funny coalescence of my personal journey and my academic education and professional experience, and what I'm interested in and what I'd like to see change in the world. I'm a person who talks about my experiences professionally and personally about my journey of mental health – depression, anxiety and my childhood.

You have a mission - masculinity is an issue you care about; violence, alcohol and drugs – these are things that matter. How did you find that?

It's all very personal for me. I've talked about it publicly, but I grew up with an alcoholic dad, and like a lot of men I know that really shaped me - my inner child for want of a better term was very wounded.

This is all retrospective learning by the way. When I look at how I developed, I gravitated towards a very structured rigid lifestyle that gave me the boundaries that I never had. Because children in their development need a clear sense of boundaries and you don't get that when you grow up in a household with any form of serious addiction or parent with mental health issues, or a combination of those things.

Dad would get sober and relapse. I was fortunate enough that in a period of recovery, he took me to a Taekwondo school and said, "I'm not doing a very good job as a dad, could you help my son out?"

I was painfully insecure, I wet the bed until I was like 10 years old and a whole bunch of issues were manifesting, but I'm fortunate that I found martial arts at a young age.

I love my dad. And that is something we need to talk about when we talk about people who struggle with addiction issues, they're just people on a journey too. And while their addiction issues and substance abuse issues can make them do painful things, it doesn't necessarily mean they're terrible people that we need to excommunicate.

Martial arts filled me up internally. So, as teenagers when my friends started doing alcohol and drugs and going down that track, I had the ability to say, "No thanks, I'm not into that." Of course, that's partly because subconsciously I'd started doing inner work, I'd been building my self-esteem through the practice of martial arts, and it was also because my dad had relapsed at that time and my household was chaos and I associated alcohol and intoxication with horrible stuff that was happening in my home life.

To be honest, the work I do now is very much trying to help other little kids not be scared. I didn't grow up feeling safe a lot of the time – it's not as though my dad was horrifically physically violent; it wasn't regular beatings or anything. But there was heaps of emotional and psychological violence and that really sticks with you. When I was a teenager, he was physically aggressive towards me, but I was a young man then and I had physical altercations with my father. Do you know how f*cked up that is? I punched out my own Dad. It's so dysfunctional. And he'll talk about it now. And he'll be like, "I deserved it."

He's repressed his feelings his whole life and they're only now coming to the surface. He'll say, "I'm so sorry for everything I put you through, I know that you struggle with depression and your mental health and I'm so sorry about everything I put you through, all the names I called you, and how I treated your mother."

The work is me sharing the lessons that I learned. I had to, I guess, do a rigorous analysis of who I am and do the things I do and come to understand that in order to articulate that to a different audience, or broader audience, I've also had to apologize to the people I have hurt emotionally myself – all the things I did when I didn't know better and come to understand my mental health and depression and anxiety, and in a way I'm kind of grateful for it.

You perceive me as an empathetic person, and maybe that's because I know what it's like to not feel very good a lot of the time; I know what it's like to have crippling self-doubt, I know what it's like to say no to things because you're scared and terrified or just anxious and have no good reason to say no. I know what it's like to never want to ask that girl out because why would she ever want to go out with you because you're ugly, and I've been on this big journey where you know I got muscular, heaps of tattoos, you know, doing all this alpha male shit but to be honest with you, being a confident person is still a journey with me.

What does it mean to be a man?

There's nothing about having heaps of tattoos, or being good at rugby, or driving a cool car, or scoring heaps of women that makes you a "real man."

Being a man is whatever you want it to be, it shouldn't matter if you're into poetry, if you're into dancing, or if you're into acting. But a lot of our culture doesn't allow us that. We can all list sports stars, myself included, you know, I could tell you some top UFC fighters, but we can't do that with authors or scientists or people who are doing more than just kicking a ball and running fast and hitting people, right?

And again, that's cultural. Those are cultural constructs.

We've given prime position to the physical, athletic pursuits for men, stoicism to men, and then we go, "Oh my god, why are kids killing themselves?" Why are boys so overrepresented in suicide and self-harming behavior? Why do men, whether it's in New Zealand or Australia, United States or England, makeup ninety per-cent of the prison population? In New Zealand, at least, in 2018, 92.2% of the prison population was male.

It's because boys are socialized to violence, we're socialized to risk-taking, we're socialized to repressing our emotions. And so that plays out.

Did you know, more men die by non-communicable diseases than women do? Why? Because there's this narrative that men are tough. "Why are you going to the doctor, bro? What are you doing? Are you a gay?"

No guy wants to go to the doctor and get his prostate checked. Prostate cancer is a very big killer in our society, and we don't have that public conversation. A lot of men are dying from diseases we don't have to die from, partly because our ideas of what it means to be a man means, the term "suck it up" means we don't ask for help.

How do you start these conversations?

The irony is, I have this 'bro pass' - because of my tatts, and my early days as a being a champion fighter it allows me to talk about these things in a way that guys kind of respect, rather than if I had just been an academic, or if I'd have been more effeminate in my appearance or whatever.

You know I'm on a level with these guys where I speak like a regular dude. I don't go in there and be like, "Hi guys, I'm here to talk about the constructs of masculinity and how that puts you in a box."

Nah, I go in and I'm like, "Hey what's up? Anyone ever call you a girl when you started crying?"

And they're all like, "Yeah bro!" and I'm like, "Is that positive??" and then we banter.

If we want to open up and be vulnerable and talk about what we don't usually talk about, then you have to meet people where they are.

I get frustrated with online culture and social justice culture and academic culture for shaming people for not having the knowledge already – like they're all going to spontaneously get it.

Change has to come from a million different places, you know? The guys get it. You brainstorm and sure, some of them will be at the back looking at their cell phones, but others will open up and be like, "Yeah, man, I started drinking cause I was shy with girls." Or "It made me more confident," or I'll ask, "When's the last time you talked about alcoholism?" and you'll see someone, they'll pause and you'll see the look on their face and they'll be like, "Damn, it's been so long."

Suicide. It's a taboo topic that no one wants to talk about. Sometimes saying "If anyone is struggling, please reach out" isn't enough. Why is that?

I think it's because we put the onus on someone who's got depression to ask for help. But by its very definition, chronic depression means you're probably not in a space to ask for help.

You're withdrawing from the world, you're in your own little world, you stay in your den. You're spending time on the internet. You stop going to the gym cause you're mentally unwell. That is an important part of the conversation. And we need to encourage people – not just men, but people – to ask their friends, "Hey man, I haven't seen you for a while." Turn up and knock on their door, don't just text and be like, "Hey man, I've brought you some bagels, let's catch up." Or like, "What's up dude, let's go out and eat some banana cake, or shall we go have a protein shake and some testosterone supplements and lift some weights together?"

We need to continue to keep our social interactions alive because they tend to get smaller as we get older and that's incredibly sad. And we need to just call people for no reason, "Why are you calling?" "I'm calling cause I like your brain and I want to hear what it's got to say."

I love it when my guy friends call me just to chat. One of my best friends was like, "I just called to talk, man." And he's like a stereotypical dude. He's a great kickboxer and runs a successful company as an electrician and as much as he's into like, partying and being a bit of a ratbag, he's a great dude. And if we allow more men to understand that even that kind of conversation is an important part of staying well and has positive ramifications and it's gonna break these cycles, it's gonna teach our sons that it's fine to ask for help, or it's fine to just hang out.

You work hard to break down the taboo but it's a controversial topic - it's challenging and confronting. Why do you think it's like this?

I don't use the term 'toxic.' I don't think it's a helpful term. Most men aren't academics, they're not activists or educators – they don't have any sort of explicit understanding of constructs of masculinity, concepts of academic masculinity, environments and all these sorts of things.

So, what most men hear when you say, 'toxic masculinity' is that 'men are bad!' and they're like, "I'm not bad, I pay the bills. I love my kids, I'm not a bad person because I like drinking beers and playing rugby."

And I totally understand that because often the way people say, 'toxic masculinity' and the way people have this conversation is very aggressive. Some regular guy will make an inadvertently sexist joke and he'll get cancelled, or everyone will pile on him on Twitter and he'll be like, "Whoa! Sorry, I didn't actually know that."

In online circles at least, there is a social validation and a social hierarchy that people get for being the one to call people out. And being the one to be seen doing the social justice work on the internet. They're not the kind of people that would go talk to people in a prison full of murderers and rapists.

No one wins from the construct of 'toxic masculinity,' least of all, men. But when you talk about it, it doesn't bring men into the conversation generally. It makes a lot of men go, "F*ck that, I don't need to hear that." So, this is just what I do. There's people like Jackson Katz that I've seen on the internet or Tony Porter from *A Call to Men* – they're like leading guys in America whose work I'm aware of. And they get sports stars – *A Call to Men* gets sports stars and old NFL players to run workshops and be educators and help men have these conversations on that level.

I guess that's what I endeavor to do in my own work. I have a workshop series called 'Level Up', that's focused on the fight scene here, bringing the men in

those gyms into the conversation. And people like Mataio from *She is Not Your Rehab* do that as well through barbering. Because if you 'other' men, then it's just as damaging as if you 'other' anyone. And we have to understand that people don't know what they don't know.

We're not born with a whole set of critical filters through which you can defend yourself against the indoctrination of masculine ideals. I've had the last few years of my adult life deconditioning myself and reflecting on my views. I love hip hop music but a lot of it is super sexist, and I'm like, "I can't listen to that anymore, but it sounds so good when I'm going for a run."

I've had to learn how to have sex differently not so much physically but emotionally. As a young person I consumed porn for a long time, because no one ever taught me otherwise. No one ever gave me that education around sex - my father tried when I was 15, he tried to give me a talk and was like, "If you ever rape anyone, I'll disown you." That's a quote from my dad. And it's a good thing to say – I mean, it's a bit blunt. But that aside, no one ever taught me about how to ask people on a date, or talk about my feelings constructively until I was much older. No one ever had conversations with me about what intimacy is.

And most men are the same. I think most people who are having these conversations are in the minority and you need to bring people into the fold. And I think often terms like 'toxic masculinity,' are weaponized. And that's the detriment of the cause. That's my personal take on things. I meet some people and they've like, got a big following on Twitter and they're saying the right things, the right phrases and the right buzzwords and the right catchphrases, and I'm like, "Yeah, but you're only getting high-fived by people who already get it." The real work is dealing with people who don't get it and then shift the degree.

You're a well read, educated guy, do you have a quote that you live by?

I have co-opted, 'PMA all day,' from my friend Toby Morse, 'positive mental attitude.' It's something people associate me with because I used to say it all the time. The concept of positive mental attitude I learned from Toby Morse who sings for a hardcore band called H2O. A positive attitude doesn't mean that we won't feel bad, or things won't happen, but we have a choice as to how we respond to things. My girlfriend can break up with me and I can go on a bender or I can go for a run and go to my therapist; I can lose my job or I can lose someone in a car accident and how I respond to that - what my actions are in response to the circumstances I find myself in through no choice of my own - can be positive or negative, and I think that's what PMA means to me, you know?

I understand what it's like being 26 and you think, "I wanna change the world," but it's like, "I'm sorry, you will contribute to changing the world, but the world is the world and you just have to accept that you're doing the best you can and don't let the perfect be the enemy of the good."

When my kids come to the gym and I'm training to fight, it's like, "You don't have to be the best today, you just need to be better than you were yesterday." If you apply that - if you take that from Muay Thai, or kickboxing and apply that to the rest of your life, then that's a good way to get ahead, I think.

"I love my dad. And that is something we need to talk about when we talk about people who struggle with addiction issues, they're just people on a journey too. And while their addiction issues and substance abuse issues can make them do painful things, it doesn't necessarily mean they're terrible people that we need to excommunicate."

Aside from the PMA, how have you dealt with adversity and failure?

Having positive actions embedded in your way of being, embedded in your lifestyle that are your fallbacks when difficult things happen. Because of that, I didn't follow my father and my grandfather and my great grandfather into alcohol as a coping mechanism and develop alcoholism.

I have met good men, specifically men, who have allowed me to channel my difficulties into physicality, which has been good for maintaining wellness, and I've had psychologists and therapists that I've seen.

When I was like, 24, my mother was like, "What's the matter?" I said, "I just hurt all the time" because I do. I did. I do sometimes, still. She said, "I'm really worried about you, would you like to see a therapist?" At 24 I was like, "Yes, sure, okay," and I still see a psychologist. I've been to a bunch over the course of my life but found an amazing psychologist about five years ago in particular who changed the game for me.

They really helped me heal from my prolonged depression after I got divorced. And has continued to allow me to unpack myself and understand my inner workings, heal my 'wounded inner child.' And those two things in tandem - the intellectual emotional curiosity and doing that were the type of physicality and catharsis that way - those were my positive tools.

Has there been a key challenge you've had to face in your life?

I got divorced seven years ago and it took me a long time to get over. I carried a lot of hurt from that, for ages. I'm no expert on relationships, so, anything I say, take it with a grain of salt

The thing is, there was much that I never got to resolve from that, and so much that I've learned now because I've gone on this explicit journey to understand myself and my place in the world and my family history and how that impacted my marriage and how that impacted how I had relationships and for a long time I wished that I could just get that closure, but I never will. And I'm at peace with that. In many ways, that whole painful journey was one of the best things, strangely, that ever happened to me. It forced me to learn and grow and that informs the work I do now. We have to learn that sometimes we never get the closure we want I guess.

I'm just grateful I've met someone now who is amazing. I get to have a second chance at a proper relationship, and apply everything I've learnt.

I would say that anyone who is going through a separation, it's like, how you separate is important. I think with a lot of us, we don't feel good in a relationship anymore and we forget that in any sort of relationship, whether it's romantic, or a friendship, the tide goes in and out.

We get busy or we get disconnected, or we grow in some different directions and we can grow in different spurts and different directions and we can pull away from each other, like the tide pulling away from the beach. And it'll probably come back in, if that person is still standing on the beach waiting for that person to come back over. But often, when the tide is out, we feel, "Oh, it's done," that we'll leave the relationship, or have an affair, or start partying, or acting out in someway that will destroy the relationship, instead of bravely trying to talk to the person we love and say, "Hey, I feel lonely in this house now. I feel like you're in a different space in life and I don't know how to reach you, or I'm in a different space from when we met, three, six, nine, twelve years ago. But I want to be on the same page as you – how do we talk about that?"

So, I think a lot of us, when we are disconnected in a relationship, really need to learn how to have brave, challenging conversations to see if there's actually still love there, and not the skills to build the relationship between the love.

Because we grow up with all these ideals and all these notions about romantic love about when we grow up: boy meets girl, they live happily ever after. When the film ends, that's when the relationship starts.

"Being a man is whatever you want it to be, it shouldn't matter if you're into poetry, if you're into dancing, or if you're into acting. But a lot of our culture doesn't allow us that."

Love is a verb and we often forget about that. It takes a whole lot of skills that most of us don't actually possess. If you're lucky enough to have grown up with great parents, who had all the skills to navigate a healthy relationship and role-model that to you, man, you're fortunate.

But most of us didn't. We grew up with our parents being passive-aggressive, or busy and walking all the time, or shouting at each other, or worse, being abusive to each other. Because of how I grew up, in hindsight, I see I had strong walls around myself that kept me emotionally distant which makes it difficult, I guess, to build a truly lasting relationship.

And I wasn't aware of any of that stuff. And when we'd argue, I would say cruel things, or she would say mean things. And I carry a lot of guilt and shame about that. We were a couple of wounded little kids on the inside, and that's what we looked like despite what our adult shells looked like. There was a wounded kid in each of us that really really deeply loved each other. But we didn't have the adult skills to keep those kids holding hands, you know?

And I think that's where a lot of adults go wrong. They fall in love with someone and they're like, "Cool." When they should be like, "Cool, this feels like it's got legs, how do we learn about one another, how do we have an intentional relationship?"

I'm grateful that I'm with a partner now who wants to have an intentional relationship. She's divorced too, I'm divorced, and for both ourselves, and for raising her son, who I love so dearly, we are intentional, and we do have those conversations now.

I think we were 36 when we met. Now we're in our 40s and we've finally learned how to have those talks and say, "I don't really feel here right now, I don't feel heard right now, I don't feel seen right now. What can we do together to keep this together because I do love you, but I'm not getting what I need out of this relationship."

She is great at those conversations but also listening in response. And I think when we're talking about these things, it's like, where do we help other people have that? I think that often, relationships aren't occurring in isolation, they're happening in the context of a friendship circle and I think friends and family have a role to play in helping us all maintain a healthy relationship. Knowing how to support your friends when they're having kids, or they're having employment difficulties or someone's drinking and doing drugs too much, or whatever it might be. Your friend has a crush on someone who's not their partner – how do you cruise through that? How do you help them see a partner or a counselor or talk to their loved one?

We are social animals and we rely on the social connections to either thrive or, the lack of the social connections to perhaps fail. That's important to consider when maintaining a healthy, long-term relationship, whether that's marriage or otherwise, and I think should you explore all of those options, it's a bit like the catchphrase of 'consciously uncoupling.'

When I was young, I didn't know how to do that. I didn't know how to consciously uncouple with someone, so I just left my marriage abruptly. Not because I wasn't in love with my wife, but because I didn't have the skills and I didn't know how to deal with my growth, my own issues, and how they manifested. Damn, I didn't know what my trauma was, and in some ways I recreated the cycles of drama I was conditioned to.

So, I think it's about learning to end a relationship in a way that doesn't leave jagged wounds that will never heal properly. And saying, "Hey, look, I love you, I have loved you, or I don't love you anymore, but this relationship – I'm not here for it any longer, I'm not doing it any longer, I need some time to leave this house, or leave this family," or leave this, whatever it is that you have, with the person that you loved, in the way that does the least harm.

It's always going to hurt and this comes more to the point that you've asked me, is now, with that hurt, you have to learn to feel it.

Looking back, the best thing, if you're dealing with a divorce or a separation or any kind of loss and failure, is to learn to be alone, you need to talk about your feelings with not just your friends, but a therapist or a counselor or someone to help you process it, you need to learn how to sleep, you need to learn how to write down your feelings, you need to learn how to eat well and not self-medicate with food, because I did that for a while, too. People do that shit with social media, and sex and drugs, it's hard to feel everything, we need to learn ways to do that. There's a phrase that might be corny but it's true, "You gotta feel it to heal it."

I realized I was playing this out when I saw that I didn't have the abs I'm accustomed to having – I looked in the mirror and was like, "What is this?" And then I was like, "Oh it's all the tiramisu and ice-cream you eat when you're sad!" So I enrolled in a marathon, and started getting myself back in order. I've found part of a happy life is finding something that you can put some of your hurt and passion and energy into.

May the conversations continue...

The true authors of *Men: Real Conversations* are the men who have opened up their hearts and agreed to be part of this book. Their biographies are distinguished and diverse.

As for the humble editors, Anthony Denahy and Emma Stirling are a husband and wife team who have created a wide range of products together via their company, Nautilus Media Group, and have three amazing children and two highly neurotic rottweilers.

Their passion is to create products that challenge the status quo in publishing, events and technology.

When possible, they can be found climbing mountains, walking through rainforests, eating good food, reciting Bill Hicks and Monty Python lines and embarrassing their children.

CPSIA information can be obtained
at www.ICGtesting.com
Printed in the USA
LVHW081211130821
695158LV00001B/1

9 780645 107234